William James on
Consciousness beyond the Margin

William James on
Consciousness beyond the Margin

_____

Eugene Taylor

PRINCETON UNIVERSITY PRESS

PRINCETON, NEW JERSEY

Copyright © 1996 by Eugene Taylor
Published by Princeton University Press, 41 William Street,
Princeton, New Jersey 08540
In the United Kingdom: Princeton University Press,
Chichester, West Sussex

Library of Congress Cataloging-in-Publication Data

Taylor, Eugene.
William James on consciousness beyond the margin / Eugene Taylo.
p.   cm.
Inculdes bibliographical references and index.
ISBN 0-691-01136-2 (alk. paper)
1. James, William, 1842–1910.
2. Consciousness.   I. Title.
BF109.J28T38   1996
150'.92—dc20   96-898

This book has been composed in Baskerville

Princeton University Press books are printed
on acid-free paper and meet the guidelines
for permanence and durability of the Committee
on Production Guidelines for Book Longevity
of the Council on Library Resources

Printed in the United States of America
by Princeton Academic Press

1   3   5   7   9   10   8   6   4   2

Dedicated to My Teachers

The late Jack Roy Strange
Professor of Psychology
Southern Methodist University

The late Frederick Streng
Professor of Comparative Religions
Southern Methodist University and
Perkins School of Theology

Sheldon White
Professor of Psychology
Harvard University

Sigmund Koch
University Professor and Professor of Psychology
Boston University

and

The late Henry A. Murray
Professor of Clinical Psychology, *Emeritus*
Harvard University

CONTENTS

PREFACE

THIS BOOK is based on analysis of primary documents in the James corpus undertaken between 1977 and 1982, when the lines of the present thesis were first laid out and before a new generation of James scholars had come upon the scene. Surprisingly, however, the materials uncovered then and the implications to which I believe they point still remain largely uncommented upon by contemporary interpreters of James's life and work. Where these materials are mentioned they seem to me to be interpreted in a different context than the one in which my own reading places them.

At that time, the first volumes of James's collected works were just coming out; the project of collecting James's letters was underway, but publishing them had not even begun; the veritable industry that James scholarship has become was just starting; and while many scholars had seen significant portions of the unpublished manuscripts, barely a fraction of these documents had appeared in the published literature. For many of these erstwhile investigators, quite apart from whether or not they really know James, the question of who claims priority for rushing each little tidbit into print has since become a puzzling standard by which reputations are made and by which careers either rise or fall on the academic ladder of success.

The truth is, however, that a vast amount of work is still left to be done on William James. In my own work, I have tried to address only a few of the pertinent questions regarding such topics as a detailed chronological sequence of James's life, the personalities of the women who had a significant impact on his work, the root of James's interest in psychical research, his interpretation of the ideas of Emanuel Swedenborg and Ralph Waldo Emerson, the complex relationship that developed between Henry James, Sr., Charles Sanders Peirce, Chauncey Wright, and William James, the vast web of relationships in James's larger family constellation, as well as James's connection to a host of personalities who did not fit into the worldview of his many later commentators.

Perhaps these are only a few of the meanings implied in the enigmatic phrase uttered by Ignace Skrupskelis, in all probability the world's preeminent James scholar with regard to the documents, who once said that the definitive James biography would not be written for another forty years. In other words, the most challenging question for

James scholars, in my opinion, remains: Do we yet have the core of James's vision of reality, from which all the rest of his life and thought radiates? My answer, merely echoing Skrupskelis, is that we have barely begun.

The present text is my second attempt to shed a little more light on this question, the first being my reconstruction of James's 1896 unpublished Lowell Lectures on "Exceptional Mental States," which first appeared in 1982 through the good offices of Jacques Barzun at Charles Scribner's Sons. Both works have been created self-consciously using a technique of primary textual analysis borrowed from the field of comparative religions. This technique cleaves so closely to the original documents that it requires additional information be considered only sparingly, and then only when it has a direct bearing on the text. My approach may be disconcerting to some readers because it omits the tremendously large corpus of literature about James that has been generated over the years. Because I have done this deliberately, I offer some further explanation of this method of doing business.

I have described the particular school of thought to which this method belongs in "Contemporary Interest in Classical Eastern Psychology."[1] This approach was communicated to me over an eight-year period, between 1968 and 1976, by the late Frederick Streng, Professor of Comparative Religions at Southern Methodist University and translator of the Indian Mahayana Buddhist texts of Nagarjuna.[2] I then adapted these methods of historical scholarship in comparative religions to archival investigation in the history of American psychology and psychiatry when I first came to Harvard University in 1977 as a Resident Graduate in Applied Theology and the History of Religions.[3] I began with a reconstruction of James's Lowell Lectures on "Exceptional Mental States"; the same year I first established a stewardship over the papers of Gordon Willard Allport and also began working in certain uncataloged sections of the E. G. Boring Papers that were not readily available to other scholars.

The method, in brief, establishes a radical separation between primary and secondary sources—much like what Hindu Sanskrit scholars have called *sruti* versus *smriti*—that which is revealed versus that which is remembered. The principal focus then becomes the primary, not the secondary, texts. In this case, the primary texts are what James himself said about a subject. The secondary texts are what the commentators have said about James and his work from his time to the present.[4]

Primary texts always exist somewhere in the form of an original document or a first edition. One must be concerned with the language in which they were written, meaning not only whether they were in English or German or Chinese but also the professional language into which they were cast—here, the lexicon of philosophy, psychology, and psychiatry in the late nineteenth century. Texts are always further situated in a particular historical time period; they belong to a particular school of thought, there are lines of influence to which the texts themselves point, and there are always particular factors surrounding their construction, including the motives and personality of the author. To allow the texts to speak for themselves is to reconstruct them in their original context, wherever possible, without the mediating influence of interpreters who have not engaged in a similar reconstruction.

The reader will further find that the method is existential, but in a uniquely American vein; phenomenological, but without being related to the Husserlian school of phenomenology; and hermeneutic, but without reference to the present hermeneutic movement in textual analysis, to which I do not subscribe. Further, it is philosophical, but does not situate James in the Western analytic tradition; rather, it places him, more accurately in my estimation, in the context of a uniquely American interpretation of pragmatism. Pragmatism, the first uniquely American philosophy to have international consequences, was, in James's hand, more a direct outgrowth of Emersonian transcendentalism and the Swedenborgian thought of Henry James, Sr., as well as a retailed version of the philosophies of Charles Sanders Peirce and Chauncey Wright, than it was a capstone to the British empiricists or in any way more closely related to the continental philosophers.

And while my method has been most heavily informed by the University of Chicago tradition of textual analysis in comparative religions, it has been further modified in its adaptation to the historical literature of psychology and psychiatry by the influence on my own thinking of Buddhist epistemology and James's radical empiricism.[5] In this adaptation the method is exegetical; that is, it is freely applied to contemporary circumstances wherever possible. It also serves a soteriologic function—namely, it presumes that historical scholarship has applications to the process of personality transformation where questions about the nature of ultimate reality are concerned.

The initial premise of the present work is quite straightforward, namely, that William James is typically thought to have abandoned psychology after publication of his *Principles of Psychology* in 1890. The text suggests, instead, that all of James's work after 1890 was, in fact, informed by his interest in psychology, but that his attention was directed toward studying "the rise and fall of the threshold of consciousness" and other phenomena related to abnormal and personality psychology, rather than toward the kind of sterile academic laboratory psychology that was becoming increasingly dominant in the United States at the time. Based upon what he believed was credible scientific evidence, James abandoned the positivist viewpoint he had taken in *The Principles* and fashioned, instead, his metaphysics of radical empiricism, which, I will claim, he meant specifically to be directed toward psychologists in the renovation of their own science. This change was to have important consequences for James's own career as he busied himself with widening the scope of psychology just when it was being narrowed by the newly arrived laboratory experimentalists fresh from the German universities.

But James held his ground, and for this reason it is understood by historians of the discipline such as Kurt Danziger that psychology in the late nineteenth century had two popes—James in America and Wundt in Leipzig. In my opinion, these two thinkers represent two radically different traditions which exist to this day and are often confused.

To assuage the misgivings of those who believe that the commentarial literature must come first, I have added an annotated bibliography at the end, in which I have tried to review what at least some James scholars have said about James and his psychology after 1890. The context in which this psychology needs to be placed, as I see it, is not the Wundtian laboratory tradition, nor is it Freudian psychoanalysis, but rather an international consortium of psychologists, psychiatrists, physicians, psychotherapists, and philosophers loosely organized into what I have since called the French-Swiss-English-and-American psycho-therapeutic alliance.

I am not the only one to hold this view, as it is also entertained to one degree or another by a small but growing band of scholars. The work of these scholars, taken collectively, suggests that this alliance played an important role in the development of subsequent trends in personality, abnormal, social, and clinical psychology in the United States in the early twentieth century; their work contributes to further understanding the origins of the split between experimental and clinical psychology, which continues to this day; their studies may even throw new light on the relevance of a flourishing medical psychology one hundred years ago to present problems in the neuroscience revolution.

Further, the work of these scholars suggests to me the outline of an alternative history to American psychology than the one promulgated by E. G. Boring and largely reiterated by most historians of the discipline after him. This newer history is uniquely Jamesean and not Wundtian and has always represented the experience of most psychologists in the United States. A major line of this uniquely American Jamesean tradition influenced the personality-social psychologists of the 1930s and 1940s and the humanistic psychologists who followed them into the 1960s, separate from the psychophysical tradition of the Germans and the behaviorism of Pavlov, Watson, Hull, and Skinner, and quite apart from psychoanalysis, although this Jamesean lineage helped in many important ways to Americanize Freud's ideas. Referring to this uniquely American Jamesean tradition, in my title I have self-consciously linked James with the idea of psychology as a person-centered science, a phrase which I have freely appropriated from the writings of Gordon Allport and Carl Rogers.

Cambridge, Massachusetts
November 1995

ACKNOWLEDGMENTS

I SUCCUMB gladly to the task of paying obeisance to the deities by acknowledging my deep debt to Max Fisch for his encouragement to persist in my thesis regarding Peirce and Swedenborg, despite all detractors; to Thomas Cadwallader for introducing me to Peirce in the first place; to David Leary, whose always good work on James seems to parallel mine so closely; to Ignas Skrupskelis, James scholar extraordinaire, for invaluable footnotes; and to Richard Wolfe, Joseph Garland Librarian in the Boston Medical Library, for research space among the unpublished manuscripts at Harvard Medical School.

This research was partially funded through the Ella Lyman Cabot Trust and the good offices of Richard Hocking and the late Peter Bertocci; the Parapsychology Foundation of New York City; the Penrose Fund of the American Philosophical Society; and the Wesley N. Gray Fund (Swedenborgian).

Acknowledgments are extended to the Library of Congress for permission to quote from the James McKeen Cattell Papers; to the Archives at Clark University for permission to refer to the G. Stanley Hall Papers; to Dr. Richard Hocking for permission to quote from the William Ernest Hocking Papers; to the Houghton Rare Manuscript Library at Harvard and the Harvard Medical Archives for permission to quote from the Papers of William James in their collections; to the Harvard College Registrar for permission to consult the Registrar's Returns; to the Harvard University Archives for granting access to the Harvard College Library Charging Records and for permission to refer to the papers of Josiah Royce, Charles Rockwell Lanman, Charles William Eliot, Gordon Allport, and Henry A. Murray; and to Harvard University Press for permission to quote from the *Works of William James.*

I am also grateful to the significant women in my intellectual orbit: Marie Santilli, Florence Weideman, the late Virginia Chancey, Sally Strange, Nina Fish Murray, Josephine Murray, Geraldine Stevens, and Lois Murphy; but particularly to my teachers: the late Jack Roy Strange and the late Frederick Streng, both of whom died prematurely from cancer within a few months of each other and thus did not live to see this book; to Sheldon White and Sigmund Koch, still two of the great figures in contemporary psychology; and to the late Henry A. Murray, who, in the years that I was privileged to know him, was for me "like the shadow of a rock to a stranger in a weary land," and who, as Gordon Allport once remarked, was more like William James than any other psychologist at Harvard.

William James on
Consciousness beyond the Margin

Chapter One

AN OUTLINE OF THE PROBLEM

WILLIAM JAMES, whether loved or reviled, looms large in the history of American psychology. He was the first to wrest control of psychology from the abstract philosophers by adapting study of mental functioning to the methods of physiology. He was the first to take up the scientific study of consciousness within the context of the new evolutionary biology. He was the first to teach the new scientific psychology in the United States in 1875; the first to open a laboratory for student instruction that same year; the first to grant a Ph.D. in the new discipline, to G. Stanley Hall, in 1878; and the first American to write a world-famous textbook, *The Principles of Psychology* (1890), from the positivist point of view. Moreover, a list of his many beloved students reads like a *Who's Who* of the discipline. As teacher, colleague, and friend, he touched the lives of James Rowland Angell, Gertrude Stein, Robert Yerkes, E. L. Thorndike, Walter Cannon, William Healy, Robert Woodworth, Boris Sidis, L. Eugene Emerson, Mary Calkins, E. B. Holt, and more.

But he fell out with the Social Darwinists when he championed the importance of the individual over the survival of the species. He scandalized the philosophers and the scientists with his theory that emotions do not follow cognitions, but rather *are* the complex of our immediate physiological perceptions. He offended the medical establishment by his eloquent and successful defense of the mental healers, and he appeared to abandon psychology altogether after 1890 when his experimentalist detractors said that professionally he had fled into philosophy and personally he had become lost in the occult.

The truth of the matter is, however, that, far from abandoning psychology, James was paying close attention to then recent advances in experimental psychopathology, a new field which historians have shown developed out of psychical research and the French experimental psychology of the subconscious, and in both lines James himself was a pioneer.[1] Experimental evidence for the pathology of the emotions and for the reality of multiple subconscious states caused James to reevaluate the antimetaphysical position he had taken in *The Principles*. This led him to his metaphysics of radical empiricism and to a sophisticated critique of experimentalism in scientific psychology after 1890.[2]

Psychologists first heard of radical empiricism, although as yet unnamed, when James delivered his presidential address to the American

Psychological Association in 1894. There James asserted that any legitimate scientific psychology must contend with the fact that no scientific
system can ever be free of metaphysics. In James's case this meant that
laboratory investigation, which was defined by strict materialism and positivist epistemology, could not possibly establish itself as the only legitimate form of knowledge-getting in psychology simply by asserting that it
was antimetaphysical. James's analysis showed that positivistic reductionism was, rather, based on a metaphysics of physicalism. James was willing
to concede that, by confining attention only to models of the external
world, replicable effects were produced that approximated normal interaction between the organism and the environment. Such modeling,
however, could not possibly apply to an understanding of the internal
phenomenological life of the person, to beliefs, attitudes, values, or to
the phenomena of changing states of consciousness. Experimentalism,
radical materialism, or reductionistic positivism, as he came to call it,
could never lead to an understanding of the whole person. Instead of
ignoring the individuality of the subject by focusing exclusively on normative scientific data, he believed that the core of the discipline should
be a scientific study of consciousness, by which he meant experience in
all its forms and manifestations.

To James this meant, among other things, that psychologists should
take an in-depth look at the phenomenology of the science-making
process. It also meant that if positivism was itself based on an implied
metaphysics, then other philosophical systems could also plausibly govern scientific psychology. James envisioned his metaphysics of radical
empiricism as serving such a function, which he developed as an epistemology, in turn, to justify his pioneering work in abnormal psychology,
psychical research, and the psychology of religion, particularly between
1890 and 1902.

But the experimentalists ignored him as a psychologist after the publication of his *Principles* in 1890. They criticized him in print for his support of the mental healers; they accused him of making a full flight into
theology; and they absolutely denied any philosophical bias to their
own definition of science. Eulogized in public for fathering the New
American Psychology, but castigated in private by the laboratory types
as irrelevant, when he died in 1910 it was nevertheless generally recognized by psychologists the world over that a major figure had passed
from the scene.

But did James really abandon psychology after 1890? After all, this is
the contention of almost all modern psychology textbooks that mention
him in any detail; it is the prevailing opinion aired by the most noted
historians of the discipline; and it was a view widely held by James's own
contemporaries who played a major role in the development of modern
psychology as an experimental, laboratory-based enterprise.[3]

My answer to the question, on the other hand, shall be a resounding "no!" In fact, as I read the evidence, James abandoned only the reigning positivist epistemology of the era. His own scientific sensibilities had been fostered under the local Harvard influences of such men as Charles Peirce, the mathematical logician and interpreter of Kant who first introduced James to the German psychophysicists; and Chauncey Wright, who had been an avid follower of the works of Comte and Mill before turning to Darwin. James had then gone on to fight his own pitched battles against the scientific pretensions of Herbert Spencer and the Social Darwinists and the political motives of medical scientists trying to infuse all of culture with reductionism. All this prepared him for the positivism of Mach and Avenarius, and for the German experimental laboratory tradition that soon came to dominate the new scientific psychology by the end of the nineteenth century.

By the 1890s, the German ideal of science, with its emphasis on determinism, materialism, and reductionism, began to gain prominence in American universities. James thought that it had created a barren brass instrument psychology, too much artificial busywork in the laboratory, and a glut of measurements carried to three decimal places, which, in the end, the experimentalists themselves admitted had no meaning except to justify their new love affair with precision. Growing more and more devoid of concrete references to human experience, psychology, according to William James, was in danger of degenerating into mere experimentalism.

James preferred instead to redefine psychology anew in terms of an evolving person-centered discipline, in vital touch as much with philosophy and the humanities as with physics and the natural sciences. At the center of this new psychology, at first only glimpsed in numerous eleventh-hour footnotes and newly written passages in his *Principles of Psychology*, was a dynamic conception of personality and consciousness, which, for the first time in his thinking, gave formal recognition to the impact of personal metaphysics in the collective enterprise of psychology as a science. His new position acknowledged the reality of consciousness as an ultimate plurality of states; it shed significant light on then current scientific studies of personality disintegration; it admitted the iconography of the transcendent as a crucial determinant of personality transformation; and it provided James with an analytic tool powerful enough to critique the unexamined assumptions of radical materialism in experimental science.

To understand his change from positivism to radical emipiricism is to throw new light on a variety of problems James took up, from experimental psychopathology, psychical research, the social psychology of crowds, the psychology of painting, our understanding of creative genius, and the psychology of education, to the experience of transcendence in religious awakening. Indeed, his psychological investigations during this pivotal phase of his career, particularly between 1890 and 1902, I shall maintain, significantly informed the development of his technical philosophy, which in turn he used to justify the possibility of a scientific psychology centered on the person rather than the laboratory.

What We Know of James's Psychology after 1890

While it is true that James's contributions to psychology after 1890 continue to be largely overlooked or misinterpreted, there is a handful of scholars who have considered James's activities as a psychologist during this era. Dorothy Ross has alluded to this period in her review of G. Stanley Hall's relation to James, but she gives greater stress to Hall's point of view.[4] Otto Marx reviewed the neurological and psychiatric journals during this time and concluded that James made no contribution to the literature.[5] Archie Baum, as well as Gardner Murphy and Robert O. Ballou, have written in defense of James's studies of psychic phenomena, but deal only with James's published materials, and they cast their interpretation against the implicit backdrop of twentieth-century definitions of parapsychology and not the nineteenth-century context of psychical research.[6] Grace Foster has given one of the most thorough analyses of James's personal and professional involvement in psychotherapy during this period, while H. D. Spoerl has reviewed with much accurate detail James's contribution to abnormal and social psychology.[7] Both these authors made their ideas known only in brief articles read by limited audiences, and they did not fully draw out the implications of James's psychology after 1890 for later developments, either in James's thinking or in the field of psychology at large.[8]

Within the history of medicine, Henry Ellenberger, Nathan G. Hale, and John Burnham have mentioned James's contribution to the rise of American psychotherapy in the late nineteenth century, but only as a prelude to the coming of Freud.[9] While they have broached James's influence on the so-called Boston School of Abnormal Psychology and pointed to his association with such lights as Morton Prince, Boris Sidis, James Jackson Putnam, and Josiah Royce, only when taken collectively does their work suggest that James played an important role in the development of a uniquely American psychology of the subconscious, now largely forgotten because it was later inundated by the flood of Freudian psychoanalysis and then politically torpedoed by the prophets of behaviorism. Norman Cameron has given a summary of James's contribution to the American reception of psychoanalysis, seconded by Barbara Ross.[10] Saul Rosenzweig in 1959 has suggested that Freud might even have been influenced by James's stream of consciousness technique, particularly as it derived from the method of automatic speaking, writing, and drawing described by James John Garth Wilkinson, a translator of Swedenborg, pastoral psychiatrist to the James family, and older colleague of William James in the field of abnormal psychology.[11]

Despite this wealth of information, historians of psychology and psychiatry continue to suggest that James was more of a philosopher than a psychologist; that his efforts in the field of psychical research were somehow not scientifically legitimate; that his dabbling in the unconscious was merely a naive precursor to Freud; and that after *The Principles of Psychology* in 1890 James was not involved in anything that could be called psychology by his more experimentally oriented colleagues. Thus, a work such as *The Varieties of Religious Experience* (1902) represents to James's most reductionistic scientific detractors a full flight into theology, even though James himself claimed that in examining religious consciousness he spoke from the standpoint of a psychologist. Clearly, to stretch a point to its limit, most experimental psychologists do not read James after 1890, if they read him at all, while theologians, ministers, and psychologists of religion tend to ignore him before *Varieties of Religious Experience.*

While James scholars generally have managed to avoid most of these problems, three tendencies are nevertheless clear: (1) James is often interpreted out of context according to an author's own more modern and oftentimes less eclectic frame of reference. James's name is then invoked as anticipating some exclusive future trend; hence, when writing about the Jamesean influence in psychology, we have James the pioneer psychoanalyst, James the pioneer behaviorist, or James the pioneer phenomenologist, all simultaneously claimed by adherents among the rival schools. (2) Most James scholars rely primarily on James's published works, on only the most accessible letters, or on only a limited reading of the vast collection on deposit at the Houghton Library at Harvard. And (3), only in certain instances has Ralph Barton Perry's initial interpretation of James and his psychology been questioned or revised. Despite Perry's eminent status as a philosopher in his own right, and despite the circumstances that he was first a student and later friend and designated biographer—and that he deserved the Pulitzer Prize he won for his life of James—he was still highly selective about what he emphasized in James's writings. Perry, ultimately a Western philosopher in the American academic tradition, tended to gloss over James's activities in psychical research, his psychology of the subconscious, the Asian influences, and the impact of the New England Mind-Cure Movement on James's thinking *as a psychologist.*[12]

Indeed, I shall maintain that even in his most positivistic phases, William James espoused a psychology which I would characterize as a person-centered science. True, he was a man of many moods and mirrors. He appeared to change his mind on an issue many times and indeed at one point said that he really didn't mind contradicting himself. But there is sufficient evidence to suggest that the general orientation toward a person-centered science was present in his work when he first entered the field of psychology in the 1870s. He may have waxed hot and cold during different decades over it as a primary focus, yet it remained hovering in the background even in his most reductionistic pronouncements. Despite his antimetaphysical claims, his *Principles* is suffused with this person-centered orientation, and it comes out most cogently in the period between 1890 and 1902, when he became intensely involved in problems of experimental psychopathology, psychical research, and the psychology of religion. As I shall also attempt to indicate, the influence of James's psychology during this period was extensive, not only in relation to the subsequent content areas and methodologies inherent in the numerous subdisciplines he covered, but also because his views on the implicit metaphysical assumptions even of the most rabid positivist epistemology continue to cast important light on the present state and future prospects of psychology.

This thesis I shall defend in five stages. First, I would like to establish that from its very inception, James's psychology, while it focused on the scientific study of consciousness, remained person-centered. Second, while James self-consciously established a positivist epistemology in his *Principles of Psychology*, even there he injected important psychological material that had clear metaphysical implications for his later philosophical critique of science. Third, using archival manuscripts as well as his published works, I would like to ask, "Just what were James's activities as a psychologist after 1890, and particularly before 1902?" and to answer by showing that his endeavors demonstrate the foundation upon which he believed a person-centered science could be built. Fourth, I would like to examine the opposition that developed in America to James's program for psychology, chiefly among a coterie of Wundt's American students who wished to displace James's influence with the rhetoric and methods of the German experimental laboratory tradition. Fifth, I intend to enunciate the grounds upon which James repudiated the positivist epistemology of these German-trained students, claiming their agenda to be an ill-conceived basis for constructing a scientific psychology. In stating my conclusions, I would like to highlight what I understand to have been James's final message to psychologists about some potential future trends in the discipline.

Chapter Two

CONSCIOUSNESS: THE FOCUS OF
EXPERIMENTAL PSYCHOLOGY
AT HARVARD BEFORE 1890

WHEN EDWIN G. BORING wrote his monumental *History of Experimental Psychology* (1929), which became required reading for almost all graduates in psychology for nearly fifty years, he already had a prearranged agenda. His aim, indeed his lifework, was to develop, largely by editorial fiat, the German experimental laboratory tradition of his mentor, E. B. Titchener, and especially the subfield of psychophysics as it had developed in the tradition of Helmholtz, Fechner, and Wundt, into what was thought of as the only legitimate standard upon which to base a science of psychology. Boring knew that he was omitting tests and measurements, developmental perspectives, and dynamic psychotherapy from his book. He even said privately that he hoped someday to do a history of those areas as well. But he publicly created the impression anyway that German experimental laboratory psychophysics was the only legitimate standard in the history of Western science, in the history of American psychology, and in the history of psychology at Harvard.[1] The birth of this movement he fixed as 1879, when Wilhelm Wundt first opened his experimental laboratory in Leipzig, which Boring declared to be the first real laborarotory of experimental psychology to be founded in the world.

Boring did not make this claim of priorities until the second edition of his *History*, which appeared in 1950, however. In the first edition of his work, he was satisfied to give James due credit for his early laboratory, which James had maintained early as 1875. But in the ensuing years between 1929 and 1950, the dates of Boring's two editions, the personality-social psychologists in the Jamesean tradition at Harvard—Allport, Murray, and others—had risen up and Boring was carrying on an ideological battle against them. In this context, using the way he wrote history as a weapon, Boring separated the experimentalists at Harvard from direct links with James, associated them, instead, with Wundt, and then proceeded to subsume James under the experimental tradition as a precursor.[2]

To make this claim, Boring had to remake William James over into a follower of the right kind of European science.[3] He accomplished this by first overemphasizing James's few weeks in 1867 as a student and auditor of Helmholtz and Wundt. He followed by cleverly outlining James's role as an empirical psychologist with a philosophical bent, but then discounted James as a serious scientist because he hated laboratory work (what James really hated, of course, was German experimental laboratory work). Boring finally dressed out the lines of the desired picture by arguing that if James was not a serious experimentalist, therefore his early laboratory of 1875 was not a real one. Boring's chief vehicle, and the denouement of his story, was to establish in the minds of succeeding generations the fiction that modern psychology really began with the founding of Wundt's laboratory in Leipzig in 1879.[4]

This assertion, however, does not explain why, in the closing decades of the nineteenth century, and at least to 1910, two popes reigned in scientific psychology, James in America and Wundt in Germany. It does not explain why experimental psychology was equated with psychical research in the minds of the American public between 1880 and 1910. It does not explain how France, America, Switzerland, and Italy differentially interpreted the new science into their own indigenous expressions. It does not even admit the history of dynamic unconscious processes. And it does not help us to see the quite separate origins of personality, abnormal, social, and clinical psychology. Nor does Boring's account help us to explain, except by its omissions, the current internecine war between academic researchers and clinical psychologists, which I believe has roots reaching back to James's time.[5]

I cannot hope in the present work to thoroughly examine all these issues. However, I would like to focus on one important aspect of their history by developing the thesis that a conceptual fusion of experimental psychology and the scientific study of psychic phenomena in the United States in the closing decades of the nineteenth century led to major developments in the understanding of consciousness and, hence, to the evolution of scientific psychotherapy by the 1890s. To do this, I would like to present evidence that reveals how experimental psychology at Harvard in the hands of William James between 1872 and 1890 was informed by early studies in experimental neuropathology, physiological psychology, and psychical research, which, in turn, significantly contributed to the development of the new field of experimental psychopathology.

EVOLUTION AND CONSCIOUSNESS: JAMES'S 1865 REVIEWS

The first piece of evidence comes from James's earliest-known statements on the efficacy of consciousness in the context of the biological evolution of humans.

Some years before details were formally published, scholars working in James's unpublished manuscript collection at Harvard University were aware of two unsigned articles authored by James that originally appeared in the *North American Review* in 1865 on the subject of Darwin's theory of natural selection.[6] The first was a review of Thomas H. Huxley's *Lectures on the Elements of Comparative Anatomy: On the Classification of Animals, and on the Vertebrate Skull,* while the second was a review of Alfred R. Wallace's *The Origin of Human Races and the Antiquity of Man Deduced from the Theory of 'Natural Selection'.*[7] These items have been of some interest, not only because they linked James with Darwin's ideas at the height of the controversy over the theory of natural selection, but also because they are the earliest-known pieces that James ever published and hence alter significantly the accepted annotated bibliographies of James's writings upon which all biographical statements about the genesis of his writing career are based. Since I have analyzed the content of these reviews elsewhere, I will confine myself to making only a few of their most salient points.[8]

In the first article, James labeled Huxley a left-wing extremist because in his writings all thought about anything was always reduced to a radical materialism. But Huxley's work was important, James said, because it supported Darwin's theory of natural selection, which was just then being taken up by so many other reputable scientists. The bulk of the article was concerned with Huxley's arguments for the theory that the skull was an evolutionary extension of the vertebral column, which James elaborated upon.

In the second article, we have a much more developed text on the theory of natural selection in which James took full opportunity to explicate, emphasizing the role of conscious choice. The question that Wallace addressed and James commented upon was why, if the creationists were wrong in believing that God created all species in their present form all at once a long time ago, do the sources of variation that one would expect to see throughout nature appear to be absent in man? The answer proposed was that they are not absent, but have been considerably slowed. This has occurred because in the course of the social evolution of the species human beings have made the decision to band together and protect the most gifted as well as the most unfortunate, especially those who would not normally survive on their own. This has changed the rate at which variation by selection is introduced into the species by significantly slowing down the selection of those unfit to continue biologically because they are being preserved for social or moral reasons. In addition, variation in the species was being further slowed because man has the ability to introduce alterations into the physical environment that far surpass any other species, thus forcing the environment to adapt to human needs, instead of the other way around. These arguments gave James a chance to develop the thought that social organization and intellectual superiority must therefore also be deciding elements in evolutionary survival, especially in humans. Consciousness, consequently, becomes an efficacious force in the biological evolution of the species.

I would say that these articles are important for three reasons. First, while other Darwinians in the 1860s were busy talking biology and the development of plants and animals, the articles show where James first staked out the problem of consciousness as his contribution to the larger discussion. He continued to develop his answers most directly against the Social Darwinists in essays such as "Great Men, Great Thoughts and Their Environment" and "The Importance of Individuals," where he argued for the evolutionary importance of individual differences and defined the principles of variation and selection that are always active in consciousness. In these texts, James maintained the position, still lost on evolutionary psychologists who remain focused on the superiority of rationality, that creative brainstorming was just as important as decision making because the widest possible number of choices allowed for the most adaptive product to be selected. The content of these essays for what they say about consciousness remains quite overlooked, however. Instead, James remains best remembered for his discussion of instinct, habit, perception, and other evolutionary topics related to the problem of consciousness which he posed in *The Principles*.

Second, the 1865 articles are also important because they reflect the influence of C. S. Peirce and Chauncey Wright on James's views.[9] At Darwin's behest, Wright had written "The Evolution of Self-Consciousness" in an attempt to identify how natural selection works in the development of language.[10] Peirce, ever the consummate scientist and logician, remained skeptical of the evolutionary hypothesis, signing neither on nor off, a fact which William, struggling with his own conception of an open universe even then, must have duly noted. Meanwhile, the Peircean influence on James's conception of pragmatism, and hence evolutionary functionalism, and on James's early conception of psychology have been well documented.[11] Subsequently, we find the influence of Peirce and Wright in James's formulations on consciousness, on evolution, on psychophysics, and on the philosophy of science. In fact, we see James's efforts to retail their work to psychologists and philosophers throughout the rest of his career.

Third, the 1865 articles are important for the light they shed on the deeper connections to Henry James, Sr., and Emerson and to the as yet unacknowledged debt of Swedenborgian and transcendentalist thought to the evolution of American pragmatism.[12] As a case in point, James's connections to Charles Eliot Norton, the editor of the *North American Review*, came through Henry James, Sr., Emerson, and the Saturday Club. These were, in fact, the same lines that William used to enter Agassiz's Lawrence Scientific School when he first came to Harvard in 1861, although he promptly sided with Agassiz's enemies, the Darwinists such as Asa Gray, Chauncey Wright, and Charles William Eliot, on the evolutionary question.

If we look more closely into the complex of relationships among these figures during this seminal period, I believe the following explanation suggests itself: When young William, the aspiring artist, abandoned the palate and brush for the Lawrence Scientific School in 1861, he was actually fulfilling a mandate as heir to the Swedenborgian and transcendentalist literary psychology of Emerson and Henry James, Sr. This was essentially a spiritual psychology of character formation which William was silently charged with carrying on and which, in the more empirical and reductionistic age in which he found himself, William transmuted into a science of consciousness and a psychology of individual differences. These events exacerbated a deep personal conflict that led James to both a crisis and recovery, but the route he took was rather circuitous.

In conflict over the suffocating influence of his father's religious metaphysics, largely through the influence of Peirce during the 1860s, William fled into the ultrapositivistic and scientific philosophy of Chauncey Wright. Peirce, meanwhile, was adopted by Henry James, Sr., into the James family as something of a spiritual son. As such, after long conversations with the senior James while William was in Brazil, Peirce converted to his idiosyncratic brand of Swedenborgianism. From there, Swedenborg's Doctrine of Use and his conception of rationality became one influence, still unaccounted for, on Peirce's later formulation of the pragmatic maxim.

For his part, by fleeing into science William successfully separated himself from continuous fusion with his father's ideas, content now to derive them indirectly through Peirce. But William could not long abide with the antiphilosophical and antireligious stance that Wright's brand of positivism represented, and William's attempt to do so literally drove him nearly to suicide by 1870. He recovered by reading Wordsworth and Renouvier and by believing to believe in free will, thus now distancing himself enough from both Henry James, Sr., and Wright, to be able to use them in his new and evolving worldview, but without the old emotional restraints. Mental science and the study of consciousness was to become his forte, and he got his first chance to teach these subjects through his old chemistry teacher, Charles William Eliot, by then presi-

dent of Harvard, who hired William in 1872 to teach anatomy and physiology. Physiological psychology, the first course so-called to be taught in
an American university, was only two years away, and from there James's
vocational course was set.

JAMES'S 1867–1868 MEDICAL SCHOOL NOTEBOOK

The second piece of evidence that helps define the origin of experimental psychology at Harvard is William James's medical school notebook,
which dates from the late fall of 1866 or early 1867.[13] The notebook is
particularly important for the glimpse it gives into the state of medical
school training at the time. There are notes on muscle and cell physiology and the differential effects of chemicals on living tissue. References
are made to the works of Huxley, Busk, and particularly Carpenter, and
chemical notations appear throughout. The most interesting feature of
the notes is the level of discourse, in that they convey extensive correlation of mental symptoms with physical pathology in diseases of the nervous system. In terms of the clinical picture of disease, no attempt was
made to reduce consciousness strictly to the language of physiology.
Rather, the signs and symptoms of the patient's mental state were presented as equally important to a description of the accompanying organic picture. Most important, a large part of this notebook contains
details of neuropathological lectures given at Harvard by Charles
Edouard Brown-Sequard. Herein, I believe, lies one of the chief sources
for William James's concept of the experimental method.

Brown-Sequard was Harvard's first professor of neurology. He had an
important influence on Henry Pickering Bowditch, James Jackson
Putnam, and William James as young medical students, and all three
came to know him in the late 1860s. Brown-Sequard was an English subject from the island of Mauritius, whose bloodline was French and Irish
American. He had received his medical training in Paris and distinguished himself for his experimental laboratory research on the nervous
system and the endocrine glands before he came to America. When he
became professor of neurology at the Harvard Medical School in 1864,
he brought with him the latest techniques of experimental medicine,
which applied laboratory research to the understanding of clinical problems important to the practicing physician. His appointment was an attempt to expose medical students to the "new physiology," that is, the
experimental (meaning surgical) demonstration of the relation of structure to function. This was the French scientific tradition of Xavier Bi-
chat, François Magendie, and Claude Bernard. In this vein, while dissection on nonliving organisms had long been a standard procedure,
Brown-Sequard was in fact the first to introduce vivisection into the med-

ical curriculum as an experimental technique.[14] James, Bowditch, Putnam, and others were the first students at Harvard to be exposed to this procedure on living organisms, which was soon to form such a vital part of the biological sciences.

One should not underestimate, in this regard, the effect that French experimental physiology had on William James's subsequent definition of scientific psychology. In Germany, experimental laboratory research became the ideal pursued in the universities, and pure science was seen as the father of clinical application. But in France, the ideal of *la clinique*, bedside teaching and the care of the patient, had held sway. Since the French Revolution, because medical schools had been founded around the Paris teaching hospitals, *la clinique* had been the focus, while scientific research, especially experimental physiology, grew up as its handmaiden. Hence, the experimental tradition in France had to fight for its own independent recognition in a way that was unthinkable for the pure laboratory sciences in Germany.[15]

In the early part of the nineteenth century, American physicians flocked to Paris to study at the patient's bedside and to tour the wards with greats such as Corvisart, Louis, Laennec, and Bouillar. Professors on the faculty at Harvard Medical School, Oliver Wendell Holmes, Sr., and Jeffries Wyman, two of James's mentors, drew their inspiration from French clinical medicine at a time when other medical institutions looked to Germany, Edinburgh, Leyden, or England. The pervasive influence of the French clinical tradition at Harvard was to continue until well into the late nineteenth century.[16] Because of this clinical emphasis on the soon-to-emerge laboratory sciences of physiology, neurology, and psychology, the French experimental tradition was also to have a significant later influence on the development of experimental psychopathology and scientific psychotherapy in Boston in a way that the ideal of German science never had.

Parenthetically, I want to add two small details about James's notebook before proceeding further. First, inserted in the flyleaf is a notation in an unidentified hand, probably Mrs. Bailey Aldrich, referring to Ralph Barton Perry, James's biographer. The notation says that Perry did not want the notebook to be a part of the William James Collection at Harvard College, ostensibly because it was "medical" and not "philosophical." Here again is a small but clear-cut example where Perry exercised his selective influence on the history of James scholarship. Second, inserted in the notebook is a letter, dated July 22, 1942, from Edwin G. Boring, the historian of experimental psychology at Harvard, to Charles Burwell, dean of the Medical School. In this letter Boring offers to give the notebook to the Medical School archives. Boring had intended to include it as part of a centenary James exhibit at the American Psychological Association meeting that year, but the meeting was canceled because of the war. With a background limited to psychophysics and engineering, Boring was unable to draw any inferences relevant to James's scientific training. He wrote: "I have gone through the notebook but do not find anything of great interest in it." By seeing the notebook as a precursor to physiological psychology, however, we gain some important clues to a direction in James's development that Boring did not fathom.

JAMES'S LABORATORY EXPERIMENTS

The third cache of evidence is actually a collection of two groups of experimental studies that James had undertaken between 1874 and 1889. The first group is indicated by two references that describe James's involvement in laboratory-oriented neurophysiology in the early 1870s, while the second is made up of what James thought of as his main contributions to experimental psychology proper.

To understand the significance of James's laboratory investigations, one should know that the physiology laboratory at Harvard Medical School, which at the time was just across the street from the Massachusetts General Hospital, had been established by Henry Pickering Bowditch as the first experimental facility in the United States for studying problems of clinical physiology. This laboratory was also the site of early collaborative experiments between Bowditch, James, Putnam, and, a few years later, G. Stanley Hall. Second, one should know that, while Bowditch had studied briefly in Paris under Bernard, Brown-Sequard, and Charcot, he was preeminently identified with Carl Ludwig in Vienna; Putnam had been a postdoctoral student under Meynert and Benedict in Leipzig. Meanwhile, in this triumvirate, James, although he remained strongly influenced by French experimental and clinical medicine, became the philosophical champion of the group because of his involvements with Peirce and Wright and the orientation toward the mind-body problem that later came to be known as American functionalism.

During the early 1870s in Bowditch's lab, James, with Putnam and Bowditch, undertook the reproduction of Meynert's experiments on cerebral localization. One of these studies, led by James Jackson Putnam with the assistance of James and Bowditch, was published in January 1874 under the title "Contributions to the Physiology of the Cortex Cerebrii."[17] The problem under investigation involved a much discussed topic in the scientific literature at the time on localization of brain function. Specific centers of the brain in live animals had been surgically exposed and then electrically stimulated, and entire maps had been drawn showing the relation of specific brain sites to bodily functions. The primary criticism of such endeavors was methodological, in that one could not definitely tell whether the superficial stimulation of surface tissue in the cortex was activating more deeply embedded brain centers.

Putnam, James, and Bowditch devised a unique approach to answer this question. Etherized dogs had a portion of their skulls surgically removed and a partial incision was then made around the area of the cortex to be tested, creating a flap of tissue which prevented electrical stimulation from penetrating more deeply into the brain at that site. Stimulation of the surface confirmed the recognized specificity of function, thus answering the questions of the critics.

An account of these Harvard activities soon appeared in the pages of the *New York Medical Record* as part of the program of the New York Society for Neurology and Electrology.[18] At the stated meeting on January 18, 1875, with Dr. Meredith Clymer in the chair, a paper "On Experimental Researches of the Motorial Functions of the Cerebral Convolutions" was discussed. Its content described Hitzig's experiments on stimulation of specific brain centers, which had produced consistent flexion and extension of the limb in five animals. James Jackson Putnam and George Miller Beard, both pioneers in the founding of American neurology, were present, along with a number of others. Putnam, by invitation of the president, was part of the program and described the aforementioned experiments, performed by himself with William James assisting. They had attempted to test, Putnam said, the degree to which feeble induction currents applied to the cerebral cortex, after the manner of Hitzig and Ferrier, acted on parts lying beneath the surface.

Putnam then proceeded to explain other experiments that William James had been doing in which Putnam had acted as assistant. Their point was to determine whether excitation of the cortex of the cervical lobes would cause a rise of blood pressure, such as had been known to follow excitation of peripheral nerves. Putnam reported that the changes in blood pressure were recorded upon a revolving cylinder through a manometer attached to some large artery. The results so far had been inconsistent, but the experiments were still in progress. In fact, they were never reported, but their role in the development of James's theory of the emotions ten years later seems quite likely.

C. K. Mills, in his historical sketch of advances in American neurology in the 1870s, referred to Putnam, Bowditch and James's experiments with faradic currents on the cerebral cortex and subcortex.[19] Ellis, a student of Bowditch's in the 1880s, recalled decades later with some reverence the importance attached to the early collaboration of these experimenters. And Cannon in the 1930s echoed this same theme as a major first step in the development of physiology at Harvard.[20]

Their significance in the present context is that Bowditch's facilities became the prototype for Putnam to develop a laboratory in neuropathology at Harvard Medical School and for James to develop the laboratory of experimental psychology in Harvard College. Their collaboration also marked the kind of mutual interaction the three would continue to have throughout their respective careers in physiology, neurology, and psychology. As a result, the history of these laboratory sciences became bound up together at Harvard. Mind-body issues around the experimental study of consciousness would come to have an important role in the evolution of the social and medical sciences, and an important era of psychological medicine in general practice would soon result.

Once his own laboratory activities got underway in 1875, James produced several studies which, in a letter to James McKeen Cattell, he labeled his only "scientific papers."[21]

The first such study, published in *The American Journal of Otology* (1882), had been undertaken as part of James's interest in the perception of space and the feeling of effort. It was an empirical verification for the hypothesis that deaf-mutes were immune to the feeling of dizziness.[22] To test this notion, James devised an apparatus for whirling each subject around rapidly.[23] An experimental group of 519 deaf-mutes drawn from various institutions was compared with a control group of nearly 200 normal subjects who were students and instructors at Harvard College. Of the deaf-mutes, 186 were totally insusceptible to being made dizzy, 134 were made dizzy to a slight degree, while 199 became dizzy as expected of normals. In the control group of 200, only one remained exempt from vertigo. From this James concluded that, along with the semicircular canals, hearing was also implicated in balance.[24]

James's second study, published in the *Proceedings of the American Society for Psychical Research*, was a replication of an experiment previously conducted by G. Stanley Hall in Bowditch's laboratory. The topic of the investigation was reaction time under hypnosis.[25] In the early 1880s, before going to Hopkins and while still in Boston, Hall had subjected "a traveling mesmerist's histrionic assistant" to a series of trials to determine the effect of trance on speed of reaction time, based on some observations of Wundt.[26] James tested the same theory by collecting data from 806 trials on three different subjects, all Harvard seniors, using reaction-time equipment and a Baltzar's kymograph. Hall had proclaimed that his data showed unequivocally that reaction time was faster during trance than when the subject was measured both before and after. By a comparison of simple mathematical averages, James showed, however, that in his subjects the trance actually slowed reaction time, which only slightly improved once the trance had ended. Rather than presuming he had established anything definite, James merely concluded that Hall's assertion was by no means proven. He implied that Hall's subject may have been acting out the subconscious desires of the experimenter; and that at the very least one "should beware of making rash generalizations from few cases about the hypnotic state."

The third study, a continuation of Wier Mitchell's observations on the phantom limb phenomenon, James also published in the *Proceedings of the American Society for Psychical Research*.[27] He based his work on interviews and questionnaires with 185 amputees and attempted to find out why some preserve consciousness of a limb after it has been lost, while others do not; why the phantom limb appears fixed in some and moves around in others; and in those that move, why some can will the movement, while with others the movement is beyond their control.

James had sent out no fewer than eight hundred circulars to addresses furnished by leading makers of artificial limbs, but he was disappointed in the results because they failed to explain the causes of the enumerated differences. He thought in a delicate inquiry such as this that a single patient carefully cross-examined would yield deeper knowledge than the answers of the average patient to an impersonal circular.

Nevertheless, he did get information that he thought might be of use to future inquirers. Three-quarters of the sample that responded, for instance, reported experiencing the phantom limb phenomenon. A much greater number, he said, had felt it immediately after the amputation, or up to years later, but the feeling had faded by the time of their questioning. About one hundred cases said they could work or wiggle their missing limbs at will. In almost all such cases there was accompanying contraction of muscle at the stump. In others, weak electrical stimulation of the stump could produce the sensation of the lost limb, and so on. In almost all cases, James was able to invoke such principles as the doctrine of specific energies to account for the neurological facts. Finally, he took up the problem of how, if telepathic powers actually do exist, it would be possible to feel an insult to a severed limb being acted on at a distance from its former owner. As for the evidence in favor of such telepathic rapport, none in his own hands, James reported, had inspired any confidence.

James's fourth study involved observation of subjects who engaged in automatic writing.[28] The typical subject would sit at a table with his or her head buried in one arm, while the other arm would be outstretched in the writing position, pencil in hand, over blank paper. If the writing hand could be made to begin to move, say through small circular motions, after some ten minutes or so, in certain developed subjects legible writing would appear of which the person would have no knowledge.[29]

The phenomenon had been extensively investigated by the British psychical researchers, and the American Society for Psychical Research had collected numerous cases over the preceding three years. James endeavored to show only some half-dozen cases. His point of departure was the assertion made by M. Pierre Janet that in a somnambulist showing double personality, during automatic writing the hand and the arm of the automatic writer were anesthetic. James resolved to look for this symptom in ordinary subjects prone to automatic writing, and, finding it, corroborated Janet's view that a true dissociation of consciousness was present.

James showed that once automatic writing began, the subject's arm and hand were completely insensitive to pin pricks and pinches. When asked directly, his head still buried, the subject reported feeling nothing. The anesthetized hand, however, wrote, unbeknownst to the subject, demanding to know why it had been stuck with a pin. James found, moreover, that it was possible to communicate with the two split halves of the subject's personality, one by speaking to the buried head, the other by speaking to the anesthetized hand, and to extract information about the subject's personality from one part that was unknown to the other.

While he found no solid evidence for any telepathic ability in the anesthetized hand, James concluded that the implications of the phenomenon of dissociation for understanding psychopathology were obviously far-reaching.

In sum, these studies show a clear focus on brain neurophysiology and the problem of consciousness. Not once did James revert to any sort of spiritualist hypothesis about life after death, nor did he presume the reality of psychic phenomena as previously given. Rather, the paradigm of psychical research became an early framework for the scientific study of the relation between mind and body and pointed the way to the later development of dynamic theories about the subconscious.

THE DESCRIPTION OF JAMES'S EARLY LABORATORY

The fourth piece of evidence I want to present is a description of James's psychology laboratory because it gives us some clues about the direction James's definition of scientific psychology had taken in its early years. The laboratory was pictured to Ralph Barton Perry by one of James's students, Ralph Waldo Black, who had been there in 1886. Black said it was the laboratory in the Lawrence Scientific School:

> Where there were some human brains in alcohol which I did not consider myself physiologist enough to cut up, also there was some electrical apparatus for measuring time reactions. We would press a key the minute we saw a spark. . . . He [meaning James] had some staples with a pin and a screw in each the width of the staple apart and we all stripped to the waist or rolled

up our pant legs and he would try them on the skin to see if we felt the contact as one or two. He said I had the most insensible calves he ever saw and thought perhaps they needed washing. If I were there now I should improvise apparatus and try experiments on my own account, but none of us seemed to realize the opportunity we had to build up a laboratory. . . . There was a sort of barber's chair at the laboratory and we would sit in it and look at a bright object on the wall preparatory to being hypnotized. . . . When it was my turn I grimaced when he approached me after I had stared a while at the object and he said "You can't be hypnotized." But with the doubts that creep into our minds with age I now recall that it occurred to me one evening that I would 'loaf over' to the laboratory and see what was going on. I was an unbidden guest and James said, "Couldn't you keep away?" So I now wonder if he 'suggested' my coming.[30]

Our first inference here is that the methodological approach in James's laboratory was one of some combination of surgical dissection, the electrical measurement of reflexes, and the use of hypnosis to artificially induce dissociated states of consciousness. Also, the student's description of the two-point threshold suggests to us the dual use of a simple piece of experimental apparatus. There are many examples of how James adapted some piece of reaction-time or psychophysical equipment to prove a point in experimental psychopathology. The staple and screw arrangement, for instance, was used in elementary psychophysics to determine when a subject could first detect two skin pricks first held closely together and then moved farther and farther apart, but it also became a way to map anesthetic and hyperaesthetic zones that would characteristically appear on the body of hysteric subjects.

And while it is true that we are given the impression that students had to be somewhat self-motivated, the fact is that they had access as undergraduates to laboratory instruction and apparatus. The point is significant, for in the claim of Wundt's laboratory as a first in 1879, Boring omitted to mention that students were not receiving credit for laboratory work even at that time, while as early as 1875 James had arranged for students to get course credit for work in both his own lab and Bowditch's as well.[31]

Finally, while we have no pictures of the lab setup in the Lawrence Scientific School, from this sketch it is apparent that physiological methods and studies in experimental psychopathology dominated the environment, with due reverence given to the German experimental laboratory methods as at least necessary to round out the picture of experimental psychology. But James did not consider the German approach as being in any way preeminent.

The Early Research Committees of the ASPR

A fifth collection of facts I would like to present is the makeup of the various research committees of the American Society for Psychical Research. In order to appreciate the significance of their impact on James's experimental psychology, one should know that the ASPR was convened in September 1884 in Boston after a visit of the physicist Sir William Barrett. Barrett had come at the instigation of certain distinguished members of the American Association for the Advancement of Science, among them Edward Charles Pickering, the Harvard astronomer; Charles Sedgwick Minot, the Harvard embryologist; Samuel Scudder, a distinguished entomologist and head of the Boston Museum of Natural History; and Alpheus Hyatt, editor of *Science*. The original Committee of Nine that worked on the organization included E. C. Pickering as chairman, plus G. Stanley Hall, William James, Henry Pickering Bowditch, William Watson of MIT, Charles Sedgwick Minot, Alpheus Hyatt, Samuel Scudder, and N.D.C. Hodges as secretary. The first official meeting of the Society was held in January 1885 at the American Academy of Arts and Sciences, with eighty-two members and one hundred associates. Among the early members of the American Society for Psychical Research were some of the great lights of American science and medicine, such as Benjamin Peirce, Asa Gray, George Fullerton, Dallas Basche, Henry Ingersoll Bowditch, Moses Allan Starr, and Charles Loomis Dana. The Society's first president was Simon Newcomb, then head of the Smithsonian Institution.

But the research committees were all clearly controlled by a tight group of Harvard professors. Charles Sedgwick Minot chaired the Committee on Experimental Psychology, which circulated questionnaires to test the prevalence of superstition in the community. The five hundred returns, tabulated by sex and age, showed by simple totals "the prevalence of a tendency toward superstition" and "the willingness to treat a certain superstition with respect, or at least a show of it," especially among women.[32]

The Committee on Thought-Transference, chaired by E. C. Pickering from the Harvard Observatory, attempted to ascertain the extent of telepathic powers in the population at large by soliciting random numbers and diagrams from individuals who believed they were reproducing what was hidden away and known only to the experimenters. Telepathy was not found to be widespread, except that numerous similarities were noted to occur frequently in people's responses. Further investigation revealed that specific individuals always chose such numbers or diagrams without knowing why, but the motifs reappeared across individuals. The committee dubbed this phenomenon the number or diagram habit and pointed out that it had no relation whatever to telepathic abilities.

The Committee on Apparitions and Hallucinations, chaired by Josiah Royce from the philosophy department, collected numerous examples of phantasms witnessed by individuals. The work of this committee was performed in conjunction with the International Census of Hallucinations, launched by the Congress of Experimental Psychology in Paris during 1889, and contributed to the idea that inner phenomena involving the subconscious were somehow related to the psychology of mental imagery.

The Committee on Mediumship, originally chaired by William Norton Bullard, the Boston physician, was eventually taken over by William James. Under James's guidance numerous individual mediums were investigated. Extensive verbatim transcripts were taken of trance sessions. James's biggest discovery here was Mrs. Leonora Piper, probably the best studied psychic medium in the early history of psychical research. Healthy, vibrant, and free of neuroses, Mrs. Piper represented for James refutation of the physicians' assertion that the ability to enter trance consciousness was a mark of psychopathology.[33]

James also chaired the Committee on Hypnotism. In the name of this committee, numerous experiments on hypnotic induction and post-hypnotic suggestion were carried on in the laboratory at Harvard. James's intent was to replicate the original observations of Charcot, Binet, Janet, Delboeuf, and Bernheim, the physicians and scientists who were at the forefront of the so-called French Experimental Psychology of the Subconscious, whose work had been further studied by F.W.H. Myers, Frank Podmore, and Edmund Gurney of the Society for Psychical Research in London.

The work of this committee was important for primarily two reasons. First, the British psychical researchers were the main conduit to the United States for the latest developments in scientific psychotherapy in England, the Netherlands, Europe, and Switzerland. Through them the earliest work of Pierre Janet on dissociation and multiple consciousness was first corroborated and transmitted to the United States in 1887, and in the early 1890s the British group, through James and his Boston colleagues, became the route through which first news of the work of Breuer and Freud on hysteria entered the American psychological literature.[34]

Second, the laboratory work on hypnotism at Harvard was the basis for the adoption of light hypnosis, crystal gazing, and automatic writing as both diagnostic and therapeutic regimes. Following James's experiments, physicians who ran the outpatient departments at the Massachusetts General and Boston City hospitals, such as James Jackson Putnam and Morton Prince, applied such techniques to large numbers of patients suffering from ambulatory psychoneuroses.[35]

Conclusions

The evidence, then, suggests the following picture. Experimental psychology in the hands of William James originated primarily in experimental physiology. But, while the emphasis with Putnam and Bowditch was on the superiority of German science, James clearly remained the exponent of the French clinical and experimental tradition. Moreover, James tempered his interpretation of European science with the more immediate and uniquely American philosophy of science put forth by Wright and Peirce. The result for James was a program that defined the new psychology as the scientific study of consciousness in ways that could be empirically explored in a laboratory setting.

Moreover, the history of James's early involvement with experimentation shows the link he developed between experimental physiology, psychical research, and experimental psychopathology. This line of thinking is further corroborated by the setup of James's laboratory in the 1880s, the focus of which was clearly on issues related to the mind-body problem. Since James still had to teach the full spectrum of methods then available in psychology, English mental testing, questionnaire methods, and techniques in German experimental psychophysics were given their due, as well as the French emphasis on hypnosis and automatic writing, which had also been taken up by the British psychical researchers.

But James's laboratory investigations, especially after 1884, were clearly harnessed in service of the scientific committees of the newly formed American Society for Psychical Research. The effect of those committees, particularly those controlled by James himself, was twofold. First, through James the ASPR acted as a conduit for introducing French and English experimental work on hypnotism and psychotherapeutics into American experimental psychology. Second, the replication of this work in James's laboratory created scientific legitimacy for the application of hypnosis and automatic writing in clinical neurology through the local hospitals. The outcome of these applications was soon to make Boston the center of developments in scientific psychotherapy in the English-speaking world between 1884 and 1920.[36]

Yet even as these developments were unfolding, by the late 1880s James's attention was focused on bringing a more all-encompassing project to completion, one that would have even larger repercussions for the establishment of psychology as a science.

Chapter Three

CONSCIOUSNESS AND THE SUBCONSCIOUS: THE CONUNDRUM OF *THE PRINCIPLES*

WILLIAM JAMES'S *The Principles of Psychology* broke upon the scientific world in 1890. Its main contribution was to take the study of mental life from the abstract philosophers and, by defining thought and feeling as physiological, to firmly establish psychology as a legitimate discipline within the domain of the natural sciences. James first signed a contract for the book in 1878 to produce the text in two years. That it took twelve showed the unswerving loyalty of his publisher, Henry Holt. But the gamble paid off handsomely, as James's *Principles* is the only pre-1900 textbook in psychology still in print after a century, and the *Briefer Course*, which immediately followed—a cut-and-paste version of the larger work—was for many years a standard textbook for most psychology courses in the United States. The long passage of time between first contract and final publication also allowed James to develop more fully some of the ideas for which he has now become most famous—the stream of thought, which in its flights and perchings bears us ever onward; the self and its biological, material, social, and spiritual aspects; habit, the great flywheel of society; and our emotions, which exist, not as abstract entities in themselves, but as the physiological complex of our immediate perceptions.

When it finally appeared in the autumn of 1890, James was relieved to get what he called "the enormous rat, which . . . ten years' gestation has brought forth" out of his hands. To his publisher he wrote: "No one could be more disgusted than I at the sight of the book . . . a loathsome, distended, tumified, bloated, dropsical mass, testifying to nothing but two facts: 1st, that there is no such thing as a *science* of psychology, and 2nd, that W.J. is an incapable."[1]

Nevertheless, as soon as *The Principles* came out, it was an instant classic. James's biographer, Ralph Barton Perry, noted that it was widely read, even by people who were under no obligation to read it, largely because it was so well written. And despite the fact that it was viewed with some shade of disapproval by laboratory experimentalists and systematizers alike, everyone of any note in psychology felt immediately compelled to get their opinion about it into print.

James Sully, the English psychologist, referred to James's "intellectual larking." He believed the book was made up only of assorted articles with no plan, and he thought the style questionable.[2] Charles Peirce, the mathematical logician, wrote in *The Nation* that it was "the most important contribution that has been made to the subject in many years." But he also said that James had indulged in "idiosyncrasies of diction and tricks of language such as usually spring up in households of great talent." G. Stanley Hall, James's former student at Harvard and by then editor of *The American Journal of Psychology*, derided the unscientific nature of the work, describing James as "an *impressionist* in psychology."

Yet the book also had its lion's share of supporters. The *Revue Philosophique* called it "*une oeuvre glorieuse.*" Carl Stumpf in Berlin, a fellow-critic of Wundt, said that James had written "the best of all psychologies, such as would make the Germans envious." George Santayana, James's younger colleague in philosophy at Harvard, said, "It would be pedantry to regret the loss of logical unity in a book so rich and living, in which a generous nature breaks out at every point." And the literary critic William Dean Howells remarked that James wrote "with a poetic sense of his facts and with an acute pleasure in their presentation." The only problem, according to Howells, was that James "had come dangerously close to writing a *popular* book."

With such diversity of opinion, we must ask, just what was significant about this definitive text, written as it was in almost the style of a psychological novel? To answer, there is significant consensus among James scholars that the primary contribution of the work was James's stated intention to define the science of mental life in terms of a strict positivist epistemology.

On the first page of the preface, James made it clear that he intended to keep close to the point of view of natural science throughout his book. According to this point of view, "every natural science assumes certain data uncritically, and declines to challenge the elements between which its own 'laws' obtain, and from which its own deductions are carried on."[3] He then proceeded to define psychology as "the science of finite minds," which assumes as its basic data three things: (1) thoughts and feelings, (2) a physical world in time and space with which thoughts and feelings coexist, and (3) what thoughts and feelings know about the physical world. While these are discussable topics, his point was that for a positivistic science, their discussion represented metaphysics and was therefore beyond the scope of his book: "All attempts to explain our phenomenally given thoughts as products of deeper-lying entities (whether the latter be named 'Soul,' 'Transcendental Ego,' 'Ideas,' or 'Elementary Units of Consciousness') are metaphysical. This book consequently rejects both the associationistic and the spiritualist theories; and in this strictly positivistic point of view consists the only feature of it for which I feel tempted to claim originality."[4]

His position, however, held the important caveat that metaphysics had its place, that it was simply inappropriate for an infant science. Positivism was necessary to launch psychology, but sooner or later "the data assumed by psychology, just like those assumed by physics and the other natural sciences, must some time be overhauled," and "the effort to overhaul them is clearly and thoroughly metaphysics."

But the problem in 1890, according to James, was twofold. Psychology needed to divorce itself from metaphysics to be launched, and metaphysics, in any case, was not yet well enough developed for its task of overhauling the sciences. By attacking associationism and spiritualism, James was, in each case, eliminating a metaphysic that was "fragmentary, irresponsible, and half-awake, and unconscious that she is metaphysical."[5] He chose instead to treat "our passing thoughts as integers" and to regard "the mere laws of their co-existence with brain states as the ultimate laws for our science." How far he achieved this agenda remains to be seen, since quite a bit of metaphysical speculation eventually crept into his text. But the scientific purists who were his detractors remained only a handful and the educated public bought his program, believing, from James's charm and style as much as from his data and his arguments, that psychology could be positivistic and still remain a human science.

James's various acknowledgments tip us off to the range of his prevailing attitude. First, he dedicated the book to François Pillon, editor of the *Critique philosophique.* The reason for this is not hard to find. At the heart of James's psychology was a person-centered science, derived largely from the influence of French experimental physiology and from a small knot of philosophers who had been instrumental, not only in James's recovery from his near-suicidal episode, but in expanding James's international reputation.[6] As editors of a widely read philosophical journal, Pillon, with Renouvier and Delboeuf (a Belgian), had arranged for most of James's early essays to be translated from the American and British literature beginning in the 1870s. This came about partly because Renouvier's ideas on free will had influenced James during his recovery from depression, and James had gratefully begun a correspondence with Renouvier thereafter. Renouvier then introduced James to Pillon. James was thus known to the French as a Frenchman from the beginning of his career, and his acclaim in France had contributed in no small part to further renown in England and America. His dedication to Pillon was a friendly acknowledgment of this long-standing debt.

We get further clues concerning James's agenda in the preface, where he extended "gratitude for the inspiration I have got from the writings of J. S. Mill, Lotze, Renouvier, Hodgson, and Wundt." As last in the line of British thinkers, from Locke through Berkeley and Hume, whose philosophy James would eventually renovate, Mill was a philosophical empiricist "unafflicted with the closed mind of the positivists."[7] James found Lotze "soundly scientific without prejudice to ulterior metaphysical considerations."[8] Renouvier was the thoroughgoing empiricist in whose pluralism James discovered "the right to believe what his moral will dictated" and "a philosophical justification of the attitude required for . . . personal salvation."[9] Hodgson, a philosophical influence equal to Renouvier, led James to see that all phenomena contain an objective and subjective aspect, "a distinction which appears, on a certain level of reflection, *within* the field of consciousness."[10] As for Wundt, "in spite of his intolerable sleekness and way of *soaping* everything on to you by plausible transitions so as to make it run continuous," James found "every now and then a compendiously stated truth . . . which is nourishing or instructive."[11]

At the same time, in his preface James lauded "the intellectual companionship (to name only five names) of Chauncey Wright and Charles Peirce in old times, and more recently Stanley Hall, James Putnam, and Josiah Royce." It would take a separate book to analyze the influences of these figures, but at least they can be roughly estimated. Wright and Peirce represented not only James's early escape from Henry James Sr.'s religious philosophy, as well as James's first introduction to science, but more importantly they stood for the prevailing mood in the developing philosophy of science at Harvard that was only reaching maturity in the 1890s, and of which James had become an integral and (according to President Eliot and professors such as Putnam and Bowditch) indispensable part. Hall had been James's intellectual companion in the new science, first as a student and then as a colleague, until Hall's own agenda had begun by the late 1880s to grate on their relationship. Putnam had drawn James into the earliest scientific experiments in neuropathology in America in the 1870s, only to convert to psychotherapeutics himself through James's work in experimental psychopathology in the 1880s. As for the great Royce, his doctrine of the Absolute provided no mere foil for James's pluralism. Royce was the arch monist and Christian apologist in a secular philosophy department that, nevertheless, stood for an ethical and teleological psychology of self-realization. There can be little doubt that he had taken Henry James Sr.'s place in the constellation of William's cosmology. Royce, in turn, had followed James into psychical research and abnormal psychology.

As for its content, Rand Evans maintains that the continuity of James's book lies in its positivistic emphasis on a naturalistic psychology in which thought itself is the thinker.[12] In my reading, *The Principles* still had at least two centers of gravity that were not easily reconcilable (probably a not inaccurate reflection of James's own state of mind at the time).

The major paradox, for our purposes, lay in James's description of the normal personality. His stated agenda for the book was to build it around traditional classifications such as instinct, sensation, perception, reasoning, discrimination, the will, and the emotions, and he tried to maintain a focus on the so-called New Science, meaning physiological psychology, or the correlation between mental states and brain states. At the same time, his text kept bursting out of these bounds because he also tried to paint a more all-encompassing picture of the whole personality in its abnormal as well as supernormal manifestations. This created a clash of epistemologies, because of the implication that "something more" lay beyond the cognitive center of attention.

To describe the accomplishments of the new laboratory science, James needed only to refer to physiological advances on localization of brain function and to the extensive psychophysical literature on vision and hearing, especially in the German language.[13] This he did in numerous places. In volume one, for instance, he refers in chapter 3 to extensive experiments in reaction time, while in chapter 9, on "Attention," he mixes pedagogic maxims with details of laboratory experiments. Ditto with chapter 13 on "Discrimination and Comparison." Chapter 14, on "Association," is one long metaphysical statement punctuated with results from the laboratory. Chapter 15, on "The Perception of Time," also contains long descriptions of experimental measurements. The results of experiments based on quantification are also densely presented in his three chapters on perception in volume 2.

But to consider the abnormal manifestations of sensations and brain states, James relied on the literature derived from the French Experimental Psychology of the Subconscious, which forms important sections of his chapters "The Relation of Minds to Other Things," "The Self," and "Hypnotism."

To consider the possibility of training human faculties beyond their normal but undeveloped range of functioning, as he did in his chapters on habit and in his discussion of double consciousness, he invoked a moral philosophy of character development. His sources here, in addition to the English moral philosophy of Carpenter and Maudsley, encompassed the psychical researches of Edmund Gurney and F.W.H. Myers.[14]

The problem was that psychophysics, abnormal psychology, and psychical research remained three historically unreconciled sources of empirical knowledge, each trying to supplant the influence of the older moral philosophy while separately claiming their own legitimacy in science. Psychophysical measurements became the back door through which psychologists attempted to identify with the German laboratory ideal in science generally. The positivist epistemology of Helmholtz and

Mach admitted no mental constructs beyond a conceptual interpretation of physical measurements. In the Jamesean scheme, this meant that
the thinker could still be the thought.

But abnormal psychology, which had arisen in the context of medicine, chiefly through French contributions in neurology, had posited
the existence of dissociated states, suggesting to James the possibility of
different fields of consciousness within mental life. If there could be
multiple thoughts, only one of which might be in the field of immediate
awareness, could there also be multiple thinkers in the same person? If
so, which one was the true self?

Meanwhile, psychical researchers in England, breaking completely
with the reductionism of the materialists, had proposed that clairvoyant
and telepathic abilities were associated with higher evolutionary states of
consciousness.[15] By presenting all three epistemologies under one cover,
James, despite his many caveats to the contrary, created an impression in
the naive reader of their unity, as if each were guided by the same underlying assumptions and methods. To the more sophisticated observer, on
the other hand, his pages seemed to abound with contradictions.

James was not unaware of this situation himself. While he maintained
his positivistic focus on the thinker as the thought, he kept injecting
metaphysics into the book, *and he said so* in numerous places.

In his chapter "The Functions of the Brain" (chapter 5) he first discussed whether or not "the cortex was the sole organ of consciousness in
man."[16] Abruptly, he then turned to restitution of function, which he
considered a "problem, not so metaphysical."[17] He spent an entire chapter on the automaton theory, only to proclaim that, "on purely *a priori*
and *quasi*-metaphysical grounds, [the theory] is an *unwarrantable imperti-
nence in the present state of psychology.*"[18] Then, he claimed that, even after
"swamping the reader with too much metaphysics" by describing the
automaton theory, he intended to follow with a chapter on "The Mind
Stuff Theory," which he states would be "exclusively metaphysical."[19]
Here, he refutes the associationists' theory of the compounding of consciousness—that more complex states are made up of smaller, simpler
aggregates. In his chapter on "The Self," he reiterates that the question
of "just who the thinker is" remains an "ulterior metaphysical inquiry,"[20]
although he says he will allow himself "to indulge in some metaphysical
reflections" on this subject at the end of the book.[21]

We also have numerous examples of James indulging in metaphysics
without explicitly telling us, although he appears to have been aware of
what he was doing. One of the most glaring examples concerns James's
mixing of different levels of epistemological discourse. In chapter 2 on
"The Functions of the Brain," for instance, while discussing the education of the cerebral hemispheres, he writes as follows:

Nerve-currents run in through sense-organs, and whilst provoking reflex acts in the lower centers, they arouse ideas in the hemispheres, which either permit the reflexes in question, check them, or substitute others for them. All ideas being in the last resort reminiscences, the question to answer is: *How can processes become organized in the hemispheres which correspond to reminiscences in the mind.*[22]

He then appends a footnote:

I hope that the reader will take no umbrage at my so mixing the physical and the mental, and talking of reflex acts and hemispheres and reminiscences in the same breath, as if they were homogeneous quantities and factors of one causal chain. I have done so deliberately; for although I admit that from the radically physical point of view it is easy to conceive of the chain of events amongst the cells and fibers as complete in itself, and that whilst so conceiving it one need make no mention of 'ideas,' I yet suspect that point of view of being an unreal abstraction.[23]

"The radically physical point of view," in other words, moves only within its own closed system of logical consistency, but the true state of affairs is that there might be no absolutely closed system. This was the common-sense position, he said, that he would later detail more fully. Until then, since "language lends itself so much more easily to the mixed way of describing," he intended to continue mixing his metaphors.

The Metaphysics of the Psychologist

This nexus between the brain and the mind was a recurring metaphysical theme. In discussing "Some General Conditions of Brain Activity" (chapter 3), for instance, James had criticized the associationists' scheme that every mental idea corresponds to a single brain cell. While this was, of course, absurd, "In some way our diagram must be realized in the brain; but surely in no such visible and palpable way as we at first suppose."[24] He then admitted in a footnote that all such schemes are ultimately symbolic. He justifies them elsewhere, however, by claiming: "Our usual scientific custom of interpreting hidden molecular events after the analogy of visible massive ones enables us to frame easily an abstract and general scheme which the physical changes in question *may* be like."[25] The wonder is that this modeling of objective reality works so often. Nevertheless, James asserts, it never is an exact duplicate. Its claims are always provisional.

What *was* the mechanism by which inner mental states and outer objects were related? The question had more than one dimension. When he said that "the word on the page does not pass from the page into the mind directly. Rather, the duplication of the object as an inner construction must take place,"[26] he as much meant to describe the phenomenon as he did point to the limits of psychology's ability to address the problem. By stating that "the dualism of subject and object and their pre-established harmony is what the psychologist as such must assume,"[27] he also felt dutybound to recognize the metaphysical boundary of this commitment:

> What must be admitted is that the definite images of traditional psychology form but the very smallest part of our minds as they actually live. The traditional psychology talks like one who should say a river consists of nothing but pailsful, spoonsful, quartpotsful, barrelsful, and other moulded form of water. Even were the pails and the pots all actually standing in the stream, still between them the free water would continue to flow. It is just this free water of consciousness that psychologists resolutely overlook. Every definite image in the mind is steeped and dyed in the free water that flows around it. With it goes the sense of its relations, near and remote, the dying echo of whence it came to us, the dawning sense of whither it is to lead. The significance, the value, the image is all in this halo or penumbra that surrounds and escorts it,—or rather that is fused into one with it and has become bone of its bone and flesh of its flesh; leaving it, it is true, an image of the same *thing* it was before, but making it an image of that thing newly taken and freshly understood.[28]

Psychologists, in other words, tend to take their categories as more objectively real than experience itself. The opposite is quite the case, however. On the proper understanding of the term "object" in psychology, James had said: "When we make a statement 'Columbus discovered America in 1492,' and are then asked what the object of consciousness is, we are likely to say it is either Columbus or America. But this is a vicious use of speech. The object is not some abstracted part, but really the entire content or deliverance, nothing more nor less." In our abstractions for experimental purposes, however, we lose almost all the whole. "The mass of our thinking vanishes forever, beyond the hope of recovery, and psychology only gathers up a few of the crumbs that fall from the feast."[29]

James in one place waxes poetic on the difference between science and the experienced world, saying that, while normative generalizations provide a basis for the rules, "each one of us," nevertheless, "dichotomizes the Kosmos in a different place."[30] Yet in other parts of the book, he becomes very reductionistic:

> In Chapter X . . . we must . . . *ask ourselves whether, after all, the ascertainment of a blank unmediated correspondence, term for term, of the succession of states of consciousness with the succession of total brain-processes, be not the simplest psycho-*

physic formula, and the last word of a psychology which contents itself with verifiable
laws, and seeks only to be clear, and to avoid unsafe hypotheses.[31]

James was aware, however, that matters of individual difference were
not excluded forever, only postponed. In his chapter on "The Self," he
writes:

> The reader will please understand that I am quite willing to leave the hy-
> pothesis of the transcendental Ego as a substitute for the passing Thought
> open to discussion on *general speculative grounds*. Only *in this book* I prefer to
> stick by the common-sense assumption that we have successive conscious
> states, because all psychologists make it, and because one does not see how
> there can be a Psychology written which does not postulate such thoughts
> as its ultimate data. The data of all natural sciences become in turn subjects
> of a critical treatment more refined than that which the sciences themselves
> accord; and so it may fare in the end with our passing Thought. We have
> ourselves seen . . . that the *sensible* certainty of its existence is less strong than
> is usually assumed.[32]

This appears to be nothing less than a change of mind in midstream, as
if there were warring worlds of meaning, struggling for control of the
same author's pen. But when one looks closely at this clash of metaphysical systems that seems to occur in *The Principles*, a pattern emerges.
James periodically reasserts his positivistic stance after making frequent
allusions to metaphysical questions. Whenever this happens, I think he
is constantly forced to reaffirm, as well, the fact that positivism and physicalism contain their own implied metaphysics.

His discussion of "The Methods and Snares of Psychology" is particularly germane to this point. In this chapter, James states the "irreducibles
of psychology." These include: the psychologist, the thought studied, the
thought's object, and the psychologist's reality.

The psychologist must become objective when he reflects on his own
conscious states, in the same way that he considers the minds of others
as a class of objects in nature to be studied. James considered it highly
important that this natural science view be understood, which he introduced at the beginning of the first volume of *The Principles*.

Erkenntnisstheorie, criticism of the faculty of knowledge, was the name
he gave to the natural science view, pointing out that the psychologist
necessarily becomes such an *Erkenntnisstheoretiker*. It was a Kantian term
which James chose to redefine. The psychologist "does not inquire
into the possibility of knowledge *überhaupt*."[33] Rather, he assumes it to
be possible and does not doubt its presence from the beginning of his
inquiry. He may on occasion, however, pronounce such knowledge
true or false and trace the reasons why it has become part of one or
the other.[34]

James goes on to define the methods of psychology. These are the introspective, which comprises the psychologist's objective assessment of the contents of his own mind; the experimental, as in the ability under certain circumstances to take direct measurements of phenomena; and the comparative, by which James meant the comparison of organisms along the phylogenetic scale as a way to place humans in their proper evolutionary perspective. To this list of methods in psychology I would also add the historical, since James himself admits as much by appending a historical note to two different sections in *The Principles*, one in his chapter on association and the other in the chapter on perception. He also claims that there are two ways to study a psychic state: (1) by its content, and (2) by its history.[35]

James then considers the sources of error in psychology. The first is misleading language. Since the language of our experience predates scientific methods, there is always the tendency to take uncritically what is merely subjectively stated. We often falsely assume that because we have named a thing it really must exist and, conversely, that if something has no name it must also have no substantive reality. Second, there is the confusion of the state of consciousness studied with the psychologists' own immediate state of awareness. Here we find the problem of looking at several different phenomena and concluding that all contain the same element, when in fact it is only the phenomenological idea of sameness within the observer and might have no real referent to the objects studied once their real differences are exposed. Third, there is the artificial limitation that all mental states studied must always be conscious. Here, one may presume that the subject should be aware of what is being observed just as the psychologist can plainly see it, but this may not always be the case.[36]

To define psychology, for James, also meant defining psychology's limits. A psychologist, in other words, is a metaphysician of knowledge who has agreed to operate only within certain rules in order to define his activity as science. He remains a philosopher nevertheless, James believes, albeit a more precise one.

HIS OTHER CENTER OF GRAVITY

Thus, two centers of gravity emerge in *The Principles*, each vying for James's attention at different times. The positivistic approach was likely the main idea he had started with in 1878, developing themes such as reasoning, instinct, and the emotions in a physiological context in order to appropriate these categories from the older moral philosophy, subject by subject. By the time he had gotten the book fully under way, James was forced to integrate, especially at the end of his writing twelve years later, the new evidence on experimental psychopathology, which called the reductionistic view of the mind, and hence positivist epistemology, into question.

James's argument against unconscious cerebration in the chapter on "Mind-Stuff Theory," as opposed to his discussion of the subconscious in his chapter on "The Self," reveals this alternative metaphysical center. In the one he takes up the issue of unconscious cerebration and presents more than a dozen points of refutation, while in the other he freely writes about dissociated consciousness. Is he merely contradicting himself on the issue of the unconscious, as some authors have assumed?[37] No, the important conceptual difference between these two chapters is that he appears to be rejecting ideas about the unconscious represented by the tradition of Schopenhauer and von Hartmann and put forward by British writers such as Maudsley, Carpenter, and Lewes.[38] At the same time, James embraces the idea of divided consciousness suggested by the French psychopathologists. For James, as well as the French experimentalists, there is no hypostatized unconscious, as if the unconscious were a thing or entity independent of other states. There are only multiple states of consciousness, each aware or unaware to some degree of the others. Actually, it was an idea that James only half-acknowledged in *The Principles* and did not develop more fully until after 1890.

Another example of this alternative center of gravity can be found in James's formulations on emotion. While the main thrust of *The Principles* is on a cognitive psychology of consciousness, that is, on the functional utility of what we hold at the center of attention, James also argued for a doctrine of relations based on feeling.

In his chapter on automaton theory, for instance, he states that no theory of brain processes is possible to conceive without being derived from a feeling. In "The Relation of Minds to Other Things," (chapter 10), he states, "Feelings are the germ and starting point of cognition, thoughts the developed tree."[39] In "The Stream of Thought" (chapter 11) he discusses the "feeling tone" of each passing thought, attributing reality even to the "feeling of 'and' and of 'if.' "[40] In his chapter on "The Emotions" he rearticulates his theory which had been hotly debated since 1884—that our perceptions of an exciting event are followed by bodily feelings, which only afterward we cognitively label as the emotion. In other words, there is no intermediary abstract entity called an emotion that is invoked between perception and bodily response. Rather, the immediate sensory and motor reverberations of perception *are* the emotions.

No thought exists independently as an isolated entity in the field of awareness. A thought is always colored by feeling tones. Feelings identify an idea as pleasant or repulsive, they link ideas to each other, and they point to a penumbra or fringe. The "halo of relations" around each thought gives richness and meaning as well as subtlety and nuance to our expression. Feelings link our primary thought with others hidden from immediate awareness beyond the margin. They are our link to other dimensions of personality. And if emotions are what give richness and depth to the passing thought, it stands to reason that they are implicated in the meaning and value schemes of the individual. Hence, the study of the emotions opens psychology up to the whole problem of motivation.

This was dangerous ground for the reductionists, as James well knew. Even the inclusion of feelings as the subject matter of a scientific investigation was abhorrent to the laboratory types, because the vagaries of emotion called into question their airtight rational schemes. Thus he also said:

> The desire on the part of men educated in laboratories not to have their physical reasonings mixed up with such incommensurable factors as feelings is certainly very strong. I have heard a most intelligent botanist say, "It is high time for scientific men to protest against the recognition of any such thing as consciousness in a scientific investigation." In a word, feeling constitutes the "unscientific" half of existence, and anyone who enjoys calling himself a 'scientist' will be too happy to purchase an untrammeled homogeneity of terms in the studies of his predilection, at the slight cost of admitting a dualism which, in the same breath that it allows to mind an independent status of being, banishes it to a limbo of causal inertness, from whence no intrusion or interruption on its part need ever be feared.[41]

Again James was recognizing the problem that psychologists avoided studying certain kinds of experience because of their implications for the very methods used in experimentation. Yet James himself did not avoid them.

One potential anomaly that he met head on was his review of various cases of multiple personality. First, there was the Reverend Ansel Bourne, whom James had studied with Richard Hodgson in their official capacity as investigators for the American Society for Psychical Research. Bourne had suddenly disappeared from his home one day and turned up a year later in another state, confused and in a daze. In the interim he had become a merchant with a separate identity and lifestyle, who had no knowledge of his former self as a minister. Upon awakening to the identity of Ansel Bourne, he had no idea where he was or who he had been in the capacity of a merchant. His circumstance had attracted the attention of the ASPR and after investigating the veracity of the man's claims and the events as reported, James was able to help the man partially recover some of his lost memories through hypnosis.

Another example was the case of Mary Reynolds, a young girl who would pass off into a second personality for months at a time. Reynolds was of particular interest because James indicated that the second personality to emerge was actually superior to the normal one. Eventually the second personality became permanent and Mary lived out the remainder of her life in this new identity.

These cases suggest the existence of multiple states of consciousness beyond the waking state, in which personal identity is not continuous within the same person from one state to another. Hence, they call into question the idea that the thinker is always continuously the same. In addition, James's examples suggest that states of consciousness have some intrinsic relation to each other. That they might be higher or lower when compared to the normal was an idea he would develop throughout the 1890s as he expanded his work on abnormal psychology and psychical research and eventually in the psychology of religion.

James's discussion of hypnotism was an important inclusion in his book because it implies a true state change from the supposed continuity of the normal, everyday, waking, cognitive condition that forms the core focus of the rest of the work.[42] This chapter, technically comprising the last discussion of the subject matter of *The Principles*, is the most cogent example of James's psychology after 1890.

James summarized first the various ways in which the hypnotic trance can be induced. Relaxation and vacancy of the the mind are the first prerequisites. Sometimes it is as simple as just telling the subject to close his eyes, relax the muscles, and think of nothing. Leave him for ten minutes, James said, and when you return he will have effectively entered the hypnotic state. The older hypnotists would make passes in a downward direction over the face to initiate and deepen the trance, and upward passes to lighten it. Fixing the gaze on an object, listening to a watch tick, or simply talking to the subject about sleep will all produce the desired results. Hysteric subjects who are particularly susceptible, he said, can be thrown into the trance by pressing on certain parts of the body, such as on the forehead or about the roots of the thumbs.

Likewise the trance may be dispelled instantaneously by commanding the subject, "All right, wake up!" or some other such declarative statement. As in induction, numerous methods for returning the person to the waking state exist. Blowing on the eyelids, sprinkling water on the face, counting backwards, anything will awaken the subject who expects to be awakened in that way. The key is that you must create the expectation before the command is executed. In other words, an appeal must be made indirectly, to states beyond the margin.

James then reviewed the current theories about the hypnotic state. The older view among animal magnetists was that a mysterious force passed between operator and subject, where the entranced person then becomes the operator's puppet. But new scientific studies had dispelled this notion. One such modern view, held by Charcot and his followers at the Salpêtrière in Paris, believed that hypnotism was a pathological state that only occurred in illness and that it had distinct neurophysiological stages. The other reigning theory, held by Bernheim and the rival Nancy School, believed that there was no special change in state of consciousness, and that hypnosis was the effect of suggestion, which occurred in all normal people to one degree or another. James's conclusion was that extreme, heightened suggestibility was obviously the mechanism at work, as Bernheim had stated, and that all of the special stages observed by Charcot were the result of suggestion. However, the Nancy School erred on the most important point, James said; namely, that hypnosis did, in fact, involve a radical change in one's state of consciousness.

James's conjecture was that this altered state was somehow related to sleep and dreaming. Hypnotism, he thought, evoked and enlarged upon the hypnagogic state, or the twilight zone between waking and sleeping through which we all pass every night. In this state, all abstract thought becomes highly pictorial; mental images rather then ideas are the rule; dream sequences, colorful visions, and constantly transforming pictures related more by association than logic dominate the field of attention. Moreover, he said, there is abundant experimental evidence to show that suggestions made during our experiences in this state tend to be immediately acted upon.

James devoted the rest of his chapter to an exposition of the symptoms upon entering the trance state. The first symptom is amnesia. In the earlier stages the patient remembers what happens, but with successive sittings the trances deepen, followed by complete loss of memory afterwards for anything that occurred within the trance. Second is suggestibility, where subjects are abnormally susceptible to all that the operator tells them, so much so that the subjects will follow the commands of no other voice. Third concerns effects produced over the voluntary muscles. In this, the operator tells patients they cannot open their eyes or mouth or unclasp their hands, and the patients are immediately smitten with impotence regarding these behaviors. All manner of symptoms of hysteria, paralysis, contractures, and aphasias for certain words or letters can thus be suggested. Fourth is hallucinations of the senses and illusions of consciousness. Here the subject can be made to think he or she is freezing or burning. Vinegar can be made to taste like champagne, complete with symptoms of accompanying drunkenness; ammonia can be made to smell like cologne, and a broomstick can become a beautiful woman and vivacious dance partner. In this, real sensations can also be abolished, as in the use of hypnosis for surgery involving even the amputation of limbs. And further, negative hallucinations can be suggested, where the subject is made blind to certain people, words, or objects. Fifth is hyperesthesia of the senses, where the sense of touch becomes extremely delicate. In one subject, for instance, it was alleged that when a dime was placed on the back of the neck the subject was able correctly to read off the date from the coin. Sixth is changes in the nutrients of the tissues, which can be brought about through suggestion, even in those physiological processes over which the subject normally has no voluntary control. Sneezing, secretions, reddening and growing pale, alterations in temperature and heartbeat, menstruation, and movement of the bowels may all occur. Even burns and blisters, and bleeding from the skin and nose, can be suggested, thus explaining, for instance, cases of stigmata among intensely devout Catholic nuns. And last is posthypnotic suggestion. Here, subjects can be given instructions in the trance which they will faithfully carry out upon awakening. Moreover, they will profess no knowledge of the order they are carrying out, but at the same time they will remain will-less to prevent it.[43]

The technique of hypnosis was to become an important tool in the development of scientific psychotherapy precisely because it was a way to artificially expose in the laboratory a host of phenomena that normally lay outside the field of normal waking awareness. For the first time investigators had the means scientifically to manipulate hidden mental processes and by so doing to verify the reality of multiple states of consciousness.

But we cannot leave *The Principles* without reiterating the point that, while James's intention had been to launch a positivistic science through a cognitive psychology of consciousness, his text also introduces at least the physiological reality of multiple states of consciousness and suggests several important means of getting at them. The positivistic agenda appears to be the product of his earlier thinking, while he seems to have appended the intrusion of multiple states in the last years of writing. Multiple states were important to consider, but had to be inserted as an afterthought to the cognitive psychology of his earlier commitment. Thus,
in the same text, even within the same chapters, James appeared to vacillate between two poles. The metaphysical dilemma this posed for the mind-body problem would force him to renovate and expand his view of psychology beyond a purely cognitive and positivistic science and lead him eventually to the birth of his fully fledged metaphysic of radical empiricism.

Chapter Four

THE REALITY OF MULTIPLE STATES:
ABNORMAL PSYCHOLOGY AND
PSYCHICAL RESEARCH

BY 1890, physiological psychology had become differentiated into experimental psychology, by which was meant experimental laboratory psychophysics and mental testing, and psychopathology, meaning the
French experimental psychology of the subconscious. German science
was fast being propounded as the universal ideal. Mental testing was recognized as the genius of the British, while psychopathology quickly became relegated to the category of French provincialism, at best a practice of medicine rather than a science of psychology.

James viewed the picture somewhat differently from America. In his
eyes, psychology was a functional science that spanned a variety of subject areas and incorporated numerous, disparate methods under an um-
brella that acknowledged the importance of evolutionary theory and empiricism, as well as the efficacy of personal consciousness. His focus was
not on science, but on the person, and the newest and most expansive
developments in the discipline were occurring through the scientific
study of the subconscious. German science, and hence German laboratory psychology, denied the evidence for the reality of the subconscious
and insisted, instead, on its own supremacy on epistemological grounds.
Psychophysical measurements, reaction-time experiments, and the controlled introspective analysis of consciousness in the laboratory were
thought to be the only legitimate methods by which psychology could
most closely identify with the natural sciences. But in James's view, the
Germans stood against the larger trend of functional psychology that
linked research activities in what can be roughly termed the French-
Swiss-English-and-American psychotherapeutic axis.[1]

Within this axis, the influence of the French on American psychopathology, especially in Boston, was extensive. Charcot's work, through his
closest disciple, Pierre Janet, became widely known as the basis for the
so-called psychogenic hypothesis, referring to the influence of the mind
on the body. According to this new view, traumatic memories could be
converted by symbolic means into both mental and physical symptoms.
At the same time, psychogenesis meant that mental diseases of no known

organic origin and the emotional component underlying all types of physical illness could be approached through the new techniques in psychology. Exposure to "psychotherapeutics," as such methods came to be called in certain medical centers both in the U.S. and abroad, became part of the routine training of certain young physicians who would later make important contributions to medical psychology.

The rise of scientific psychotherapy in America received its impetus from rapid developments in experimental psychopathology throughout the 1890s. Some items on these subjects occasionally appeared in the pages of the *Journal of Nervous and Mental Disease* and the *American Journal of Insanity*, but the emphasis of the psychiatrists remained largely biological. G. Stanley Hall's *American Journal of Psychology*, begun in 1888, continued to report on the latest developments in psychology and psychiatry from abroad, except that Hall increasingly began to favor reporting from the German literature on laboratory subjects. James Mark Baldwin and James McKeen Cattell launched the *Psychological Review* in 1894, which tried to give a more balanced view of the new developments in psychology and to report on the latest American work that was not filtered through Hall's particular scientific and philosophic bias. Here, at least, psychotherapeutic topics received a regular hearing, largely through articles and reviews by William James.

This was also the period when psychology, psychiatry, and medicine began to organize against the spiritualists and mental healers. The irregular practitioners, already a large and thriving community, were making fantastic but unsubstantiated claims about their faith cures. Yet, by their advocacy of psychosomatic ideals, the spiritual healers attracted large numbers of the psychologically ill ready to pay almost any price to be cured, and *patients appeared to get better under their care*. Again, William James emerged as their strongest advocate. To them, he became something of a folk hero. James's own motives led him to become involved, not because of issues concerning the question of life-after-death, or clairvoyance and telepathy, but by virtue of the fact that the irregulars were the only ones dealing directly with problems of the subconscious.[2] Scientific laboratory psychologists, meanwhile, because of their epistemological constraints, continue to ignore these issues even today. As a result, most of James's contributions to experimental psychopathology and to practical psychotherapeutics remain little known.

At the same time, James's various essays and reports have remained scattered throughout a wide expanse of literature from the period not readily accessible to any but the most ardent devotee of James scholarship. Their recovery shows the inextricable relationship between abnormal psychology and psychical research during this period; they indicate a climate of psychotherapeutic practice that was at once thought to be scientifically legitimate while remaining rich in religious overtones; and they point to a psychology of character development that incorporates the iconography of the transcendent into a scientific model of personality.

THE HIDDEN SELF

The first piece that needs to be recovered from this little-known era of James's psychology is his essay "The Hidden Self," originally published in *Scribner's Magazine* in 1890, and thereafter lost to historians in the international roar of acclaim James received from publication of his long-awaited *Principles* at about the same time.[3]

In "The Hidden Self," James introduced the American reading public to the scientific advances of the French Experimental Psychology of the Subconscious; he acknowledged the preeminence of Pierre Janet in the field of psychotherapeutics; and, in a popular and widely read format, he set forth the experimental evidence for the reality of subconscious states.

Anticipating numerous objections beforehand, James first took up the strangeness of his topic. This strangeness, he felt, occurred because normal waking consciousness remains forever familiar only with itself and is fearful of anything beyond the margin of the known. But by paying attention to the "unclassified residuum," James said, one sets in motion not only changes in consciousness but also scientific revolutions. Such a revolution in thinking was then underway, James pointed out, with regard to phenomena called "mystical" and "occult," now made more understandable to consciousness by the new scientific study of hypnotism.

It is only natural, he continued, that we should see these advances coming from France, always the home of character. French literature had already established itself as a genre in which the expression of all variations of human nature was possible. Thus, where the minute and faithful observation of abnormal personality was concerned, French science should take the lead. In particular, since the work of the Salpêtrière and Nancy schools was already so well known, James proposed to introduce some new observations by summarizing Pierre Janet's doctoral thesis, "L'Automatisme psychologique" (1889), which had caused such a commotion abroad when it was first published the previous summer.

In the same breath, James also proposed to review the work of Alfred Binet. Binet had been the foremost exponent of the the Salpêtrière School in the mid-1880s, but he had not weathered well the intense public criticism of Charcot's theories. His reputation had been somewhat eclipsed in France, but he nevertheless had established a following in the

United States when Paul Carus, editor of the *Monist* and the *Open Court*, opened the pages of his journals to translations of Binet's work on dissociation and multiple consciousness. Binet's then most recent contribution in the American literature had been a widely read monograph entitled "On Double Consciousness."[4]

Both Janet and Binet, James maintained, "may be called contributors to the comparative science of trance-states,"[5] and the description of their various cases was highly suggestive. But in the end, James focused mainly on Janet, indicating by editorial fiat Janet's ascendency in Charcot's circle.

Janet's most important contribution was experimental evidence for the emergence of multiple states of consciousness in hysteric patients. Hysteria in its extreme form consisted of pathological alterations in the perception of the senses and in the functioning of physical organs. One or both eyes may become blind, or half the field of vision in each eye may disappear. The patient may report tunnel vision or the total loss of sensation for colors. Hearing, taste, and smell may be similarly effected. Most striking are the cutaneous anesthesias, James said. These appear as patches of insensibility all over the body, a phenomenon well known to the old witch-finders. Anesthesia can effect an entire lateral side of the body from head to foot. Indeed, the entire skin, mucous membranes, hands, face, feet, muscles, and joints can be effected without the other vital functions being disturbed.

Janet found that by throwing the hysteric into a deeper hypnotic trance a completely different personality seemed to emerge, one that had none of the defects of the normal diseased condition, but appeared much healthier and also knew all about the troubles of the waking personality. At yet a deeper level, a third type would emerge that had still other characteristics and had knowledge of the other two personalities. It was as if separate states existed within the person, each with partial characteristics of the whole. Whenever one type emerged, the individual identity, and hence all the memories and experiences of the others, disappeared. With this new type, the developmental stage of the person at the time of the original trauma would also emerge, hence the frequent appearance and demeanor of a child in cases of multiple personality. These different selves, moreover, not only succeed one another, but actually coexist simultaneously.

Citing the case of Léonie, James quoted Janet, *in extenso*:

This woman, whose life sounds more like an improbable romance than a genuine history, has had attacks of natural somnambulism since the age of three years. She has been hypnotized constantly, by all sorts of persons, from the age of sixteen upwards, and she is now forty-five. Whilst her normal life developed in one way in the midst of her poor country surroundings, her second life was passed in drawing-rooms and doctor's offices, and naturally took an entirely different direction. To-day, when in her normal state, this poor peasant-woman is a serious and rather sad person, calm and slow, very mild with everyone, and extremely timid; to look at her one would never suspect the personage which she contains. But hardly is she put to sleep hypnotically than a metamorphosis occurs. Her face is no longer the same. She keeps her eyes closed, it is true, but the acuteness of her other senses supplies their place. She is gay, noisy, restless, sometimes unsupportably so. She remains good-natured, but has acquired a singular tendency to irony and sharp jesting. Nothing is more curious than to hear her, after sitting when she has received a visit from strangers who wished to see her asleep. She gives a word-portrait of them, apes their manners, pretends to know their little ridiculous aspects and passions, and for each invents a romance. To this character must be added the possession of an enormous number of recollections whose existence she does not even suspect when awake, for her amnesia of them is complete. . . . She refuses the name of Léonie, and takes that of Léontine (or Léonie 2), to which her magnetizers had accustomed her. "That good woman is not myself," she says, "she is too stupid." . . . To herself Léontine (or Léonie 2), she attributes all the sensations and all the actions; in a word, all the conscious experiences, which she has undergone in somnambulism, and knits them together to make the history of her already long life. To Léonie 1, on the other hand, she exclusively ascribes the events lived through in waking hours. I [Janet] was at first struck by an important exception to the rule, and was disposed to think that there might be something arbitrary in this partition of her recollections. In the normal state Léonie has a husband and children. But Léonie 2, the somnambulist, whilst acknowledging the children as her own, attributes the husband to "the other." This choice is perhaps explicable, but it followed no rule. It was not till later that I learned that her magnetizers in early days, as audacious as certain hypnotizers of recent date, had somnabulized her for her first accouchements, and that she had lapsed into that state spontaneously in the later ones. Léonie 2 was thus quite right in ascribing to herself the children—since it was she who had had them—and the rule that her first trance-state forms a different personality was not broken. But it is the same with her second state of trance. When after the renewed passes, syncope, etc., she reaches the condition which I have called Léonie 3, she is another person still. Serious and grave, instead of being a restless child, she speaks slowly and moves but little. Again she separates herself from the waking Léonie 1. "A good but rather stupid woman," she says, "and not me." And she also separates herself from Léonie 2. "How can you see anything of me in that crazy creature?" she says. "Fortunately I am nothing for her!"[6]

It was even possible, James said, for the field of associations to become so widened in one of the deeper somnambulistic states that the patient would recount to the hypnotist some traumatic incident, long forgotten by waking consciousness, immediately after which the hysteric symptoms began. By this means the therapist now had a clue to the origin and hence the cure of the malady.

James then gave the details of Janet's case of Marie, a nineteen-year-old girl who had come to the hospital in desperate condition. Her symptoms included monthly convulsive crises, chills, fever, delirium, and attacks of terror, together with various shifting anesthesias and contractures and a fixed blindness in the left eye. During her first seven months, Janet had taken little notice of her as she underwent the usual course of treatment, including the water cure and ordinary hypnotic suggestion.

When she fell into a despair, Janet attempted to throw her into a deeper trance, hoping to uncover the remote psychological antecedents of her disease. He succeeded beyond his expectations, for both her early memories and the internal memory of her crisis came flooding back in deep trance. From this condition, Janet learned three important things: the periodic chill, fever, and delirium were the effect of a foolish immersion in cold water when she was thirteen. The subconscious self repeated the episode as a hallucination at regular intervals, which the waking personality experienced only as periodic chills and fever. Her periodic attacks of terror came from another experience. When she was sixteen she had seen an old woman killed by falling from a height. The subconscious self, James explained, saw fit to believe itself present as the lady fell whenever the other crises came on. As for the hysterical blindness in her left eye, Marie revealed that this came from an episode when she was six. At that time she had been forced against her will to sleep in the same bed with a child who bore a disgusting eruption on the left side of her face. Marie had subsequently developed a similar eruption of her own, which disappeared after a few years but was replaced with anesthesia of the skin and blindness of the eye.

To alleviate these symptoms, James told his audience, Janet hypnotized Marie and took her back in her imagination to the earlier dates. He took her back to the bed at age six, and, once the hallucination was evoked, he altered it in the girl's mind. The young companion in the bed was made to appear without the eruption and was described as charming until Marie was able in her mind to caress without fear this new object of her imagination. Likewise, the scene of the cold immersion was given a different and harmless result. And the episode of the old woman's fall was changed into a comical ending. After these episodes in subconscious reeducation, all of Marie's previous symptoms disappeared as if by magic. No symptoms reappeared at the writing up of Janet's case. The woman had, in fact, gained weight, became physically changed in her well condition, and was also no longer hypnotizable.

James then ends the essay with some important observations. He asserts first that the American mind-curers and Christian Scientists unquestionably get results no less remarkable than this, although by very different methods. Second, he links the British psychical researchers with the French neurologists, all of whom, he said, had made the most scientific progress in fathoming the real power of the imagination and harnessing it for healing. James differed with Janet only in that the French investigators were willing to acknowledge only the reality of the waking state and various subliminal ones. But for James:

> There are trances which obey another type. I know a non-hysterical woman who, in her trances, knows facts which altogether transcend her *possible* normal consciousness, facts about the lives of people whom she never saw or heard of before. I am well aware of all the liabilities to which this statement exposes me, and I make it deliberately, having practically no doubt whatever of its truth. My *own* impression is that the trance condition is an immensely complex and fluctuating thing, into the understanding of which we have hardly begun to penetrate, and concerning which any very sweeping generalization is sure to be premature. *A comparative study of trances and subconscious states* is meanwhile of the utmost urgent importance for the comprehension of our nature.[7]

James ended by saying that Janet's work was pathbreaking and would fast become "the center for the crystallization of a rapid accumulation of new knowledge." He then issued a call to arms: "And I confidently prophesy that anyone who may be induced by this article to follow the path of study in which it is so brilliant a pioneer will reap a rich reward."

THE PHENOMENA OF TRANCE MEDIUMSHIP

A second piece that helps to define his psychology after 1890 was James's report for the *Proceedings of the ESPR* on his early years of experimentation with the Belmont medium, Mrs. Leonora Piper. He had written this report at the request of F.W.H. Myers in 1890.[8]

Born in Nashua, New Hampshire, in 1859 into an English family of Congregationalist descent, Leonora Simonds was raised in Methuen, Massachusetts, and in 1881 married William R. Piper of Boston, who held a variety of occupations from manufacturer to salesman and superintendent. The Pipers moved to Boston shortly after their marriage and began to have children.

Mrs. Piper belonged to a family that was reportedly free from a history of nervous maladies. During her childhood, however, she suffered occasional episodes such that she lost consciousness and had visionlike experiences, suggesting a knowledge of distant events. Otherwise she enjoyed perfect health, until sometime between 1882 and 1883. At that time, she developed a tumor, which followed a blow from a sledge, and she feared cancer. Her husband's parents advised her to seek medical consultation with a medium, and to oblige them she went to a blind man, J. R. Cocke. Here, she had her first experience of being entranced. Later, in a group meeting with the same medium, she entered into a deep trance and supposedly communicated a message from the dead son of a group member.

From this public display, Mrs. Piper received numerous requests for sittings, one of which came from Elizabeth Gibbens, mother-in-law of William James. Mrs. Gibbens's housemaid spoke to the James' housemaid about the matter. When word about Mrs. Piper eventually got to James, he was initially skeptical. He sent his sons around to Mrs. Piper's neighborhood, and the boys returned with news that she was a perfectly normal mother who was well thought of by her neighbors. A sitting was arranged and James brought his wife, after which both became quickly convinced of Mrs. Piper's extraordinary powers. Soon, James introduced Mrs. Piper to the American Society for Psychical Research, saw to it that she received some remuneration for her efforts as a subject of investigation, and for the next eighteen months personally arranged her sittings.

The most remarkable aspect of her trances at this time was the appearance of Dr. Phenuit, a masculine-sounding voice that claimed to be a French physician who acted as Mrs. Piper's control, or the intermediary between this world of the sitters and the other world of the dead. Once Mrs. Piper entered the trance, Phenuit would speak through her, answering questions and making statements. Later in Mrs. Piper's career, Phenuit would disappear and other controls would replace him.

Almost everyone of any consequence in Cambridge and Boston held a séance with Mrs. Piper—Bowditch, Pickering, Putnam, Prince, President Eliot, Silas Weir Mitchell, even Charles Sanders Peirce. Mrs. Piper soon became the most extensively studied medium at the time, although others were investigated as well. Stenographers were hired, verbatim reports were collected, and much traveling was undertaken. Eventually, the cost of these reports would strain the American Society for Physical Research to its limit, but historically the great value of the transcripts is that they are some of the earliest and most complete records of the interchange between a scientific observer and a subject in a somnambulistic state.[9]

In responding some five years later to Myers's request for an account of his experiences with Mrs. Piper, James admitted that he had kept no notes of his early sittings, preferring instead to verify her trances for himself, and then turned the task of detailed documentation over to others. He was thus able to furnish only an account from memory as to Mrs. Piper's powers.

James gave a summary of his early contacts with her by referring to his report of 1886, which he had originally presented as head of the Committee on Mediumistic Phenomena to the American Society for Psychical Research.[10] There, he had reported on about one dozen sittings with Mrs. Piper that he had personally conducted and added the testimony of twenty-five other sitters. He also reported on a series of demonstrations he had undertaken to test the relationship between Mrs. Piper's mediumistic trances and the ordinary hypnotic trance. His results showed that she was at first not an easily hypnotizable subject, but after numerous trials he succeeded in partially inducing the hypnotic condition. Here she showed all the physical signs of being entranced, except that he could not influence her consciousness by suggestion.[11]

He mentioned other characteristics as well. Her muscular reactions were at first very weak under hypnosis, but could be made stronger by practice. Her pupils contracted in the mediumistic trance, and suggestions that she would remember what she had said in the trance state upon awakening did not succeed, whereas in hypnosis, posthypnotic suggestion produces a memory for all that has happened. There was no sign of thought transference, tested through card guessing in both the hypnotic trance and the mediumistic state. These and other tests showed James that "so far as the evidence goes, then, her medium-trance seems an isolated feature in her psychology," although he admitted that this had not been firmly established.

James admitted that he had no explanation for Mrs. Piper's trance phenomena. The theory of spirit control was hard to reconcile with the extreme triviality of the productions, except that occasionally Mrs. Piper's control did engage in long lectures about the sitters' inward defects and outward shortcomings, which, James said, "were very earnest, as well as subtle morally and psychologically, and impressive in a high degree."[12]

Here, we have a hint of the most important function of the mediumistic trance, namely, as a reservoir for the uncovering of self-knowledge. The majority of demonstrations with Mrs. Piper, however, focused on information about others that was allegedly obtained independent of the normal sensory channels. The distinction had not yet been made between knowledge of outwardly corroborated facts and projective information about the inner dynamics of the self which could be used for personal growth. Such an interpretive framework would have to await the evolution of Jung's psychology after 1900.[13]

Eight years supervened before James again wrote about Mrs. Piper. Then, in 1898, he reviewed the report released by Richard Hodgson on "A Further Record of Observations of Certain Phenomena of Trance," which had appeared in the British *Proceedings of the Society for Psychical Research* in February.[14] Hodgson's report was based on some 500 sittings, 130 of which had been with unnamed strangers introduced to Mrs. Piper for the first time. By then she had given up her previous control, "Phenuit," for a new one called "G. P.," who purported to be the returned spirit of the recently deceased youthful New York literary man, George Pellew.

James also included a graphic description of the steps involved in trance induction:

> The medium waits passively for the trance to come on, which it now does quietly, though formerly there was a good deal of respiratory disturbance and muscular twitching. 'Phenuit' used to communicate entirely by speech, but G.P. early manifested himself by seeking to write on a pad placed on the medium's head. He now writes on the table. 'Phenuit' may talk whilst the hand is writing on other subjects, often under controls different from G.P., and purporting to be deceased friends of the sitters. After two hours, more or less, the communications grow 'weak' and confused, and Mrs. Piper emerges from the trance, often with an expression of fear or distress, and usually with incoherent expressions on her lips, which Dr. Hodgson ascribes to her own subliminal consciousness, as distinguished from her consciousness under complete control.[15]

The main feature of the trances, James said, was the display of supernormal knowledge, although most of it was trivial and pertained only to the intimate details of the personal lives of the sitters. The memory in particular seemed to have a profound capacity. Mrs. Piper could sit with someone after an interval of several years, and, according to the stenographic notes, take up the conversation just where she had left it off, despite the fact that many thousands of sittings with others had supervened. And while her trance memory was acute, her waking memory showed no such extraordinary signs. Of particular interest to James was the extensive cross-correspondence of minute facts that the entranced medium could keep in mind and weave together over the years. Here we have "no ordinary memory, and we have to explain its singular perfection either as the natural endowment of her solitary subliminal self, or as a distinct collection of memory systems, each with a communicating 'spirit' as its vehicle."

James then fielded three possible theories to explain the phenomenon. There was, first of all, the explanation of fraud, but this had been ruled out in Mrs. Piper's case because she had been studied for such a long and close period. Then there was the spirit hypothesis, which seemed unlikely because the communications were so trivial. Then there was the theory that the "subliminal" extension of Mrs. Piper's own mind masqueraded in this way, and played these fantastic tricks, using preternatural powers of cognition for the basest of deceits, "but what a ghastly and grotesque sort of appendage to one's personality is this, from any point of view."[16] Finally, James said:

> We may fall back on the notion of a sort of floating mind-stuff in the world, infra-human, yet possessed of fragmentary gleams of superhuman cognition, unable to gather itself together except by taking advantage of the trance states of some existing human organism, and there enjoying a parasitic existence which it prolongs by making itself acceptable and plausible under the improvised name of a 'spirit control.'[17]

James concluded that Hodgson's skeptical attitude of the scientist, patiently collecting the facts firsthand, was the only possible approach to understanding the great complexity of these matters, as compared to that of the science-mongers, who surveyed the phenomena from a distance and summarily disposed of it as mere fraud.

The Statistical Inquiry into Hallucinations

A third indication of James's psychology during this period comes from his report, made with Richard Hodgson in 1892, on the prevalence of hallucinations within a sample of the American population.[18] The study was part of a much larger international census on hallucinations commissioned by a group of investigators at the First International Congress of Experimental Psychology, which had convened in Paris in 1889. The census had originated with the work of Edmund Gurney, who had undertaken to study a small-scale statistical sample of subjects for the Society for Psychical Research in England. Gurney was particularly interested in spontaneous imagery in healthy individuals who experienced the hallucination of a relative or dear friend just at the moment of death, when the dying person and the hallucinator were separated by great distances. His results had indicated a greater prevalence for this phenomenon than would be expected by chance alone, and, as a result, a much larger study was initiated by investigators at the Paris Congress.

William James was appointed to take charge of the American census. A questionnaire was drawn up and widely circulated. The purpose of the inquiry was to "scientifically describe . . . hallucinations of sane persons, including under this term phantasmal appearances which some deny to be hallucinations because they believe them to be ghosts."[19] Specifically, the instructions asked, "Have you ever, when completely awake, had a

vivid impression of seeing or being touched by a living being or inani-
mate object, or of hearing a voice; which impression, so far as you could
discover, was not due to any external physical cause?"[20]

The study sought: "1) to ascertain approximately the *proportion of persons* who have such experiences, and 2) to obtain details as to the experiences with a view to examining into their cause and meaning."[21]

Each person who was sent a questionnaire was instructed to survey at
random all persons until they had garnered a cohort of twenty-five who
would answer whether or not they had experienced a hallucination. Of
those who said yes, the questioner was to get firsthand details, including
name and address, and then send the materials back to the experimenters. The experimenters then contacted the yea-sayers themselves for further inquiries.

James published the call widely, and responses began pouring in at a
rate beyond his immediate capacity to acknowledge. In the meantime, a
series of controversies arose within various camps over not only the definition of terms, but also the implicit assumptions of the entire effort.
Spiritualists, on the one hand, objected to the term "hallucination" because it immediately implied that what was seen was not real. When a
spiritualist sees a ghost, it was thought to be the real embodiment of a
departed soul, not simply a psychological product of the human imagination. Reductionistic purists in science, on the other, claimed that the
whole enterprise was flawed because it originated with individuals who
were biased toward the supernatural. Instead of having an open mind,
they were pursuing the study only for selective corroboration of their a
priori beliefs.

Nevertheless, in 1892, William James and Richard Hodgson were able
to report that answers had been received from 6,311 persons. Of this
total, 3,745 were men and 2,566 were women. Of these, an equal number
of men and women, 441 in each class, respectively, answered yes for a
total of 852, or 13.50 percent of the total.

By 1896, when James had made his final report to the International
Committee, the numbers had risen slightly. The total number of answers
came to 7,123. The number of yeses stood at 1,051, or 14.75 percent of
the total. James noted seventy-one cases of visual hallucination of some
recognized living person, of which twelve were reported to have occurred on the day of death of the person seen. By comparing the number of deathbed cases to the whole sample with the number that would
occur by pure chance in the entire U.S. population, using the annual
death rate, James was led to the conclusion that *"apparitions on the day
of death are, according to our statistics, 487 times more numerous than pure
chance ought to make them."*[22]

These figures were eventually shown to be in agreement with the international averages, which were based on 17,000 responses and tabulated by the Society for Psychical Research in England. James was thus led to the conclusion that the census data

> affords a *most formidable presumption* that veridical hallucinations are due to something more than chance. Now this means that the telepathic theory, and whatever other occult theories may offer themselves, have fairly conquered the right to a patient and respectful hearing before the scientific bar; and no one with any real conception of what the word 'Science' means, can fail to realize the profound issues which such a fact as this may involve.[23]

THE 1894 REVIEW OF BREUER AND FREUD

We find another clue to the direction of James's psychology during this period in the inaugural issue of James Mark Baldwin and James Mckeen Cattell's *Psychological Review*, which appeared in March 1894. In this maiden volume, William James purportedly gave the first notice of Breuer and Freud's work, "Ueber den psychischen Mechanismus hysterischer Phenömene," to appear before the American psychological public.[24]

Not to deny James his accolades, the real purport of his review was twofold. First, he concluded that Janet deserved all the credit for the most sophisticated articulation of the psychogenic hypothesis; that all Breuer and Freud did, at most, was provide corroboration for Janet's already old findings. Second, James reiterated his belief, but now to professionals in psychology, that these French and German sources clearly showed that the American mental healers had been practicing sound methods of scientific psychotherapy all along.

Evidence for these conclusions is to be found in the work itself. If we look back into the issue of *Psychological Review* in question, we see that James's review of Breuer and Freud occurred in tandem with two other reviews.[25] In fact, the Breuer and Freud review was sandwiched in between them in such a way that they were clearly meant to be taken as a trilogy.

The first, by no means insignificant, was James's review of Pierre Janet's medical dissertation under Charcot, *État mental des hystériques*, a work which, according to James, "set the seal on the revolution which during the last decade has been going on in our conceptions of mental disease."[26]

Naming Charcot, Janet, Pitres, and Gilles de la Tourette as pioneers, James said that male and female hysterics alike who were previously burned at the stake were now more benevolently treated like any other patients suffering from a medical disease, but in this case one involving a weakness of the intellect.

He then summarized the hysterical constitution by reiterating the psychogenic hypothesis. In the first place the threshold of the principal consciousness is not fixed but movable. Physical and moral shocks cause both sensations and ideas to become "subliminal," that is, buried and forgotten, where they exist parasitically. A subconscious nucleus consists of memories of the original shock, around which are drawn other related but subsequent traumatic memories, as well as numerous accidental associations. Their total effect is manifested to the principle consciousness through hallucinations, motor impulses, anesthesias, amnesias, aboulias, and confusions, and they also have a direct effect on numerous bodily functions.

Janet proves their existence, James says, by a variety of methods, including hypnosis, automatic writing, by hallucinations that come out during crystal gazing, by the patient's talk during sleep, by utterances during the attack, and by what Janet calls the "method of distraction."[27]

During these experiences, the patient reveals obsessive memories and ideas and will explain in detail the origin of their symptoms, all of which are now owned by the subliminal self and of which the principal consciousness is totally unaware. The main malady of the hysteric is a *narrowing of the field of consciousness*, which causes the usual vacillation, inconsistency, revery, lack of will and attention, poor memory and ennui, and which accounts for their extreme suggestibility.

In a few pages, James then packs in a multitude of examples. In the end, praising Janet for his lucidity and his concrete cases, James faults him only for not being more general, and for confining himself only to asylum cases, when one wonders if the milder cases met with in private practice also suffer from split-off ideas. While his theories would certainly undergo modification, James concluded with the hope that Janet would remain at the forefront of the newest developments.

James then turned to Breuer and Freud's little piece, "On the Psychical Mechanism of Hysterical Phenomena." As if to show that there was absolutely no doubt where his sympathies were located, James opened with a quote from F.W.H. Myers and invoked Janet's preeminence: "'Hysteria is a disease of the hypnotic stratum,' wrote Mr. F.W.H. Myers many years ago, and this important paper," James says, referring to Breuer and Freud, "is a comment on his dictum and an independent corroboration of Janet's views reported above."[28] We are at a loss as to whether James just does not understand the discrepency between Breuer & Freud and Janet, or whether, at that early date, as Ellenberger

has so cogently asserted, there was in reality very little difference between them.[29] By 1893, Freud had already translated Charcot and
Bernheim and abstracted them for his own purposes. At the same time,
however, he had not yet sufficiently differentiated himself from Breuer's
theories and from the method of hypnosis.

James only notes that the two "distinguished Viennese neurologists . . .
stumbled accidently on cures which enable them not only to give a
general formula for the disease, but a general method for its treatment." James then alluded to the mechanism where shocking memories
fall into the subconscious and can be discovered only in hypnoid states.
The cure, according to Breuer and Freud, James said, is to draw out
the psychic traumata in hypnotism, and "let them produce all their
emotional effects, however violent, and *work themselves off* [James's ital-
ics]. They make then (apparently) a new connection with the principal consciousness, whose breach is thus restored, and the sufferer
gets well."[30]

Here, at least, is the germ of Freud's doctrine of abreaction, which
Janet did not articulate (Janet felt that emotional venting in the hypnoid
state did not automatically lead to changes in the principal consciousness). Breuer and Freud neglected to tell us just how, then, the breach
is restored, and this is likely the meaning of James's use of the adverb
"apparently," to describe the alleged new connection. James finishes off
by saying that Janet's case of Marcella, which he had already mentioned,
was a perfect example of what Breuer and Freud describe.

James then completed the trilogy with a review of Leander E. Whipple's *Philosophy of Mental Healing*. His point was that the American mental
healers had known for years that morbid symptoms sprang from unconscious fixed ideas, and he was glad that scientific evidence had finally
come forth to justify what was the basis of successful mental therapeutics.
While James thought Whipple's theoretical exposition lacked technical
sharpness, it was much more "assimilable" than any previous statement
James had read. By getting into the patient's inner subconscious life and
dispersing the fixed ideas, all sorts of cases, from neuralgias, rheuma-
tism, bronchial catarrh, debility, nervous agitation, chronic diarrhea, in-
somnia, dyspepsia, and chills respond with amazing success. This approach surpasses even that of the asylum doctors, whose main regimes
were restraint and forced feeding. James regretted that Whipple did not
give more details of the method by which fixed ideas were to be pulver-
ized away. The author seemed to suggest only that most metaphysical
healing involved the telepathic action of one subliminal self on another,
"But with this," James concluded, "we navigate in full wonderland, where
without safe guidance we had better not proceed."

JAMES'S DEFENSE OF THE MENTAL HEALERS

While he remained skeptical about their metaphysical claims, James still believed the mental healers had uncovered important facts about human experience, and it was the duty of experimental psychologists to investigate these claims if their assertions about scientific impartiality were actually true. One incident, in particular, that brought this argument to light in print was James's ardent defense of the mental healers against unwarranted attacks by the medical profession.

In March 1894, the same month that his reviews of Janet, Breuer and Freud, and Whipple came out, James wrote to the editor of the *Boston Evening Transcript*, strenuously protesting a bill then before the Massachusetts legislature that would have required all persons practicing medicine in the state without "reputable degrees" to take out a license.[31] The license could only be issued after an examination proving their skill in medicine and surgery, and the examination would be given by already licensed M.D.s appointed by the governor.

James agreed that the public needed to be protected against unprincipled or unskilled doctors, but he thought the bill should be resisted for three reasons. First, it restricted individual citizens' right of free choice regarding the kind of practitioner they would like to treat them. Such a restriction, James said, was un-American. Second, the law is not sufficient to regulate the healing art of medicine in the same manner as plumbing or apothecary. Medicine, in addition to the concrete ministrations of the doctor, requires more impalpable psychological skills that harness the healing resources of the total person. Third, the suppression of certain practitioners will hinder the progress of therapeutic knowledge as a whole. James dispensed with his first two objectives in a few paragraphs and then focused his energies on the third.

He wished, he said, elaborating on this last point, to confine his comments to a branch of knowledge with which he was most conversant, that of "diseases of the nervous system and the mind." All of our knowledge, he continued, including anatomy, symptomatology, classification and diagnosis, and the various hypnotics, anesthetics, sedatives, and stimulants of various sorts, are sufficient at least to effect temporary relief, but they often bear little relation to the patient's permanent cure. He chastised science for lecturing incessantly over the bedside of the dying patient, meanwhile ignoring practical interventions that have a direct pedagogical and moral action on the patient's character, which would have long-term effects for healing. "He who can influence the patient's mind in the direction of health holds the key." This endeavor as a science is but in its infancy, having begun in Europe only some

fifteen years earlier. While the medical establishment only tardily admitted the facts of mesmerism, in America "they have been carried on in a
much bolder and more radical fashion by all those 'mindcurers' and
'Christian scientists' with whose results the public, and even the profession, are growing gradually familiar."[32]

James held "no brief for any of these healers" and confessed he could
not assimilate any of their theories. But he believed that they had
produced a mass of facts that were patent and startling. It would thus be
a public calamity to interfere in the progress in this area. The mind-
curers would refuse to take the medical examinations, would court jail
willingly, and a public outcry would follow that would be embarrassing to
those who put up the bill, simply because it would show the glaring
deficiencies of regular medicine to address the psychological aspects of
physical illness:

> And whatever one may think of the narrowness of the mind-curers, their
> logical position is impregnable. They are proving by the most brilliant new
> results that the therapeutic relation may be what we can at present describe
> only as a relation of one *person* to another *person*; and they are consistent in
> resisting to the utter-most any legislation that would make 'examinable'
> information the root of medical virtue, and hamper the free play of per-
> sonal force and affinity by mechanically imposed conditions.[33]

According to William James, if the chief task of a science of human nature in the next generation is to understand the phenomena of the
mind-curers, then the present bill would clearly obstruct the progress of
medical knowledge.

True, he said, "vampire quacks who live by preying on the victims of
sexual disease" must be punished, but "it is a poor policy to set fire to
one's house to broil a mutton chop, or to pour boiling water over one's
dog to kill his fleas." The bill at any rate would not protect the public
from just those same vampires who hold the medical license. "It will be
hard to regulate those creatures effectively under any legislative device;
but to regulate the whole delicate mechanism of the relations between
physician and patient in the State of Massachusetts, for the sole purpose
of making it easier for the police to descend upon a few such miscreants,
is simply preposterous."[34]

In the end, James prevailed. That section of the bill requiring licensure
through examination by the M.D.s was gutted. In its place a provision was
inserted stating that no persons in the state could append the initials
"M.D." after their name who had not qualified for the title by a state
examination. James wrote in favor of the new provision and it passed.

Nevertheless, there was also a price to pay. It is generally understood
by James scholars that his defense of the mental healers further tar-

nished his reputation among medical men as well as the new laboratory-oriented scientists in psychology, chiefly because James had appeared publicly to oppose the presuppositions of legitimate science. As a result, during the 1890s, as James appeared to become more of a popular American folk hero, his scientific reputation went into eclipse and he slowly became disenfranchised from the disciplines in which he had originally made a name for himself. His public lecturing increased dramatically, even though he said he only expanded these activities to augment his income. By his own accounts, he ceased to keep up with developments in the most recent literature on brain neurophysiology, and he seemed to abandon the laboratory altogether.[35] These may be further contributing reasons why modern psychologists suppose that James was no longer a practicing "scientist."

But, these were only appearances. Actually, James's interest and contributions to psychology remained very much alive and well, as his publishing and lecturing activities attest.

JAMES'S DEFINITION OF PERSONALITY

Not the least of his interests, which gives us another clue to the scope of his psychology after 1890, comes from an important conceptual definition James made of personality. That he may have defined the term at all is interesting, because James presented no systematic conception of personality in his *The Principles of Psychology*, but rather linked the sense of self with our experience of consciousness. He advocated a psychology of the individual, but nowhere did he appear to hypostatize personality into a category for psychologists to organize as a subfield of their endeavors. The focus on the person was, rather, implied as a given at the core of James's worldview. Personality theorists such as Gordon Allport, Henry Murray, and Gardner Murphy looked back decades after James's death and saw James as a forerunner of their efforts.[36] But, because there was no systematic theoretical frame of reference defining the limits of the person, they believed they had to define a scientific study of personality anew.

Now, one of the more interesting tidbits culled from the critical edition of the *Works of William James* project is a little-known article that James published in *Johnson's Universal Cyclopedia* for 1895, reprinted each year to 1897, defining "Person and Personality."[37]

James began, like any good lexicographer, with an etymological derivation, noting that the word "person" comes to us by way of Old French, from the Latin *persona*, as in a theater mask and as a loan word from Greek, adapted to *per* (through) plus *sona're*, sound (i.e., speak). In the common parlance of the 1890s, "person" meant "an individual man in his typical completeness as uniting a human body to a free and rational soul." Thus, personality was usually denied to pure spirits and to the departed, because they had no body. It was also denied to idiots because they were irrational, to maniacs because they were not free, and to animals because they were not human. James further pointed out that the various fields of psychology, ethics, law, and theology, by emphasizing only one aspect or another, have defined personality in completely different ways.

In psychology, he said, personality as it was then defined in the 1890s, was designated as individuality, or personal identity. Some saw it as an ultimate and self-subsistent core, others as derived from other principles.

James then compared this modern contrast with a similar one found in the Hindu system. Here he described the absolute plurality of the Samkhya with the ultimate monism of Vedanta. He noted, as well, that the modern theosophists' doctrine was derived from the Vedanta.

James then analyzed the spiritual principle of personality among the Jews (*Rauch*) as the warm breath of life which animated the dust, when breathed thereinto by Jehova. Breath-spirit, he said, which was generic to all primitive thought, developed into the animal and theological spirits with the Greeks. He mentioned the *pneuma*, or fiery air-current of the Stoics. Plato and Aristotle subordinated the principle of the breath to the immaterial and rational psyche, he said, from which is derived later spiritualistic conceptions of personality. Man is composed of two warring principles: the soul, immortal, preexisting, superior to Nature; and the body, the soul's vessel or prison, simultaneously the soul's servant and the source of its errors and faults. For Aristotle, this duality was expressed in terms of soul as form and body as matter, a conception which dominated Christian philosophy until the time of Descartes. Scholasticism hardened this doctrine into the soul and body as incomplete when separate and whole as a concrete substance only when the body and soul were united.

Not until Descartes, James continued, do we find the distinction so common today between consciousness and the unconscious. The person, a purely spiritual entity, became separated from the rest of nature, including the body, which was material. Personal identity was, nevertheless, real for Descartes, but as a principle, not a result.

James pointed to Locke's *Essay Concerning Human Understanding* as the true beginning of empiricism. Locke explained personality as a result, not a principle. It does not lead to consequences by simply being, but is made from moment to moment by causes. Ontological self-identity, while real, is not a person until there are memories, Locke said. Consciousness is what makes a person when it remembers past experiences as having been its own. For Locke, transcendental identity was unimportant; personal identity was the only thing of practical consequence because it was directly verifiable and an empirical phenomenon. Hume went beyond Locke, James said, by abandoning all reference to substances, spiritual or material. By personal identity, Hume meant our sense of gradual change in the succession of our ideas. Both their views were developed in England and Germany by the associationist psychologists, often dubbed "a psychology without a soul."

Since Kant, James continued, subjection to moral law and the autonomy and freedom it implies have become the specific marks of personality. A person has inner ideal ends for which he or she takes responsibility. Here psychology becomes ethical and juridical.

James then claimed that recent psychology rests on Locke. All schools refer to the empirical self as the succession of associated ideas held together by memory. For some, the compound of these units is the person, which is thus secondary, with no unifying principle. Others claim a spiritual soul which owns the ideas, or a transcendental ego, which performs their synthesis.

Thus far, James had gotten through about half the article, during which he had fielded a contemporary working definition of personality and sketched the philosophical history of conceptions of the self, at least in the West. Having set the stage, he then devoted the rest of his discussion exclusively to dissociation and multiple personality. These conceptions he put forward as the current revolution in psychology in the 1890s, saying that they raised a host of questions about the basic nature of personality that demanded attention.

Studies in multiple personality suggested that something more was needed beyond the mere contemporaneous connection of many ideas with one organism. Such phenomena show us that we have successive or simultaneous selves not in communication with each other. He then outlined familiar examples, such as ordinary forgetfulness, absentmindedness, and rapid forgetting of dreams, where subsequent recollection shows the lost idea has been there all the time.

In somnambulism and hypnosis the rule is for the person to forget when coming to, and to re-remember when again entranced. Thus, two separate lives with separate memories for each may appear in the same personality. Edmund Gurney of the Society for Psychical Research in England had shown through automatic writing that both memories coexist. Pierre Janet, Alfred Binet, and others associated with the so-called French Experimental Psychology of the Subconscious had found that when waking consciousness was anesthetic, other dimensions of personality registered its experiences. F.W.H. Myers has called these other dimensions "subliminal selves." James then gave credit again to Pierre

Janet for originating the psychogenic hypothesis—that hidden memories, split off from the waking state, are the cause of hysteric symptoms.

From there, James passed to cases of alternating personality. He cited Janet's case of Léonie. He also cited Laurancy Vennum, a case he had developed in *The Principles*. He reviewed his own study of Ansel Bourne, and the classic French case of Louis V., who had been identified with five different personalities. In all these cases, progressively deeper levels of personality revealed hidden dimensions unknown to the more superficial strata, again suggesting to James that what we call the person is actually an ultimate plurality of selves. Unity was only a characteristic of a single narrow band of consciousness attached to waking material reality.

One of the means we have to penetrate into these other dimensions, James said, was through automatic writing. All persons are automatic writers to some extent. The writing hand becomes sometimes anesthetic, sometimes not, and all degrees of detachment from consciousness are shown. Automatic writing passes off into the mediumistic trance and may be succeeded by speaking under the influence of a control. As before, nothing is usually remembered upon awakening.

Demon possession seems to be the same as trance mediumship, obeying, however, a different inspiration as to its moral content. In both, attacks are short, no memory remains, and between attacks the patient is entirely well. While such subjects have nothing in common with the insane, it is curious, James pointed out, how they all have a generic similarity, which suggests a common cause that at present remained unknown. They at least plead for more rational study.

Such facts have again brought forward the question, "What is the unifying principle of personality?" It is certain that one body may be the home of multiple consciousnesses, and hence, in a Lockean sense, of many persons. But they are more like accidental selves made up of ideas grouped together and leading a quasi-independent life.

It is also clear that the margins and the outskirts of what we take to be our personality shade off into unknown regions. Cures and blisters under hypnosis show this, as does occasional surprising knowledge of facts in mediums. While their significance is yet to be understood, he concluded, their investigation is urgent.

Classical Eastern Psychology[38]

James was also keenly aware that certain non-Western cultures had developed a sophisticated psychology of inner experience, particularly the Asian traditions that taught meditation and yoga.[39] But he also believed that, like the literary psychologists of the earlier transcendentalist era, the Asian systems were based on an intuitive psychology of character formation. This meant that from an epistemological standpoint, their methods and results were not directly translatable into the language of scientific empiricism; rather, an extrapolation was necessary to make their ideas useful.

Toward this end, James was no stranger to Asian ideas. Reipe, for instance, a scholar from the State University of New York, has written on James's interest in Indian philosophy.[40] Characterizing James's attitude toward Indian thought as one of attraction and repulsion, Reipe saw Indian philosophy as basically uncongenial to James's pragmatic emphasis on concrete experience. James, however, was more well versed than Reipe supposed.[41]

References to Sanskrit terms can be found scattered throughout James's writings as early as the late 1860s. *Maya*, "*nirwana*," *Tat Tvam Asi*, and comments on the oriental philosophy of negation are examples. Their mere appearance suggests a literary sophistication beyond that of a normal student educated in the Western analytic tradition. Indeed, we know that James's introduction to such concepts came chiefly through American literary sources, especially from Emerson's library and the transcendentalist circle, of which Henry James, Sr., had been a working part.

We also know that as a young medical student traveling in Europe, James had heard an outline of Buddhist history recited by Wilhelm Dilthey at the dinner table of Hermann Grimm (James had been introduced to Grimm by Emerson).

We also know that James had a collection of books on Eastern religions in his personal library. While he had very few textual translations, he had a number of works on technical philosophy, chiefly on Hinduism, but he was most attracted to eyewitness accounts of religious experiences from various Asian cultures.

James was also in close touch with developments in comparative religions at Harvard. He knew, for instance, Charles Carroll Everett, dean of the Harvard Divinity School and professor of comparative religions, who also taught courses on the psychology of religion in the philosophy department. The Everetts and the Jameses had been friends of long social standing. The families had first met in the 1860s, and Everett had been a member of the Cambridge Metaphysical Club with James, Peirce, Chauncey Wright, and Oliver Wendell Holmes, Jr., out of which the philosophical movement of pragmatism was spawned. James also had been good friends for several decades with Everett's colleague in comparative religions, C. H. Toy.

James Houghton Woods, another member of the history of religions circle at Harvard, had ascended to an eminent position in his field through James's inspiration. Woods had been an instructor in anthropology in the late 1890s until James suggested that he should begin the study of Indian philosophy. Woods went abroad to study with the Vedantic scholar Paul Deussen, and returned with a Ph.D. from Leipzig. He soon distinguished himself by translating the *Yoga Sutras of Patanjali,* an important text on the Samkhya philosophy and the psychology of meditation, which appeared as part of the Harvard Oriental Series under the editorship of Charles Rockwell Lanman.

Lanman was a neighbor of the Jameses, and William James was his hero. Lanman's daughter, who was eleven when James died, remembers James attending meetings of the Harvard History of Religions Club. Here, James came into contact with the latest ideas defining scholarship in comparative religions, one probable source for his knowledge of non-Western religious texts in the *Varieties of Religious Experience.*

Both William James and Josiah Royce shared an interest in Asian thought. Royce had studied Sanskrit at both Johns Hopkins and at the University of Leipzig, and his language studies must have in some way informed his later interest in symbolic logic, as Sanskrit grammar is among the most complete and precise in the world. Royce was also well versed in monistic Hindu philosophies akin to his own theory of the Absolute.[42]

James also had numerous encounters with Eastern meditation teachers, among them Anagarika Dharmapala, the Theravada monk from Ceylon, and the eminent Hindu monk and disciple of Ramakrishna, Swami Vivekananda. Vivekananda seems particularly important because his ideas appear regularly in James's writings.

Although there is every reason to believe that they had known of each other through mutual friends since 1893, James encountered Vivekananda when the swami came to Harvard on March 25, 1896, to lecture on "The Vedanta Philosophy." The talk was sponsored by the Graduate Philosophical Society,[43] and Vivekananda was introduced by Charles Carroll Everett.[44]

In substance, Vivekananda began his Harvard lecture by outlining the different schools of orthodox Hindu philosophy that are based on the teachings of the Vedas, the most sacred of the Hindu religious scriptures. The system that he wished to emphasize to his audience was that of Advaita Vedanta, or nondualism, which claimed absolute identity between the true nature of the individual self, the *jiva,* and *Atman,* or the Divine. Advaita, Vivekananda told his audience, was considered the highest philosophical expression of Vedic teaching.

It was a classical exposition that conformed exactly to the traditional view of the Hindu schools. Vivekananda did admit, however, that the psychology of the different systems was drawn in every case from the

Samkhya, meaning the general description of states of consciousness attributed to the Samkhya-Yoga texts of Patanjali.

From the Advaita standpoint, the aim of spiritual practice is the complete cessation of sense attachment to illusory phenomena in the material world, a goal that Vivekananda expressed as self-abnegation for the sake of others. These ideas were of particular interest to the philosophers at Harvard, who were concerned with the relation of the One to the Many, with the issues of monism and pluralism, and with the links between individual character development and social evolution.

Of greatest interest was Vivekananda's definition of psychology. By it, he meant the spiritual evolution of consciousness, not simply the description of sense data and its analysis by the mind. The very impetus for our perceptions, Vivekananda said, was not stimulation from external sources, followed by the organism's response, but rather the active spiritual principle in each of us using consciousness to reach out and apprehend objects in the external world, thus giving them life and meaning. In external science, he said, concentration of mind means putting attention on an object defined within the context of the material physical world. With internal science, concentration of mind means drawing the attention inward toward one's self. This is yoga, which means, literally, yoking the mind and body.

James had a private meeting with Vivekananda a few days after the lecture, and he made numerous references to him at various times in his writings. An analysis of these passages suggests the angle that James took on classical Eastern psychology as a whole.

James was, first of all, impressed with the Hindu emphasis on an inner tranquility that could be systematically cultivated. In his *Talks to Teachers on Psychology and to Students on Some of Life's Ideals* (1899), he said:

> We have lately had a number of accomplished Hindoo visitors at Cambridge, who talked freely on life and philosophy. More than one of them has confided to me that the sight of our faces, all contracted as they are with the habitual American over-intensity and anxiety of expression, and our ungraceful and distorted attitudes when sitting, made on him a very painful impression. "I do not see," said one, "how it is possible for you to live as you do, without a single minute in your day deliberately given to tranquility and meditation. It is an invariable part of our Hindu life to retire for at least half an hour daily into silence, to relax our muscles, govern our breathing, and meditate on eternal things. Every Hindu child is trained to do this from an early age.[45]

James went on to lament that American education incorporated no such practices into the experience of either teaching or learning. So James concluded: "From its reflex influences on the inner mental states, this ceaseless over-tension, over-motion, and over-expression are working on us grievous national harm."

Another reference James made to Vivekananda occurred in *The Varieties* (1902). There, in the context of discussing the higher faculties of the hidden mind, James cited the ultimate monism of the Vedanta as embodied in Vivekananda's London lectures of 1897, "Practical Vedanta and the Real and Apparent Man." James's conclusion was that interpretations regarding the nature of ultimate reality may vary from individual to individual, but the underlying psychological mechanisms seem to be the same, and in this continuity James saw the basis for a truly objective science of religions.

James also made extensive references to Vivekananda in his *Pragmatism* (1907). Vedantic Hinduism, James said, illustrated the extreme form of monistic doctrine that characterizes most religious descriptions of ultimate reality. But he pointed out there that such pronouncements as "We all are One" can be read two ways: first, as a dogmatic statement about the way reality is that everyone should adopt as the right explanation of things; and second, as a phenomenal description about the inner experience of someone making such a statement. In this second way, unity can be equated with higher consciousness in the individual, while pluralism is still preserved for the radically different descriptions of religious experience that characterize humanity as a whole.

Finally, James did not confine himself solely to an interest in ideas. He was also acquainted with two of Vivekananda's Western disciples, the Irishwoman Margaret Nobel, and the eccentric Polish philosopher Wincenty Lutoslawski. Nobel had taken the vows of a *sanyasi*, or nun, with Vivekananda, and under a new initiated name, Sister Nevidita, she had embraced Hindu philosophy as her own religion. James had at least one of her books in his personal library, and ran into her occasionally while traveling abroad.[46]

The other disciple of Vivekananda, Wincenty Lutoslawski, exerted an important influence on James's philosophy beginning in the late 1890s. James wrote a preface to Lutoslawski's *World of Souls*, and Lutoslawski's ideas appealed to James's philosophy of pluralism at a crescent moment in the formulation of this doctrine.[47] Their relationship dated from the time Lutoslawski first introduced himself to James by letter and came to visit the Harvard Psychological Laboratory in 1893 on his way to the World Parliament of Religions in Chicago. Later, Lutoslawski tried to interest James in the practice of yoga, meditation, and fasting. James admitted only to experimenting with breathing exercises. Meditation, for James, was too much like the morbid brooding on ideas that so plagued him during his near-suicidal depression of 1870. He had an aversion to fasting, probably because Henry James, Sr., had voluntarily fasted to death in 1882. As for yoga, James preferred walking in the Adirondacks; and as to discipline, James flatly stated that writing was *his* yoga.

But Lutoslawski's miraculous recovery from a serious physical illness through intensive fasting and meditation became for James a major example of the hidden powers dammed up in each of us. Just out of reach are always those reserves of energy held in abeyance by our lazy habits. Such reserves must be released if we are to experience any renewal in life—physically, morally, and spiritually. James gave expression to these ideas using Lutoslawski's yoga as a prime example in "The Energies of Men," his presidential address to the American Philosophical Association in 1906.[48] James would later call the liberation and eventual harnessing of these important inner forces the moral equivalent of war.[49]

JAMES'S LOWELL LECTURES ON EXCEPTIONAL MENTAL STATES

The most important collection of evidence we have that gives us some substantial clues about James's psychology after 1890 is assembled in the recent reconstruction of his 1896 unpublished Lowell Lectures on "Exceptional Mental States."[50]

James first proposed his lecture series in a letter to Augustus Lowell on April 18, 1896. He said: "I wrote to you some six weeks ago with reference to Mr. C. H. Hinton of Princeton as a possible Lowell lecturer. I am now taking the liberty of annoying you in a similar way with regard to another candidate, namely *myself*."[51] He offered Lowell "a mass of floating matter that is hardly yet codified and organized, but that is becoming more and more so, and that has great practical and historical importance, to which for some years past I have been giving a good deal of attention, and which I think I could bring together in an instructive way." He then listed ten subjects, later shortened to eight, namely: Dreams and Hypnotism, Automatism, Hysteria, Multiple Personality, Demoniacal Possession, Witchcraft, Degeneration, and Genius.

The purpose of the lectures, James later wrote to a friend, was specifically to avoid developing psychic or occult themes, and rather, by bringing together the newest insights of psychotherapy, medicine, neurology, and psychiatry, to deal with decidedly morbid subjects, but "to shape our thoughts about them toward optimistic and hygienic conclusions." Too long had morbidity been treated as something somehow fixed, unalterable, and so much different from the normal. Long before Freud, it was James who claimed, "We are of one clay with lunatics and criminals." His import was to destroy the untouchability surrounding our view of the insane. In the end, however, he could not resist making frequent allusions to the occult.

The actual content of the lectures revolved around James's concern to show that morbidity is in fact a manifestation of what we call normal, except that in psychopathology, common ways of thinking, feeling, and acting are blown out of proportion. His first four talks—on dreams and hypnotism, automatism, hysteria, and multiple personality—constitute James's understanding of a dynamic psychology of the subconscious within the individual, while his second four, on demoniacal possession, witchcraft, degeneration, and genius, constitute the same dynamic psychology, but now seen at work in the social sphere. Morbid symptoms in the individual are paralleled by instances of mass contagion within groups. Change can come by strengthening the individual psyche, through reeducation and efforts to promote character development, and by manipulation of the group mind through social cohesion or dispersion, as the need may be.

James began by comparing sleep and dreaming with those states brought on under hypnosis. Both sleep and the hypnotic trance are contrasted with the waking state. When we are in these altered conditions, they seem like all there is, when in reality they also form a part of the total picture. Thus, the sound mind is a system of ideas in gear, integrated, with a field of awareness, a focus at the center, and a margin or periphery. What is on the *margin* controls meaning and links our primary idea at the center of attention with all other possible dimensions of awareness.

To demonstrate his point, James reviewed Gurney's work on the relation between posthypnotic suggestion and automatic writing. How was it possible, for instance, that a subject could be made to *not* see a certain line among many others like it? Didn't some form of perception and discrimination have to take place *before* the individual became so selectively blind? And what of the subjects who have had deafness suggested under hypnosis, and in the middle of their deafness are commanded to hear again, and do so? Were they really deaf? Or shamming? James concluded that while the hypnotized subjects could genuinely not hear, it was a special kind of sensorial blindness and deafness, just as we would normally forget a name, or accidentally "cut" an acquaintance.

Is consciousness split, or is it rapidly alternating? James's conclusion was that there were two simultaneously conscious systems operating at once. One represented waking consciousness and the other a vast subliminal region that lay buried within, a concept developed by F.W.H. Myers. On this subject Myers had said:

> . . . that the stream of consciousness in which we habitually live is not the only consciousness which exists in connection with our organism. Our habitual or empirical consciousness may consist of a mere selection from a

multitude of thoughts and sensations, of which some at least are equally conscious with those that we empirically know. I accord no primacy to my ordinary waking self, except that among my potential selves this one had shown itself the fittest to meet the needs of common life. I hold that it has established no further claim, and that it is perfectly possible that other thoughts, feelings and memories, either isolated or in continuous connection, may now be actively conscious, as we say "within me,"—in some kind of coordination with my organism, and forming some part of my total individuality. I conceive it possible that at some future time, and under changed conditions, I may recollect all; I may assume then various personalities under one single consciousness, in which ultimate and complete consciousness, the empirical consciousness which at this moment directs my hand, may be only one element out of many.[52]

Within us we have innumerable streams of consciousness. We are each greater than we really know, Myers claimed, and yet within us we also have a dark bestial and undeveloped side. We are capable of experiencing both psychopathology and transcendence.

James adapted this view to the psychogenic hypothesis, arguing for the reality of the "buried idea." Within us we hold a plethora of mental images representing our experiences, from the worst to the best. Of those formed from traumatic shock, we have no memory. But they persist in the subliminal region, floating around in the subconscious, acting according to laws of their own. Often such ideas, James claimed, reiterating what he had said elsewhere, become parasitic, drawing other similar ideas into a constellation of subliminal memories. Thus we see the transition from the isolated symptoms of the hysteric, the tics, contractures, anesthesias, weaknesses of will, to the full-blown hysteric attack. Lost memories from the subconscious then force their way into waking life and totally dominate the field of consciousness. In their most extreme and well-developed form, such parasitic constellations can emerge as separate, independent personalities, and more than one may appear in a single person. Hence, the phenomenon of multiple personality.

But consciousness beyond the margin, James said, can be tapped in hypnosis, through dreams, by automatic writing, or by a new technique, "Breuer's method of talk-cure." He was here referring to Breuer and Freud's method of inducing a psychological purge of these malignant ideas.[53] By handling the buried idea, memories of a traumatic experience can be reintegrated back into the network of associations that form the framework for the normal, integrated personality.[54]

In addition to this interpretation, James also added F.W.H. Myers's perspective. Most medical definitions of multiple personality had assumed that the secondary personalities which emerged were mere undeveloped fragments or else appeared to be totally independent of the primary consciousness, when they were not really. Myers considered this only one interpretation and countered with the possibility that the actual invasion of one personality by another, either extraterresterial from the after-death plane or one that was earthbound, could not be ruled out. James subscribed to these ideas as well, believing that the after-death hypothesis had neither been conclusively proven nor disproven.

More importantly for James, however, was Myers's observation that almost all cases of multiple personality that had appeared in the medical literature assumed that the secondary consciousness was more primitive than the primary waking state. In fact, its very appearance was a sign of psychopathology. Both James and Myers, however, cited cases where the secondary personality was far wiser than and greatly superior to primary consciousness. In certain instances, as we have seen in James's *Principles*, the superior secondary personality would emerge to become the dominant self for the rest of a person's life.

Having established the reality of the subliminal region of consciousness and concluded that it not only had a psychopathic but also a transcendent aspect, James proceeded to focus on the way the morbid side takes control of personality and begins to infect others, which can lead to true social epidemics of a functional and psychogenic variety.[55] His examples of demon possession showed clearly that one powerful and charismatic individual who gives evidence of possession in the trance state can induce a similar experience in large numbers of people with whom he or she had both direct and indirect contact. There were also many positive instances of demon possession, particularly where possessed persons performed oracular and healing functions within an accepted cultural framework.

History shows, James claimed, that demon possession was equated with mediumship. In his own modern time, James noted that mediumship of a very optimistic variety flourished among the New England mental healers because it promoted religious awakening. Thus, mediumship seems to become more benign, the less pessimistically it is regarded, he concluded. In fact, there is evidence that it is another example of alternating personality: "Not by demons but by a fixed idea of the person that has dropt down," he said, quoting Pierre Janet.

In another example of this mass psychology of the subconscious, James cited the European Inquisition and the Salem witch trials. They were both similar, he asserted, to the sham cholera epidemics in Italy and France that had appeared in the early 1880s. The symptoms subsided when whole villages were scattered and the most volatile individuals were resettled away from each other. In the Inquisitions, evidence indicates that the accused witches in many cases were suffering from hysteric symptoms. At the same time, James felt that the accusers themselves were insane, weak-minded individuals who had great power in their hands. Many victims and accusers suffered from what we would call today mass hysteria.

James then turned his attention to true insanity. Instances of acute degeneration, especially from disease and heredity and from severe traumatic shock, represented examples of a complete break with material reality. But the fact that the genuinely morbid might be related to the normal personality, James pointed out, was a novel idea. He suggested further the somewhat audacious idea that the morbid may be closer to the real truth about the human circumstance, only they cannot effectively communicate it to us.

His various solutions to the problem of insanity remain highly suggestive. In one place he had said earlier in his career:

> There can be little doubt that in the capacity for self-formation which each one of us has in greater or less degree, there lies a power over himself to prevent insanity. Not many persons need go mad, perhaps,—at any rate from moral causes,—if they only knew the resources of their own nature, and how to develop them systematically.[56]

And in another:

> As the asylums are spreading in size, the very atmosphere within the walls may be said to be saturated with lunacy. They are becoming centers for the condensation and aggregation of the malady rather than places of cure, just as the crowding in at a fever hospital makes the disease more malignant. We are convinced that this is an evil that has been too much overlooked. The insane not only require more physical support than the sane to keep them from going back, but also more healthy mental stimulus; they cannot lean upon themselves without deteriorating. Hence the true principle of cure for the curable and of support for the incurable, *is an association with healthy minds.*[57]

By the mid-1890s, for James, the modern dynamic theories about the subconscious, theoretically at least, proposed an entirely new way to gain access into the inner world of troubled lives, and as such, seemed to hold out new hope for the insane.

As a final example of mass psychology, James took up the role of the genius in society.[58] The common stereotype was that the genius represented a superhuman, perfected being. Scientific medicine had destroyed this idea by showing that genius was, in fact, allied with insanity. But the medical view, erred, in James's opinion, by asserting that the genius was *nothing but* a morbid type. Examples of healthy-minded individuals who were also geniuses were all too numerous. What got a man into the biographies was usually the caprice of the judges or the man's overemphasis on one skill or idea alone. Genius was, James concluded, a *social* conception. What made the instance of genius psychological was *first-class superiority of intellect*. While it is true, he said, quoting Lombroso, that "madness ferments in the dough of which great men are made," the superior intellect of the genius took the morbid and eccentric qualities of his personality and turned them to creative ends in a way that he and society were the better for it. In this way, the solitary men and women of genius impacted positively on the continued social evolution of the species.

The real lesson of the genius books is that we should welcome sensibilities, impulses, and obsessions if we have them, so long as by their means the field of our experience grows deeper and we contribute the better to the race's stores; that we should broaden our notion of health instead of narrowing it, that we should regard no single element of weakness as fatal—in short, that we should *not be afraid of life*. He said, "all these geniuses and their mental peculiarities are the organs by which mankind works out the experience which is its destiny." He then drove the point home by saying:

> Who shall absolutely say that the morbid has no revelations about the meaning of life? That the healthy-minded view so-called is *all?* . . . A certain tolerance, a certain sympathy, a certain lack of fear, seem to be the best attitude we can carry in our dealing with these regions of human nature.[59]

And in thanking the audience for their attention, James expressed the hope that they would leave with this more positive attitude increased and confirmed.

James's Graduate Course in Psychopathology: 1893–1898

Regarding scientific psychotherapy during this time, two great independent streams in neurology and psychiatry surged forward that occasionally intermingled. The evolution of psychotherapeutic techniques within neurology and psychology were used to treat the ambulatory psychoneuroses in general hospital outpatient clinics. Meanwhile, experimental laboratory methods, borrowed by clinical psychiatrists from psychology, were first introduced onto the wards of the insane asylums. That these streams developed separately suggests why psychotherapeutic methods, which existed within neurology in the 1880s and 1890s, did not actually enter the practice of psychiatry until the early twentieth century.

An instructive case in point was the situation at Harvard. Between 1893 and 1900, because of new links formed between psychology, neurology, and psychiatry, several generations of students were exposed to unprecedented opportunities for learning about the latest advances in experimental psychopathology. Overall, the mental sciences at Harvard were all intertwined. Faculty who taught neuropathology, psychology, psychiatry, and philosophy were all on intimate personal terms; they shared each other's formulations about the mind-body problem; they used each other's writings in their course materials; and class rosters show that a small knot of the same students would often be enrolled simultaneously in their classes.

James Jackson Putnam and his assistants at the Harvard Medical School, E. W. Taylor and Morton Prince, developed courses in neuropathology that taught medical students how to differentiate between functional and organic disturbances of the nervous system. Their materials were later incorporated into Putnam and Waterman's *Studies in Neurological Diagnosis* (1902), the first textbook in neurology used at Harvard that answered Walter Bradford Cannon's call for adoption of the case teaching method.[60]

Edward Cowles, superintendent at the McLean Asylum, which had recently been moved from Somerville to Belmont, had pioneered the introduction of laboratories into the mental hospital environment which studied pathology, chemistry, and psychophysics. Nevertheless, he had also taken a keen interest in the new psychoneurotic cases, especially the diagnosis of neurasthenia, or nerve weakness. William James, it has been rumored, had even been one of his patients. Cowles also offered courses to medical students in clinical psychiatry with case studies that made use of formulations about the nature of consciousness and personality taken from James's *The Principles of Psychology*.[61]

Meanwhile, over at Harvard College under the aegis of the philosophy department, Josiah Royce was developing conceptions of the self that had a direct bearing on the alterations of self-identity experienced in psychopathic states.[62] Royce's ideas would soon have a direct effect on the development of social milieu therapy for the treatment of psychoneurotics at the Massachusetts General Hospital after 1900.[63]

At the same time, William James, between 1893 and 1898, began teaching the first graduate course offered at an American university in the new mental pathology.[64] Here, students learned about the modern dynamic psychology of the subconscious, they heard the latest controversies over the mechanisms at work in the psychotherapeutic treatment of the neuroses, and over the forms of insanity that might be influenced by psychogenic means.

The catalog first described James's course in 1893–94 as "Philosophy 20b, a Psychological Seminary," the equivalent of what we would call today a small seminar. It dealt with "Questions in Mental Pathology, embracing a review of the principle forms of abnormal or exceptional mental life." By 1896 it had been upgraded in the catalog as a full-fledged course, Philosophy 15, involving lectures and special presentations.

The textbook James used was Henry Maudsley's *Pathology of Mind.* Originally published in 1867 as the *Physiology and Pathology of Mind,* the third edition had abstracted from it just the section on mental pathology, which was then published as a separate text, *The Pathology of Mind,* in 1879.[65]

The book had four parts: the nature and causes of insanity, symptoms, clinical varieties, and treatment. Causes included an analysis of physiological, psychological, and social forces in the development of insanity. Symptomatology detailed the traditional classification scheme of psychiatric diagnosis—the melancholias (depressions), mania, delusions and hallucinations, idiocy, imbicility, and dementia. Of the clinical varieties, childhood and adolescent insanity were considered first, followed by insanity in childbirth and the insanities accompanying old age, general paralysis, epilepsy, and alcoholism, as well as those associated with gross brain disease.

After a brief section on pathological anatomy came recommendations for treatment. Two major strategies were put forward: prevention of the insane from procreating and techniques for maintainence of psychological self-control. The text stressed particularly the development of a quiet mind and a strong will in those with a predisposition toward insanity in order to keep the disintegration of personality in check.

Unfortunately, a search has failed to turn up any student notebooks for James's course, so that we are deprived of direct knowledge about what was actually taught. Instead, we must infer the course content indirectly from a variety of related archival sources. These include James's numerous journal reviews, the content of his published books, records showing the pattern of his reading during this period, related correspondence, and various references made by James's students.

NOTES ON JAMES'S READING FROM 1889 TO 1896

Some evidence showing the probable content of James's graduate course in experimental psychopathology comes from the Harvard College charging records from 1889 to 1896. These were the ongoing records kept by the Harvard College librarian that showed which titles a member of the Harvard community checked out and for how long.

The common procedure was for the borrower to record the date a book was due, then list the author, title, and date of publication, followed by a signature, all on a single line. When the book was returned, the entire line was crossed out with a pen, showing the transaction had been completed.

A problem for contemporary scholars interested in these materials has been that, for several decades before the introduction of the Dewey Decimal System, a succession of library classification systems was in effect which appear to be idiosyncratic to the needs and perceptions of individual librarians.[66] Only after a painstaking reconstruction have these cryptic entries been decoded.[67]

In James's case, the charging records show a rich and varied exploration of specific psychological and philosophic topics relevant to his concerns at the time, and they reveal as well his broad-ranging interests across many disciplines and in a variety of languages, principally English, French, German, and Italian. These include works by Spinoza, Leibnitz, Descartes, and Schopenhauer in philosophy; Hughlings Jackson in neurology; Golgi, Zeihen, and DuBois-Reymond in physiology; Ranvier and Hoppmann in anatomy; Newton, Maxwell, and Planck in physics; Laplace in mathematics; Galton, Spencer, and Wundt in psychology; and Ideler, Krafft-Ebing, Esquirol, Pinel, Falret, Magnan, Prichard, Winslow, Clouston, and Maudsley in psychiatry.

The most frequently renewed books over a seven-year period include Descourtis's, *Du Fractionnement des opérations cérébrales, etc.*; W. S. Evans's, *Memory Training*; Calmeil's *De la folie*; Griesinger's *Mental Pathology*; Hammond's *Nervous Derangement*; Bucknill and Tuke's *Manual of Psychological Medicine*; Beard's works on *Nervous Exhaustion* and *Sexual Neurasthenia*; Lombroso's studies on genius and insanity; Sully's *Teachers' Handbook of Psychology*; Wynter's *Borderlands of Insanity*; Constans's *Relation sur une epidémie d'hystéro-démonopathie*; Chiap and Franzolini on *L'Epidemia di Istero-Demonopatie in Verzegniss*; Pitres's works on hysteria; Binet's on multiple personality; Mercier's *Sanity and Insanity*; Sprenger and Kramer's *Maleus Maleficarum*; and numerous books by Braid on trance.[68]

The range of James's reading was both broad and detailed as he surveyed a variety of different disciplines, narrowing in where necessary on the most recent materials.

DEVOTED STUDENTS

Another way of inferring the content of James's course comes from an examination of famous students who either worked under James and were influenced by his subject matter, or who actually took his course.[69]

James Rowland Angell, at the suggestion of John Dewey, had gone to Harvard to study with James in 1891. While working on a master's degree, Angell took over collating the American data from the census on hallucinations that had come out of the 1889 Paris Congress on Experimental Psychology. Angell went on to become a pioneer in the scientific study of mental imagery for fifteen years before becoming president at Yale University and later head of the Carnegie Foundation.[70]

Elmer Ernest Southard first heard about Freud from James when he took the mental pathology course in 1896. Southard went on to become the Bullard Professor of Neuropathology at Harvard, a pioneer in the autopsy of mental patients, founder of the Boston Psychopathic Hospital, and, as a result of his connections to James and Royce's circle, the man who would later coin the term "psychiatric social work."[71]

Harry Linenthal was a young medical student who took James's course in 1898. Linenthal became a voluntary assistant physician at the Massachusetts General Hospital and in 1904, along with Boris Sidis, began translating Freud and Pavlov for the neurological staff under James Jackson Putnam, who was just then embarking on experiments with different psychotherapeutic techniques. Linenthal went on to become a state health inspector before returning to the MGH to head up the Industrial Medicine Clinic in 1912. Eventually, he became the chief medical officer at the Beth Israel Hospital in Boston and an important example in Boston medicine of a family physican who had an extensive knowledge of psychotherapy.

George Arthur Waterman, who helped implement James's ideas on psychotherapy, became an assistant neurologist under Putnam at the Massachusetts General Hospital, published on non-Freudian methods of dream interpretation, and later distinguished himself as a private psychotherapist to such exclusive clientele as Robert Frost and General George Patton.[72]

Mary Whiton Calkins, after studying with James, went on to found the first laboratory of experimental psychology at Wellesley. The first woman to become a president of the American Psychological Association and the American Philosophical Association, Calkins was best known for the first thoroughgoing, systematic psychology of the self, a result of the influence of James and Royce.[73]

William Healey, who took James's course in psychopathology, went on to head the Juvenile Psychopathic Institute in Chicago. After that he became the first director of the the Judge Baker Guidance Clinic in Boston in 1917.[74]

William B. Parker took James's mental pathology course in 1896. Parker went on to develop the first home-study course in psychotherapy in New York around 1908.[75]

Boris Sidis's dissertation, *The Psychology of Suggestion* (1897), undertaken in the Harvard Psychological Laboratory under William James, became an influential text in the development of French social psychology in the late 1890s. Sidis wrote numerous texts on psychopathology and multiple personality. He first trained William Alanson White in psychotherapy at the New York Psychiatric Institute. Before he died he had attracted enough wealthy patrons to establish his own private hospital for psychoneurotics in Portsmouth, New Hampshire.[76]

Gertrude Stein did poorly in French prose and poetry as an undergraduate but was superb in physics and psychology. Under James's direction, she studied automatic writing in the Harvard Psychological Laboratory, published two experimental studies on the topic, and, at James's suggestion, went on to medical school at Johns Hopkins. She never finished, however, but went to France to be with her brother, Leo, to collect paintings and to write.[77]

Stein's laboratory partner, Leon Solomons, took James's mental pathology course in 1894. In their first experimental studies together, Stein and Solomons alternated in the roles of subject and experimenter, so that both became adept at the technique of automatic writing. Solomons, however, eventually died of a disease he had contracted in the laboratory.

W.E.B. DuBois, a fiery and rhetorical graduate student in history, was influenced by James's psychology of the subconscious long before he ever read Marx or Freud, and he incorporated the idea of double consciousness into his metaphor of the veil in his *Souls of Black Folk* (1904). In exchange, he gave both William and his brother, Henry James, a glimpse into the Afro-American religious experience.[78]

Two other students were E. L. Thorndike, later the famous learning theorist and educational psychologist, and Robert Sessions Woodworth, later the head of psychology at Columbia, who once said that together he and Thorndike had taken all of William James's courses at Harvard in the second half of the 1890s. Both were enrolled in James's lectures on mental pathology during the academic year 1896–97.[79]

Finally, there was Walter Bradford Cannon, who was also influenced by James during this period. While he went on to become a pioneer in experimental physiology and followed in Bowditch's footsteps, the Jamesean influence was still evident in his career. Cannon is best known for his work on the physiology of the emotions, and the origin of this interest most obviously came from William James. As an undergraduate, Cannon had written a summary of the James-Lange theory of the emotions and outlined all of the major criticisms against it, ostensibly for James's use in "What Is an Emotion?"(1894), which was James's final statement on the theory as stated in *The Principles*.[80] In addition, a recently discovered Harvard Medical School student notebook belonging to Ralph Larrabee from 1902 shows that, once Cannon began teaching medical students, he included in his course on general physiology at least one session on hypnosis and suggestibility. The content of this lecture is thoroughly Jamesean in both language and style.[81]

There were others. Suffice it to say that numerous young students passed through the interface of activities in psychology, neurology, and psychiatry at Harvard in the 1890s, and several of these went on to become pioneers in various aspects of modern psychotherapy in the next century.

Using these bits of evidence, we can conclude that James was widely read in the contemporary literature on psychiatry and experimental psychopathology. His database was at once anecdotal, physiological, and statistical, while he also drew from his own experience; he even had direct contact with several patients and experimental subjects. From a theoretical standpoint, he well understood the differentiation between clinical psychiatry and the new medical psychology of the psychoneuroses. His chief contribution appeared to be as an interpreter for the reigning dissociation model of Janet, Myers, and Flournoy.[82]

James's course was historic for several reasons. Not the least of these was that it defined the core of his vision of psychology at the middle of the 1890s. It also influenced several generations of Harvard students, some of whom would apply James's psychology of the subconscious to their own respective fields in the arts, sciences, and humanities, while others were encouraged to become practitioners and theorists who would become pioneers in the development of scientific psychotherapy in the early twentieth century. The content of this ongoing course also became the basis for James's later contribution to the psychology of religion movement, where he linked active exploration of the subconscious to religious awakening. But perhaps most important, it marked the unofficial beginning of the so-called Boston School of Abnormal Psychology, which was central to developments in scientific psychotherapy in the English-speaking world for more than a quarter of a century.[83]

EDUCATION AND PSYCHOLOGY

A final piece of evidence showing James's psychology during the 1890s is *Talks to Teachers on Psychology: and to Students on Some of Life's Ideals* (1899).[84] No more restrained example of Jamesean thought exists than this work, for the reason that all references to psychopathology were deliberately omitted. James did this self-consciously, he said, because teachers were too impressionable. He stated emphatically that once teachers got an impression in their mind about a student, it became almost permanently fixed. For this reason alone, it was better to steer teachers directly on the course of psychological growth rather than illness. *Talks to Teachers* thus became a book primarily about the application of psychology to character development in an educational setting.

Grounded in the new evolutionary biology, James's *Talks to Teachers* was the application of various chapters from *The Principles* to the problem of how children learn. It presented the stream of consciousness as a succession of fields within which one had to capture the interest of the child. It focused on shaping thoughts toward appropriate behaviors. It counseled teachers to build on the student's native reactions first and then proceed to appeal to the acquired ones. It emphasized the plasticity of habit, the association of ideas, and problems of interest, attention, memory, acquisition, apperception, and the all-important will.

James's main message was for teachers to take the child as an integrated whole. Character development and the maturation of personality were the desired ends, in the good teacher as well as the good student. Science was not going to tell you what to do, he told them, for "psychology is a science, and teaching is an art; and sciences never generate arts directly out of themselves. An intermediary inventive mind must make the application, by using its originality."[85] As to students, he cautioned teachers to be more sympathetic toward those who might do poorly on examinations, for, unlike the glib and ready reproducers, they usually succeed better in the larger test that life sets for us.

James's chapter on habit was particularly full of lively maxims. He enjoined both teachers and students to "make our nervous system our ally instead of our enemy." In the acquisition of a new habit, "[we must] launch ourselves with as strong and decided an initiative as possible." One should "never suffer an exception to occur till the new habit is securely rooted"; "Seize the very first possible opportunity to act on every resolution you make, and on every emotional prompting you may experience in the direction of the habits you aspire to gain"; "Keep the faculty of effort alive in you by a little gratuitous exercise everyday." Thus, "Let no youth have any anxiety about the upshot of his education, whatever the line of it may be. If he keep faithfully busy each hour of the working day, he may safely leave the final result to itself." These are still profitable thoughts today.

But the most compelling of his chapters in this volume, ones that have been often overlooked, are his talks to students on some of life's ideals: the ability to relax in a fast-paced environment, the need to open ourselves to the views of others in order to see the whole, and the importance of purpose and commitment, not just to ideals, but to acts. From especially these, James says, one can find the germ of a pluralistic and individualistic worldview.

Dissociation Theory and the Myerian Subliminal

Before closing this section of the discussion I must emphasize the importance that James attached to two guiding themes of the decade: the French model of dissociative consciousness, and F.W.H. Myers's ideas about the subliminal.

Dissociation, also referred to variously as disaggregation, somnambulism, and double, or multiple, personality, was the primary model that emerged in the late nineteenth century to explain the psychoneuroses. Dissociation as a psychological concept seems to have come into vogue in the late 1870s and early 1880s and was derived from a combination of at least three sources: the philosophy of the association of ideas, experimental advances in brain neurophysiology, and the rise of the French experimental psychology of the subconscious.[86]

Dissociation, according to the British associationists, meant the process by which we come to discriminate within a whole, composite elements not yet discriminated in previous experience within this whole. William James and Carl Stumpf were credited with describing the Law of Dissociation.[87] According to this law, where *a* and *b* occur together as part of a whole without being discriminated, the occurrence of one of them, *a*, in a new combination, *ax*, favors the discrimination of *a*, *b*, and *x,* from each other.

Within this philosophical endeavor to understand normal thinking processes, dissociation was not a negative trait of mental activity. While most physicians and psychologists were empiricists who were trained in the Western rationalist tradition to understand their sensations by logical categories, there were a few bright minds throughout who maintained that important scientific discoveries could be made about the potential of the mind, once the normally conditioned habits of rational thought were suspended. Dissociation, for instance, was one explanation for how personality change might come about. Such a view would soon have an important impact on new ways of looking at psychopathology.

The concept of dissociation, as it arose in experimental psychopathology, was a way to understand abnormal states of consciousness. As the converse of evolution, it was seen to break down more highly developed structures into simpler ones, but in the sense of a retrogression to a less well developed state. The abnormalities might be slight, as in a momentary lapse of consciousness, or more grave, as in cases of hallucination, illusion, or severe disorders of personality. In mental illness, the main trend of associative thought processes was believed to disintegrate, and a portion of the stream of thought and feeling would then be dissociated from the rest. The subject, in a normal state, became unaware of what took place in the abnormal or dissociated condition, and while in the dissociated state might or might not have knowledge of normal functioning. In all, the process of dissociation was thought to run through every possible state of consciousness. It was, in fact, the basis for James's claim that consciousness in its natural but undeveloped condition is an ultimate plurality of selves.

Dissociation was a useful explanatory model for several reasons. It could be generally applied to many observed clinical cases. It was the product of the most recent advances in brain neurophysiology. It guided the evolution of an entire generation of psychotherapeutic techniques that were applied in the early treatment of the ambulatory psychoneuroses. It held out hope for the development of new interventions in the treatment of the most severely insane. Finally, as dissociation was the explanatory device for psychopathology, so too could dissociation and association serve to help us understand the processes of normal functioning. And beyond the theory of the normal personality was the possibility of supernormal functioning. Here the doctrine of the association of ideas pointed to a higher-order integration, a perception of the interrelatedness of all things, characterized alike by the mystics and the mental healers in the transcendent experience.

But the materialistic and positivistic philosophy of French science precluded any such metaphysical formulations. For the iconography of the transcendent, James, who had been so used to hearing it from Emerson and Henry James, Sr., in his boyhood, had to turn to the conception of subliminal consciousness put forth by F.W.H. Myers.

Myers's formulations were, in fact, central to the development of James's psychology and philosophy in the 1890s, and they form the epistemological core of James's scientific activities in abnormal psychology and psychical research. James expressed this influence in a eulogy just after Myers's death in 1901: "Frederick Myers was a psychologist who worked upon lines hardly admitted by the more academic branch of the profession to be legitimate; and as for some years I bore the title of 'Professor of Psychology,' the suggestion has been made (and by me gladly welcomed) that I should spend my portion of this hour in defining the exact place and rank which we must accord to him as a cultivator and promoter of the science of the Mind."[88] Speaking about human immortality as Myers's main concern, James said, "His contributions to psychology were incidental to that research, and would probably never have been made had he not entered on it. But they have a value for Science entirely independent of the light they shed upon that problem."[89]

Both Myers and James believed that until their own time all of psychology had been written along classic and academic lines. As a consequence, the mind was treated as an abstraction in which only its normal adult traits were recognized:

A sort of sunlit terrace was exhibited on which it took its exercise. But where that terrace stopped, the mind stopped; and there was nothing further left to tell of in this kind of philosophy but the brain and other physical facts of nature on the one hand, and the absolute metaphysical ground of the universe on the other.

But of late years the terrace has been overrun by romantic improvers [he calls Myers "the radical leader of the romantic movement"], and to pass to their work is like going from classic to Gothic architecture, where few outlines are pure and where uncouth forms lurk in the shadows. A mass of mental phenomena are now seen in the shrubbery beyond the parapet. Fantastic, ignoble, hardly human, and frankly non-human are some of these new candidates for psychological description. The menagerie and the madhouse, the nursery, the prison, and the hospital, have been made to deliver up their material. The world of mind is shown as something infinitely more complex than was suspected; and whatever beauties it may still possess, it has lost at any rate the beauty of academic neatness.[90]

This stereotyped view of academic neatness, James further elaborated, was based on "social prejudices which scientific men themselves obey."[91]

Myers has made much of the inner domain respectable to psychology, James went on, through the coordinating power of his thought, that is, through his ability to see relations and connections among different phenomena and to arrange them in an understandable series.

Myers's greatest contribution, however—one that is destined to transform psychology in the twentieth century, James said—was his conception of the subliminal consciousness. *"What is the precise constitution of the Subliminal?*—such is the problem which deserves to figure in our Science hereafter as *The problem of Myers.*"[92] He said, "Post-hypnotic suggestion, crystal gazing, automatic writing and trance speech, the willing game, etc., are now, thanks to him, instruments of research, reagents like litmus paper or the galvanometer, for revealing what would otherwise be hidden."[93]

His most sympathetic detractors claim that supernormal cognitions form no part of the subliminal region. Myers would say, James claimed, that the subliminal is composed of innumerable discrete regions, levels separated by critical points of transition, and no one formula holds true for them all: "Any conscientious psychologist ought, it seems to me, to see that, since these multiple modifications of personality are only beginning to be reported and observed with care, it is obvious that a dogmatically negative treatment of them must be premature, and that the problem of Myers still awaits us as the problem of far the deepest moment for our actual psychology, whether his own tentative solutions of certain parts of it be correct or not."[94]

Myers also outlined various ways in which the subconscious communicates to consciousness: namely, through sensory and motor automatisms and through the symbolic hypothesis. Subliminal states showed themselves to consciousness through automatic and reflexive behavior as well as through energy-laden imagery within the field of consciousness. "Obsessive thoughts and delusions, as well as voices, visions, and impulses, thus fall subject to one mode of treatment. To explain them, we must explore the Subliminal; to cure them we must practically influence it."[95]

From these formulations Myers went on to develop "his brilliant conception, in 1891, of hysteria." He defined it as "a disease of the hypnotic stratum." And here James again emphatically states that Binet and Janet were the first to corroborate Myers, followed by work "in Germany, America, and elsewhere."[96]

Myers's theory is epochal, James explained, "not only in medical, but in psychological science, because it brings in an entirely new conception of our mental possibilities." Psychopathology and transcendence express themselves to consciousness through the self-same channels, and thus are logically confused as "the same." Once we can discriminate between the two, our ability to actualize the higher rather than the lower then becomes possible through the exercise of our will.

Psychologically, this seemed plausible to James, except for one difficulty inherent in Myers's scheme, namely, "his conception of mental evolution is more radical than anything yet considered by psychologists as possible." The cornerstone of his conception was the fact that consciousness had no essential unity. "It aggregates and dissipates, and what we call normal consciousness, the 'Human Mind' of classic psychology,—is not even typical, but only one case out of thousands," which caused James fittingly to say, in conclusion, that "it looks to me like one of those sweeping ideas by which the scientific researches of an entire generation are often moulded."[97]

Chapter Five

MYSTICAL AWAKENING: AN EPISTEMOLOGY OF THE ULTIMATE

PSYCHOLOGY of religion has had a checkered history. Abandoned as an unwanted stepchild of scientific psychology in the early part of the twentieth century, it became, and mostly remains, an unwanted orphan within the field of religion. There was a brief time, however, just around 1900 and before the onslaught of psychoanalysis and behaviorism, when the psychological study of religious experience had its heyday in American psychology. G. Stanley Hall was an important figure in this movement. He encouraged an empirical approach to religious behavior, especially around such topics as conversion; he supervised a few doctoral dissertations in the psychology of religion; and for a number of years he edited the *American Journal of Religious Psychology*. He remained indelibly wedded to the Christian scheme of salvation, however, as his *Jesus the Christ in the Light of Psychology* (1917) shows. In the end he never produced more than a psychology of his own Christian religious experience.[1]

But it was William James at Harvard who stood at center stage in the psychology of religion, partly because of his international reputation as a psychologist, partly because of his broadminded approach to studying all aspects of human experience, and partly because of his philosophy of pragmatism, which he put forward as a way to evaluate claims of ultimate truth and to reconcile conflicting belief systems.

THE INGERSOLL LECTURE ON IMMORTALITY

James's first major foray into the field of religious life was his Ingersoll Lecture of 1897. His talk was entitled "Immortality: Two Supposed Objections to the Doctrine," which he delivered at Harvard and published in 1898.[2] James was the second incumbent to the endowed lectureship and fancied he had been asked, not because he had a volume of messages about the future life to give to his audience, but because he was an officer of the inviting institution. The question of immortality itself, he said to his audience, was just not a burning question with him.

Nevertheless, he promised to rise to the occasion. In order to limit himself because he had only the scope of a single lecture, whatever else immortality might mean he intended only to elaborate on two points.

The first was to address the relationship between the brain and the mind. In modern biology, he explained, it is presumed that consciousness is a product of physiological brain functioning, and that when the brain dies, consciousness ends with it. The brain, therefore, produces the mind. It is not incompatible with the tenets of biology, however, to conceive that the brain, rather than being a mere producer, might actually be a *transmitter* of consciousness. To make his point, he used the analogy of the relationship between radio waves and the Marconi wireless. If this second view were true, it meant that when the brain died, consciousness would also cease, *but only in the sense of no longer being transmitted through that particular unique organ.*

The important point about the transmissive view is that something existed prior to and something persists after the demise of the unique transmitter, upon which the life and experiences of the transmitter makes its mark. He referred to this something as an "infinite Mother-Sea" of consciousness that surrounds us at all times and can be made visible only during unique moments when there is a rending of the veil that separates waking consciousness from it.

The benefit of this view, he said, is that it allows the biological relation of the brain and the mind to remain intact while opening up the possibility that religious and spiritual explanations of the ultimate might not be entirely incorrect.

His second point was to address the supposition in most people's implied definition of the afterlife that Heaven had a finite capacity and could, therefore, hold only a limited number of souls. As far as the common person's uncritical reflection on the matter went, of course, only those souls would be there who were most like ourselves. Hence, Heaven would be peopled with all of our family and friends, for instance, but not our neighbor and his family, whom we never liked anyway, and certainly there would be no room for our enemies.

The idea of Heaven's capacity was a new one, James said, brought about "due to the strain upon the quantitative imagination which recent scientific theories, and the moral feelings consequent upon them, have brought in their train."[3] Moreover, it bred one of the greatest fallacies of the age, "the result of nothing but an invincible blindness from which we suffer, an insensibility to the inner significance of alien lives, and a conceit that would project our own incapacity into the vast cosmos, and measure the wants of the Absolute by our own puny needs."[4]

On the contrary, James maintained, if immortality were really true and Heaven really did exist, it would not be a physical place, but rather like a state of inexhaustible being. The old concept of capacity would not obtain, and everyone who had been on earth, by virtue of their simply being there, would find a place.

Many voices were raised when James's little book first appeared, both in praise and in criticism. But one of the strongest collective objections concerned his transmission theory of cerebral action. If finite personality in normal life was due to transmission through the brain of a higher and more vast ocean of consciousness, then after the death of the brain all that would be left was this larger undifferentiated consciousness. Such a pantheistic idea of survival ran contrary to the Christian idea of immortality, which means survival in strictly personal form.

James asserted in his preface to the second edition that he was no pantheist of the monistic pattern, and conceded only that he had oversimplified for brevity's sake. He answered the objections by saying "there might be . . . many minds behind the scenes as one. The plain truth is that one may conceive the mental world behind the veil in as individualistic a form as one pleases, without any detriment to the general scheme by which the brain is represented as a transmissive organ."[5]

To take the extreme individualistic view, he asserted, "One's finite mundane consciousness would be an extract from one's larger, truer personality, the latter having even now some sort of reality behind the scenes."[6] The smaller self, James said, might still leave behind impressions on this larger consciousness.

He also admitted that all this "would seem to have affinities rather with preexistence and with possible re-incarnations than with the Christian notion of immortality." But he countered by saying that he did not mean to take up immortality in general, only to show that the transmission hypothesis was not incompatible with the brain-function theory of our present mundane consciousness.

THE VARIETIES OF RELIGIOUS EXPERIENCE

There is no more influential book in the field of the psychology of religion than William James's *Varieties of Religious Experience*. First delivered as the Gifford Lectures on Natural Religion at the University of Edinburgh and published in 1902, James's work continues to be the most widely used textbook in psychology of religion courses taught throughout the United States.[7] Its impact can partly be gauged by the wide range of responses when it first appeared.

Royce got the first advance copy but had it in his hands for only a few hours before it was stolen from him by President Eliot. Eliot gobbled the book up and found it "interesting and instructive," but he was, he wrote James, "quite unable to accept as records of actual experience some of the narratives which you print."[8] James replied that, be that as it may, one cannot dispute the evidence for *changed lives* as a result of such experiences. Barrett Wendell called the book "divinely shameless," and James himself joked that his lectures "seem to add fuel to the fire which burns in the hearts of God's enemies as well as that which burns in those of his friends," because, like it or not, so many people seemed to be reading it. And not all were theological types. Ernst Mach, the physicist, wrote to James: "Your fine and remarkable book . . . has gripped me powerfully. Religious inspiration is certainly very similar to the scientific inspiration which one feels when new problems first present themselves in a form which is as yet not wholly clear. There is an as yet unmeasured depth into which one is gazing."[9]

To understand its staying power, we must look a little into the content and direction of this remarkable work. In the first place, James made it absolutely clear that this was a text in psychology. At the outset he informed the members of his Edinburgh audience: "As regards the manner in which I shall have to administer this lectureship, I am neither a theologian, nor a scholar learned in the history of religions, nor an anthropologist. Psychology is the only branch of learning in which I am particularly versed. To the psychologist, the religious propensities of man must at least be as interesting as any of the other facts pertaining to his mental constitution. It would seem therefore as a psychologist, the natural thing for me to do would be to invite you to a descriptive survey of these religious propensities."[10]

James's main thesis centers around the subconscious and its exploration as a doorway to the awakening of mystical religious experience. Religion he defined at the outset as "the feelings, acts, and experiences of individual men in their solitude, so far as they apprehend themselves to stand in relation to the divine."[11] He omitted theologies and ecclesiastical organizations, claiming they were secondary growths superimposed on what was to be his main focus, that of immediate personal experience. He took as his basic data, neither graphs nor numerical figures, but *documents humains*, that is, written testimony to the value of different kinds of religious experience given by unique personalities.

He then proceeded to establish the reality of the unseen. Within us, beyond the threshold of waking consciousness, we have dimensions of experience not readily understood by the normal self. The unseen is quite familiar to those particularly oriented toward the spiritual life through a pervasive sense of religious presence that is simply known from within. It is in fact so certain to those who have it that it remains impervious to denial through mere logic. James says, "Please observe, however, that I do not say it is *better* that the subconscious and nonrational should thus hold primacy in the religious realm. I confine myself to pointing out that they do so hold it as a matter of fact."[12] Religious life, in other words, is known by deeply felt emotions that expand and contract within us, not by purely abstract concepts.

The general basis of all religious experience, James said, is the fact that man has a dual nature, and is connected with two spheres of thought, a shallower and a profounder sphere, in either of which he may learn to live more habitually. The shallower and lower sphere is that of the fleshy sensations, instincts, desires, egotism, doubt, and lower personal interests. The spiritual in man, especially according to the American Mind Cure philosophies, is considered partly conscious, but largely subconscious, and through the subconscious part of it they believe that we are already one with the Divine without any miracle of grace or any abrupt creation of a new inner man.[13]

These and other optimistic types, James said, absolutely deny evil. They are the once-born personalities who came into the world already having access to visions of perpetual goodness. In contrast are the twice-born, those who must sink into the abyss of mental darkness before becoming transformed and reborn into a newer, higher light. Both kinds of personality, James said, are necessary for a complete picture of religious life. The once-born, he said, are exemplified by men such as Ralph Waldo Emerson, Edward Everett Hale, Walt Whitman, and the mind-cure doctors. The optimistic creed of the mental healers is that through the practice of breathing, relaxation, and guided mental imagery they will be led to bliss. The sick soul, on the other hand, lives by the philosophy that it is his business to continue to fail in good spirits. But James wrote: "There is no doubt that healthy-mindedness is inadequate as a philosophical doctrine, because the evil facts which it refuses to positively account for are a genuine part of reality. They may, after all, be the best key to life's significance, and possibly the only openers of our eyes to the deepest levels of truth."[14]

For the subconscious, he reiterated, contains a plurality of selves, heterogeneous personalities all acting at once in the background of our attention, exerting their influence to varying degrees and highly pronounced in pathological types as well as in religious genius. Only on rare occasions do we find within ourselves one unsuspected depth below another, as if the possibilities of character lay disposed in a series of layers or shells, of whose existence we have no premonitory knowledge.

Subconscious incubation was the idea James put forward to explain religious conversions in the adult, while self-surrender is the key to admittance into these deeper regions of our inner life. It was also in his discussion of conversion that James spoke at greater length on the psychological conception of subliminal consciousness. He called it the "field formula," referring to the current psychological conception through which the ultra-marginal zone of experience was being investigated:

> I cannot but think that the most important step forward that has occurred in psychology since I have been a student of that science is the discovery, first made in 1886 [by F.W.H. Myers], that, in certain subjects at least, there is not only the consciousness of the ordinary field, with its usual center and margin, but in addition thereto in the shape of a set of memories, thoughts, and feelings which are extra-marginal and outside the primary consciousness altogether, but yet must be classed as conscious facts of some sort, able to reveal their presence by unmistakable signs.[15]

The discovery of this region, James said, has revealed to us an entirely unsuspected peculiarity in the constitution of human nature and casts light on many phenomena of religious biography. And if there were indeed higher spiritual agencies that can directly touch us, "the psychological condition of their doing so might be our possession of a subconscious region which alone should yield access to them. The hubbub of the waking life might close a door which in the dreamy subliminal might remain ajar."[16]

James also dealt with the qualities of the religious personality. Saintliness, he said, is the collective name we give to the ripe fruits of subconscious incubation. He was particularly referring to persons with unstable nervous systems, who, because of their wide subconscious life, are prone to temporary alterations of consciousness, shifting excitements, and rapid falls of the threshold of normal awareness. They are religious types precisely because they seek spiritual insights and are guided by the higher emotions. They are examples for the rest of us of faith, self-sacrifice, obedience, devotion, and voluntarily accepted poverty. (James mentioned chastity as well, but omitted a discussion of it.) Such qualities, when taken to extremes, can become pathological. Thus James warned against what he called "theopathic absorption." The great value of saintliness, he said, is the emphasis on individuality and on the importance of individual differences. Such personalities are models for our own realization of the higher life. Thus James presented the ideal of ascetic discipline in the midst of wealth as one stirring example of what he would came to call the moral equivalent of war.

This brought James to a discussion of the deepest source of religious emotions, in which he blatantly declared that "personal religious experience has its root and center in mystical states of consciousness."[17] He gave four characteristics of the mystical state: its ineffability, its noetic quality, its transiency, and the passive attitude required for its onset. Mystical consciousness, he said, defies expression in normal terms. It is a state of insight into depths of truth unplumbed by the discursive intellect, carrying a sense of authority with it for all after time. For even though it lasts only a brief moment in the temporal frame of the experiencer, the sense of timelessness makes its influence permanently enduring. It comes only when we are ready to surrender completely to it. Its onset may be facilitated by preliminary voluntary operations. But once the characteristic sort of consciousness has set in, mystics feel as if their own will were in abeyance and that they are grasped and held by a superior power.

James then gave personal accounts from Martin Luther, J. A. Symonds, Richard Maurice Bucke, Swami Vivekananda, St. Ignatius, St. Theresa, St. John of the Cross, Dionysius, Jacob Boehme, Plotinus, Angeles Selesius, and Helena Blavatsky. He further cited passages from Max Müller's translations of the *Upanishads*; C. F. Koeppen's *Die Religion des Buddha*; Schmolder's translation of the Sufi mystic, Al Ghazzali; and he recommended V. L. Mitra's *Yoga Vasishta Maha Ramayana* as a definitive text on yoga. He also took up a discussion of ultimate states, in which he compared the Christian experience of *orisen* with the *samadhi* of yoga, the *Atman* of Vedanta, and the state of *nirvana* described by the Buddhists. Such personal accounts, textual studies, and conceptual examples suggested to him that in the psychology of the subliminal or subconscious region one finds the foundation of religious experience.

JAMES'S RELIGIOUS EPISTEMOLOGY

Numerous writers have attempted to capture the essence of James's vision of religious experience, the general consensus being that he preached a naturalistic theism.[18] God exists as a belief in people's minds and hearts and this belief has definite consequences in shaping a person's response to the environment. "God, to be real," he once said, "must have consequences." But he was informed enough to realize that whatever one's conception of the ultimate, it probably came through the subliminal. A psychology of the subconscious thus became the generic blueprint for understanding how each person evolved his or her conception of what was ultimately real.

James's own epistemology of the ultimate was revealed in a number of other places besides *The Varieties*. Among these are sources such as his correspondence with Henry William Rankin; James's published accounts of nitrous oxide intoxication; the contents of recently recovered notebooks from the only graduate course he ever taught at Harvard on psychology and religion; and the manuscript lecture notes of his Harvard Divinity School lectures on "Intellect and Feeling in Religion," delivered in 1902.

THE JAMES-RANKIN LETTERS

Henry William Rankin, an invalid writer on religious topics from East Northfield, Massachusetts, had first written to James in the mid-1890s, offering several copies of *Demon Possession and Allied Themes* by John Livingston Nevius. Rankin had been born and raised in China, the son of a Presbyterian missionary, and Nevius had been another missionary stationed in China who had become a family friend. Nevius had accidentally cured a few cases of demon possession among the Chinese peasants by invoking the passages in the Bible where Jesus had done the same. Heartened by the peasants' adoption of Christianity once they had been cured, Nevius endeavored to canvass the other Christian missions in China for similar cases of possession. To these he added numerous literary accounts of possession from China and Japan, and, once the material was all together, brought his manuscript back to the United States to be published. He died shortly after arriving, and it fell to Rankin to bring the book to light.

After painstakingly seeing the work through the press, Rankin sent three copies to James. James, in turn, read the book, produced two reviews, and incorporated the material into both of his graduate lectures on psychopathology and his 1896 Lowell Lectures on "Exceptional Mental States."[19]

A continuing correspondence then developed between the two, and when James first received his invitation to give the Gifford Lectures on Natural Religion in 1897, Rankin further provided a number of books on religious autobiography. James carried these books around for almost six years before returning them, after duly acknowledging Rankin's aid in the preface to *The Varieties*.

As he carted the books around, James would write an occasional postcard to Rankin, and Rankin would reply with a twenty-page letter, attempting all the while to convert James to Presbyterian missionary Christianity. James, in turn, would always counter with some diverting comment, at one point admitting that he remained pretty firmly fixed in the line of Henry James Sr.'s Swedenborgian approach to religious experience.

One gets the impression in reading the letters that James was striving to articulate his own personal theology in drafting his lectures. This interpretation finds confirmation in an oft-quoted letter that appeared in Henry James Jr.'s collection of William James's *Letters* in 1920, and which the psychologist of religion, Walter Houston Clark, identified as the seminal statement by which James finally broke loose from his father's theological apron strings.[20] Not coincidentally, this letter is also one of James's epistemological statements on the nature of the ultimate:

To Henry W. Rankin

Edinburgh, June 16, 1901

Dear Mr. Rankin,—I have received all your letters and missives, inclusive of the letter which you think I must have lost some months back. I profess-ed you because I had read your name printed with that title in a newspaper letter from East Northfield, and supposed that, by courtesy at any rate, that title was conferred on you by a public opinion to which I liked to conform.

I have given nine of my lectures and am to give the tenth tomorrow. They have been a success, to judge by the numbers of the audience (300-odd) and their non-diminution towards the end. No previous "Giffords" have drawn near so many. It will please you to know that I am stronger and tougher than when I began, too; so great a load is off my mind. You have been so extraordinarily brotherly to me in writing of your convictions and in furnishing me ideas, that I feel ashamed of my churlish and chary replies. You, however, have forgiven me. Now, at the end of this first course, I feel my "matter" taking firmer shape, and it will please you less to hear me say that I believe myself to be (probably) permanently incapable of believing the Christian scheme of vicarious salvation, and wedded to a more continu-ously evolutionary mode of thought. The reasons you from time to time have given me, never better expressed than in your letter before the last, have somehow failed to convince. In these lectures the ground I am taking is this: The mother-sea and fountain-head of all religions lie in the mystical experiences of the individual, taking the word mystical in a very wide sense. All theologies and all ecclesiasticisms are secondary growths superimposed; and the experiences make such flexible combinations with the intellectual prepossessions of their subjects, that one may almost say that they have no proper intellectual deliverance of their own, but belong to a region deeper, and more vital and practical, than that which the intellect inhabits. For this they are also indestructible by intellectual arguments and criticisms. I at-tach the mystical or religious consciousness to the possession of an ex-tended subliminal self, with a thin partition through which messages make interruption. We are thus made convincingly aware of the presence of a sphere of life larger and more powerful than our usual consciousness, with which the latter is nevertheless continuous. The impressions and impul-sions and emotions and excitements which we thence receive help us to live, they found invincible assurance of a world beyond the sense, they melt our hearts and communicate significance and value to everything and make us happy. They do this for the individual who has them, and other individu-als follow him. Religion in this way is absolutely indestructible. Philosophy and theology give their conceptual interpretations of this experiential life. The farther margin of the subliminal field being unknown, it can be treated as by Transcendental Idealism, as an Absolute mind with a part of which we coalesce, or by Christian theology, as a distinct deity acting on us. Something, not our immediate self, does act on our life! So I seem doubtless to my audience to be blowing hot and cold, explaining away Christianity, yet defending the more general basis from which I say it proceeds. I fear that these brief words may be misleading, but let them go! When the book comes out, you will get a truer idea.

Believe me, with profound regards, your always truly,

Wm. James

The two key statements here are (1) that James attaches the mystical or religious consciousness "to the possession of an extended subliminal self, with a thin partition through which messages make interruption"; and (2) *The farther margin of the subliminal field being unknown,* it can be treated in a variety of ways consonant with the tenets of an individual's belief system, whether socially sanctioned or not.

Anesthetic Revelations

Another source for statements on the ultimate is the collection of references James makes throughout his writings to drug-induced mysticism. James had undertaken experiments of his own as early as twelve years old. He had indulged, along with the other medical students, in numerous episodes of self-medication in the 1860s. He continued his experiments with chloral hydrate as a young professor at Harvard; he carried on a correspondence with Benjamin Paul Blood in the 1870s and 1880s on the philosophy of so-called anesthetic revelations; he tried peyote as late as the mid-1890s when he was over fifty; and he wrote on several occasions about his experiences with nitrous oxide.

Quoting Blood, he had said:

> After experiments ranging over nearly fourteen years I affirm—what any man may prove at will—that there is an invariable and reliable condition (or uncondition) ensuing about the instant of recall from anaesthetic stupor to sensible observation, or 'coming to,' in which the genius of being is revealed; but because it cannot be remembered in the normal condition it is lost altogether through the infrequency of anaesthetic treatment in any individual's case ordinarily, and buried, amid the hum of returning common sense, under that epitaph of all illumination: "this is a queer world."[21]

James expanded on the nature of mystical revelations under nitrous oxide in *The Varieties,* where he again affirmed Blood's contention that "in the nitrous oxide trance we have a genuine metaphysical revelation."[22] James there referred again to his own personal experiments:

Some years ago I myself made observations on this aspect of nitrous oxide intoxication, and reported them in print. One conclusion was forced upon my mind at that time, and my impression of its truth has ever since remained unshaken. It is that our normal waking consciousness, rational consciousness as we call it, is but one special type of consciousness, whilst all about it, parted from it by the filmiest of screens, there lie potential forms of consciousness entirely different. We may go through life without suspecting their existence; but apply the requisite stimulus, and at a touch they are there in all their completeness, definite types of mentality which probably somewhere have their field of application and adaptation. No account of the universe in its totality can be final which leaves these other forms of consciousness quite disregarded. How to regard them is the question,—for they are so discontinuous with ordinary consciousness. Yet they may determine attitudes though they cannot furnish formulas, and open a region though they fail to give a map. At any rate, they forbid a premature closing of our accounts with reality.[23]

Here, James affirms that the drug is merely a vehicle for opening the inward doors of perception, as a later author has called it, and by inhaling the substance, James confirmed that consciousness appears to be an ultimate plurality of states, the transcendent realities awakened being one of an important class that points to a higher condition possible in human beings.

JAMES'S GRADUATE COURSE ON THE PSYCHOLOGY OF RELIGION

Yet another source for James's epistemological statements on the ultimate come from recently discovered notes showing the content of the graduate course on the psychology of religion which James conducted at Harvard in 1902. From this evidence we may take note of an interesting relationship between psychology and religion at Harvard between 1896 and 1902, when courses in philosophy, sociology, experimental laboratory psychology, and comparative religions were all taught under the aegis of the philosophy department. One of these was this graduate course on the psychology of religion, the only one on that subject that James ever taught at Harvard.

The course itself, however, had an earlier history. From 1896 to 1899 Charles Carroll Everett had taught Philosophy 6 for undergraduates on the philosophy of religion. This course combined philosophy, psychology, and comparative religions together. It was offered for a number of years in the philosophy department and cross-referenced in the Divinity School catalog. At the same time, and in the same department, among others, Münsterberg taught courses in experimental laboratory psychology, Francis Greenwood Peabody taught "The Ethics of the Social Question," and James taught undergraduate courses on Kant, philosophical problems in psychology, and his graduate course in psychopathology.

James went on sabbatical in 1899 and Everett's Philosophy 6 course had its title changed to "Elements of Religious Faith."[24] Everett also began teaching Philosophy 13, "The Comparative Study of Religion." This course was described in the catalog as "Studies in the Comparative History of Religions, particularly the Vedic religion, the Hindu Philosophers, Buddhism, Mazdaism, and the Chinese Religions." Philosophy 6 and Philosophy 13, the catalog recommended, could be taken together. Both courses were offered in the academic year 1900–1901, but in the spring, unexpectedly, Everett died. James was away preparing for his Gifford Lectures, the first half of which he had delivered from May to June of 1901. James Houghton Woods evidently took over Everett's teaching duties at the time.

During the spring semester of 1902 the college catalog states that Woods was now teaching Philosophy 13, renamed "The Science of Religions," with the same description as Everett's course, except with the addition of primitive forms of animism. For the academic year 1901–1902, James is listed as teaching Everett's Philosophy 6 course, now entitled "The Psychological Elements of Religious Life." Twenty-three students enrolled in the course and five of these were also taking Woods's "Science of Religions" course.

We are intensely curious about the content of the courses taught by both James and Woods, as they would seem to throw additional light on James's references to a "science of religions" in *The Varieties*. Certain clues about them are available to us.

While pursuing his studies in philosophy and psychology at Harvard, for instance, Woods had published a valuable little book, *The Value of Religious Facts* (1899), and James's copy of this work is still extant.[25] There can be little doubt that James's ideas on psychology are contained in it, and that James, in turn, was influenced by Woods's interpretation of a science of religions. Such a science, Woods says, proceeds by the empirical methods of any other science—by observation, deduction, hypothesis testing, and generalization. Its two great branches are psychology and history. Psychology probes the value of religious experience within each person, and history accounts for the diversity of religious forms from one culture to another over time. Both are needed to construct a science of religions.

As for James's course in the psychology of religion, of the twenty-three people enrolled only one was an undergraduate; the rest were graduate students in the arts and sciences, divinity students, or students from the

medical school.[26] One was Horatio Dresser, Swedenborgian minister and
a Ph.D. student of James's whose parents, Julius and Annetta Dresser,
were followers of Phineas Parkhurst Quimby, the spiritual healer who
had cured Mary Baker Eddy. Also present was Arthur Whittlesley Towne,
who later became a well-known New York social worker. Also present was
William Ernest Hocking, a young engineering student who had switched
to philosophy because of James's influence and would later become a
professor at Harvard and chair of the philosophy department. A search
of Hocking's papers at Harvard has produced his notes for this graduate
course.

Hocking's notebook yields a gold mine of important facts. First, it
shows that the content of the course came directly from James's soon-to-
be-published Gifford Lectures, which means that these students were the
first American audience to be exposed to *The Varieties* before it appeared
in print. Second, in his discussion of healthy-mindedness versus the pessimistic types, James gave an important comparison of Buddhism and
Christianity, lauding them both as religions which transform the vision
of evil, making them seem deeper and more adequate than other religious traditions. Third, James again lays great stress on the importance
of individual differences. "Here is the hopelessness of psychology,"
James says, "—that the various temperaments see the conflict under such
different categories." Fourth, Hocking notes that James does not see the
necessity of any higher formulation than the naturalistic worship of the
divine in the self. Finally, Hocking's references to the science of religions
are suggestive, for he says, "[A] Science of Religions in the critical sense
is the proper work of philosophy," and "the resulting nucleus may be
abstract and dry enough, but in each the individual becomes clothed
with his own *aberglaube* and acquires reality again. Arguments, unless
they find some backing in your heart, will not pass as good arguments.
[A] Science of Religions cannot force religion on you any more than
philosophy can. But it can show the relevance of certain forms of experience and thus furnish a certain ground for being believed in." Hocking's
notes for the course then end with references to "The definite Hypothesis," "The subliminal self is the mediating term required," "Religion and
Science," "The exploration hardly begun."[27]

So we see from the content of James's course the important link he
continued to pursue between a psychology of the subconscious and religious awakening. At this interface, he found not only what he believed to
be psychology's true contribution to the religious sphere, namely the
construction of a cross-cultural comparative psychology of trance states,
but also the grounds for a potential dialogue between the radically different epistemologies of those who spoke for science and those who
spoke for religion.

JAMES'S HARVARD DIVINITY SCHOOL LECTURES

Another source for understanding his psychological approach to the ultimate is a series of lectures James gave for the Harvard Divinity School during the summer of 1902.[28] The Summer School of Theology had been launched by President Eliot in 1899 for the purpose of cross-fertilizing the disciplines with honored scholars and educating an enlightened clergy and lay public in the most advanced knowledge of the times. The theme of the eighteen-day session in 1902 was devoted to current problems in theology. Among the speakers were George Herbert Palmer, George Foote Moore, William W. Fenn, and Francis Greenwood Peabody. While announced as a Divinity School activity, the lectures were held in a large lecture hall of the Semitic Museum on Divinity Avenue. James spoke at noon on a Monday and Tuesday.[29]

James's lecture title had been widely announced as "Intellect and Feeling in Religion," but, having just published his Gifford Lectures, he felt compelled, he told his audience, to consider his original title as only provisional and, instead, to connect the program with his book. Among others, there were two principal themes that he again took up from *The Varieties*. The first was the problem of individual differences in religious experience and the other was a Science of Religions.

Religious experience always involves the life history of individuals. What is the function of normative religion for life, he asked? His answer was that science communicates facts and religion communicates values. Both are needed for a healthy, normal life. The dialogue between different religions is one of constant acrimony and argumentation, he noted. Meanwhile, we live in an age in which science has discounted the significance of religious experience altogether. The problem is not deciding which religion is superior to the others or whether science is true and religion is false. The heart of the matter is recognizing that there are different types of personalities who have different tendencies, needs, and ways of taking the world. Any true science of religions, James said, must not take sides on these issues. Such a science must deal with facts, by which he meant the facts of history and the facts of human experience.

The facts of experience interested him the most as a psychologist, James said. He was specifically referring to the observations on subconscious life made by "F.W.H. Myers, Pierre Janet, Theodore Flournoy, Morton Prince, Richard Hodgson, and James Hyslop." Here he defined again the outlines of the so-called French-English-Swiss-and-American psychotherapeutic axis, which included the French Experimental Psychology of the Subconscious, the Society for Psychical Research in England, experimental psychopathology in Switzerland, and the Boston

School of Abnormal Psychology. The prevailing model was that of dissociation, with the added coda that personality contained within it the
possibility of both psychopathic and transcendent states. The greater
portion of us that lies perpetually buried, our higher nature, as well as
agencies of superior intelligence that may express themselves through
us, all come to consciousness through the subliminal, he said.

James admitted, however, that his idea of the supernormal entering
through the subliminal was just a hypothesis, "a mere program for study,
a suggestion." He said that he only wished to press it upon his audience's
attention because it gives dignity and backbone to witnessed facts; the
theory heals a historic breach between science and religion; it confirms
tolerance and respect for personal secrets; and it leaves room for science
to study the facts of human experience.

In collating the ideas from these varied sources, we can allow James to
sum up his own position:

> If the word 'subliminal' is offensive to any of you, as smelling too much of
> psychical research or other aberrations, call it by any other name you
> please, to distinguish it from the level of full sunlit consciousness. Call this
> latter the A-region of personality, if you care to, and call the other the
> B-region.[30] The B-region, then, is obviously the larger part of each of us for
> it is the abode of everything that is latent and the reservoir of everything
> that passes recorded or unobserved. It contains, for example, such things as
> all our momentary inactive memories, and it harbors the springs of all our
> obscurely motivated passions, impulses, likes, dislikes, and prejudices. Our
> intuitions, hypotheses, fancies, superstitions, persuasions, convictions, and
> in general all our non-rational operations come from it. It is the source
> of our dreams, and apparently they may return to it. In it arise whatever
> mystical experiences we may have, and our automatisms, sensory or motor;
> our life in hypnotic and 'hypnoid' conditions; our delusions, fixed ideas,
> and hysterical accidents, if we are hysteric subjects; our supranormal cogni-
> tions, if such there be, and if we are telepathic subjects. It is also the foun-
> tainhead of much that feeds our religion. In persons deep in the religious
> life, as we have now abundantly seen,—and this is my conclusion—the
> door to this region seems unusually wide open; at any rate, experiences
> making their entrance through that door have had emphatic influence in
> shaping religious history.[31]

Chapter Six

THE ANTI-JAMESEAN MOVEMENT

WHEN WE SEEK to find the origins of the idea that William James abandoned psychology after 1890, one of the most obvious sources is the opinion of James's own contemporaries who had much to gain politically by debunking Jamesean psychology as unscientific. Indeed, one might speculate that, as the move toward the social legitimization of the sciences gained momentum in the late nineteenth century, significantly reinforced by the rise of the graduate schools and with increasing specialization in the disciplines, the identification of psychology with the natural sciences increasingly meant power, money, and prestige.[1]

Recently, historians of science have made the case for the unique character of the natural sciences in the United States.[2] Because American science had made such great strides in astronomy and chemistry, the emphasis was on situational observation and the solution of practical problems.[3] Science as practiced in the European tradition, however, was quite different. Particularly in Germany, where the state traditionally supported laboratory investigation in the universities, the natural sciences were ordered around advances in physics. The ideal of German experimental laboratory science rigidly defined the relation between pure and applied research, claiming laboratory investigation as superior.

It is easy to see, therefore, that James's psychology did not exactly flourish in a vacuum, but, through the earlier influences of Peirce and Wright and through the laboratory programs of Bowditch and Putnam at the Harvard Medical School, James's psychology actually was more representative of the tenor of American science in general than the type of psychology that was being imported into the United States from German laboratories beginning in the early 1880s.

Since Boring had deep allegiances to Titchener and the German experimental laboratory tradition, the near pathological focus of historians since Boring's time has been on Wundt's laboratory at Leipzig.[4] It is instructive to note that James's psychology predominated in the United States from the mid-1870s at least into the mid-1890s and probably well into the first decade of the twentieth century, at least up to the time of James's death in 1910.[5] In this endeavor James had numerous compatriots in American academic psychology. Among them, to name only a few, were such lights as Josiah Royce, John Dewey, James Mark Baldwin,

George Trumball Ladd, Edward Thorndike, Robert Woodworth, James Angell, Boris Sidis, and Mary Calkins.

The establishment of the laboratory ideal in American psychology, on the other hand, was largely effected by a succession of Wundt's returning American students (Titchener, an exception, was a British émigré) who established themselves in universities around the country, founded laboratories, began to edit journals, reviewed the literature, convened professional societies, and wrote textbooks to promote their views. To a man (and to a woman), their agenda was to establish the German experimental laboratory tradition as the proper standard for scientific psychology, and to do so they each had to go to great lengths to justify their efforts in the face of the prevailing definitions of American psychology, which were more Jamesean, more experiential, and more person centered than they desired. This meant debunking the older Jamesean tradition, especially the legitimacy of psychical research. Four such personalities who figured prominently in this anti-Jamesean movement were G. Stanley Hall, James McKeen Cattell, Edward Bradford Titchener, and Hugo Münsterberg.[6]

G. STANLEY HALL

Granville Stanley Hall, the man who allegedly received the first Ph.D. in American psychology at Harvard in 1878 under James and Bowditch, was later president of Clark University, founder of the Child Study movement, and inviter of Freud and Jung to America.[7] In 1879 he was the first student from the United States to enter Wundt's laboratory, but he did so unofficially. He did some work there, but never produced a publishable study; he heard Wundt lecture on psychology, and he attended one of Wundt's seminars. When he returned to America in 1881, he lectured briefly at Harvard on educational subjects before going on to the Johns Hopkins University in Baltimore to take a half-time professorship in logic and psychology. He did no experimental work during the eight years he was in Baltimore, and while he did appropriate some apparatus for doing experiments, the historian of psychology Thomas Cadwallader has recently unearthed correspondence between Hall and the Hopkins trustees, which showed that money was given to Hall to buy equipment, but, the trustees stated in writing, "as long as it was not to be used to expressly *found* a laboratory."[8]

Hall had his own idiosyncratic agenda for defining scientific psychology. He never really abandoned the moral philosophy of his mentor Mark Hopkins, and somewhere deep in his soul he remained to the end of his life an ordained Christian minister. He thoroughly digested Hegel's philosophy, first becoming a staunch apologist, but finally rejecting it, yet he never could really get it out of his system.

When he first turned his attention to the new experimental psychology, Hall had intended to study with Wundt in Germany but claimed he was waylaid in Cambridge, Massachusetts, by an offer from President Eliot to teach English at Harvard. While there, he studied the new experimental psychology under William James. By the time he actually got to study with Wundt, as he wrote back to his old mentor James, he had become enough of an experimental laboratory technician in his own right to look askance at Wundt's agenda, and so he spent most of his time in Ludwig's laboratory of physiology.

But when he returned to America, Hall appeared to do a complete about-face. He became evermore distant from James. At first he joined the newly founded American Society for Psychical Research as a vice president, but quickly dropped out to oppose both the methods and the conclusions of the Society. He founded *The American Journal of Psychology*, and from that vantage point became a vocal exponent of psychology as a German experimental laboratory science after the work of Helmholtz, Fechner, and Wundt. He would soon became president of Clark University, and within a few years (while James was away in Europe) convene the first meeting of the American Psychological Association. In all these endeavors, he as much rewrote the history of American psychology as lived through it, scoring James out of the narrative as an experimental psychologist whenever possible.

One episode, in particular, shows the extent to which Hall attempted, and in large measure succeeded, in creating history by editorial fiat. The incident in question had to do with who founded the first laboratory of psychology in America. Namely, in 1895, Hall made the claim in his journal that *he* had founded the first laboratory in the United States devoted to experimental psychology. This event, Hall claimed, occurred at Johns Hopkins in 1885, and it was subsequently his various students at Hopkins who graduated and went off to found all the other laboratories in the United States.

A great hue and cry immediately went up from several quarters, and James McKeen Cattell, as editor of *Science*, the main organ of the American Association for the Advancement of Science, found himself at the center of an exchange among G. Stanley Hall, William James, James Mark Baldwin, and others.

James's letter is dated October 19, 1895, from the Psychological Laboratory, Harvard University:

> To the Editor of *Science*: *The American Journal of Psychology* began a new series last week with an 'editorial' introduction, in which some most extraordinary statements appear. As an official of Harvard University I cannot let one of these pass without public contradiction. The editorial says (on the top of page 4) that the "department of experimental psychology

and laboratory" at Harvard was "founded under the influence" of some unspecified person mentioned in a list of President Hall's pupils. I, myself, 'founded' the instruction in experimental psychology at Harvard in 1874–75, or 1876, I forget which. For a long series of years the laboratory was in two rooms of the Scientific School building, which at last became choked with apparatus, so that a change was necessary. I then, in 1890, resolved on an altogether new departure, raised several thousand dollars, fitted up Dane Hall, and introduced laboratory exercises as a regular part of the undergraduate psychology course. Dr. Herbert Nichols, then at Clark, was appointed, in 1891, assistant in this part of the work; and when Professor Münsterberg was made director of the laboratory, in 1892, and I went for a year to Europe, Dr. Nichols gave my undergraduate course. I owe him my heartiest thanks for his services and 'influence' in the graduate as well as the undergraduate department at Harvard, but I imagine him to have been as much surprised as myself at the statement in the editorial from which I quote—a statement the more remarkable in that the chief editor of the American Journal studied experimental psychology himself at Harvard from 1877 to 1879.[9]

I shall confine myself only to a few major points brought out by James's response. One is that James never laid any claim to being the first to found a laboratory, and it was only when driven to the wall by the absurdity of Hall's assertion that he felt compelled to state his view of the matter for the record. It seems clear enough that in Hall's mind, James was not to be considered an experimental scientist and that the Harvard laboratory was never official until 1891, when Nichols came in anticipation of Münsterberg's arrival a year later. James, on the other hand, saw his lab in the 1870s as an entirely legitimate enterprise that deserved recognition, and he saw himself as teaching Hall experimental psychology at the time.

Another point is that, despite loud caveats to the contrary by James, Baldwin, and others in the pages of *Science*, a surprising number of historians and psychologists continue to believe Hall's version to this day. When inaugurating the newly founded experimental laboratory at Wittenberg College in 1927, Cattell himself gave Hall credit for founding the first laboratory in America.[10] Gardner Murphy's *Historical Introduction to Modern Psychology* (1929) states the same, and in 1985 Johns Hopkins celebrated the centennial of the "founding" of its psychological laboratory by Hall, with a self-congratulatory symposium of papers, subsequently published as a book.[11]

Finally, Hall had his own confused and complex political agenda for establishing himself as a representative of the new science in America. His problem was not so much that he succumbed to German science, but that he became one of the earliest victims of scientism in American psychology, albeit through the Germanic influence. American moral philosophy, he believed, was being displaced by German idealism, which was less religious and more analytic in its claims.[12] True, his genetic psychology was hardly a copy of German psychophysics, and he later even became enamoured with Freud, but when Hall produced his own history of psychology in 1912, it was all about Fechner, Helmholtz, and Wundt.[13] There was no James in it, and no recognition that there was a truly scientific psychology in America before Hall had founded it. With this subterfuge, in all likelihood perpetrated with great feelings of pride and innocence, Hall thus deserves the dubious honor of being the first American student of Wundt beginning in 1888 to publicly repudiate the reigning Jamesean psychology in America.

JAMES MCKEEN CATTELL

James McKeen Cattell was actually the first official American student of Wundt to receive the doctorate, and his subsequent experimental work on reaction time and word association "brilliantly exemplified" the spirit of the Leipzig School.[14] He arrived in Leipzig in 1880 and soon became Wundt's assistant. Eight years later, he returned to the United States as a professor of psychology at the University of Pennsylvania, where he founded a laboratory and trained a number of prominent students, among them Lightner Witmer, and where he first became known for his emphasis on quantification and laboratory research.[15]

By the early 1890s, Cattell managed to acquire the journal *Science* from the family of Alexander Graham Bell. The publication had been previously edited by N.D.C. Hodges and Samuel Scudder, two distinguished scientists in their own right who were friends of William James and ardent supporters of the American Society for Psychical Research. Charting a completely new course after its purchase, Cattell affiliated with the American Association for the Advancement of Science, making his journal the main organ of that premier scientific body in the United States. Thereafter, as Sokal has pointed out, Cattell more and more became a spokesman for the broad field of American science generally, and gradually moved away from his original interests in German experimental psychology. His *American Men of Science* (1906), for instance, was based on rating methods more reminiscent of Galton. In the end, historians of psychology have judged him by his success in interweaving the Helmholtz-Wundt tradition with that of English mental testing, even though he is perhaps better known for this later role as a chronicler, spokesman, and editor of American science in the opening decades of the twentieth century.

The James-Cattell correspondence in the Library of Congress is extensive and spans almost two decades, from the early 1890s to James's death in 1910. The general impression one gets from reading through it is that Cattell idolized James, following after him like a puppy dog.[16] Nevertheless, professionally Cattell showed himself to be a man of principle regarding what he thought was legitimate science, and he judged much that was called psychology at the time as unscientific, especially where it was associated with psychical research and the name of William James.

In 1896, for instance, Cattell reviewed William James's presidential address before the British Society for Psychical Research. There Cattell concluded that the strongest argument on behalf of psychic research was not the anecdotes and other evidence, but the distinguished nature of leaders such as James and Sidgwick, although why such men took an interest in the subject seemed a mystery.[17]

Moreover, while James's address was admirably written, and his review of the work of the psychical research society one of skill and moderation, Cattell judged James's discussion of the census on hallucinations and his arguments in favor of clairvoyance to be illogical. In Cattell's view, a mass of merely suggestive evidence without definite repeatable proof was worthless. And, even if there was a white crow, such as Mrs. Piper, it proved nothing, and only "belonged in a museum."

A few years later, James and Cattell had a public exchange over the issue of psychical research, this time on the occasion of Richard Hodgson's article, "A Further Record of Certain Phenomena of Trance," which had appeared in the *Proceedings of the Society for Psychical Research* in England during February 1898. Hodgson admitted after almost fourteen years of skepticism, during which time he had investigated virtually thousands of sittings with Mrs. Piper, that finally he had been converted to spiritism by the evidence. He pronounced Mrs. Piper's trances absolutely genuine and concluded that she indeed showed clear evidence of supernormal powers.

Cattell, as editor of *Science*, took it upon himself in the April 1898 issue to comment sarcastically about Hodgson's conclusions and to associate William James's name with what reputable scientists could only conclude was a charade.[18]

James was quick to reply. He believed it his duty to make a comment because "any hearing for such phenomena is so hard to get from scientific readers that one who believes them worthy of careful study is duty bound to resent such contemptuous public notice of them in high quarters as would still further encourage the fashion of their neglect."[19] He clarified himself by saying "any hearing," since he well knew it would be impossible to get a fair hearing. Still less could he expect fair treatment: "The scientific mind is by the pressure of professional opinion painfully drilled to fairness and logic in discussing orthodox phenomena. But in such mere matters as superstition of a medium's trances it feels so confident of impunity and indulgence whatever it may say, provided it be only contemptuous enough, that it fairly revels in the untrained barbarians' arsenal of logical weapons, including all the various sophisms enumerated in the books."[20]

James chided Cattell for making just such comments. He faulted him first for quoting Hodgson as saying that "many of Mrs. Piper's trances show supernormal knowledge," but then picking from Hodgson's report five instances in which they showed nothing of the kind. James said that Cattell then jubilantly proclaimed, "We have piped unto you but ye have not danced," and then signed his name with an air of finality, as if this were all the refutation that was needed. James thought Cattell's comment "an extraordinarily perfect instance" of *"ignoratio elenchi."*

When Cattell ignored the large part of the report showing how Mrs. Piper seemed to have inexplicably accurate knowledge about a sitter, but cited instead only those cases where five sitters announced Mrs. Piper's revelations as preposterous, James accused Cattell not only of unfairness, but of suppressing the truth: "I am sure that you have committed these fallacies with the best of scientific consciences. They are fallacies unto which, of course, you would have been in no possible danger of falling in any other sort of matter than this. In our dealing with the insane the usual moral rules don't apply. Mediums are scientific outlaws, and their defendants are quasi-insane. Any stick is good enough to beat dogs of that stripe with. So in perfect innocence you permitted yourself the liberties I point out."[21]

In James's view Cattell had not argued on the merits of the case, but rather created a controversy with his poor form. James asked the reader to judge for himself by going directly to Hodgson's report of the most recent five hundred sittings.

Cattell responded that he had not meant for his comments to be taken as an editorial, but rather:

> I gave my individual opinion, Professor James gives his, and I fear that our disagreement is hopeless. I could not quote the 600 pages compiled by Dr. Hodgson, but I gave the concluding sentences written by *all* the men of science whose seances were reported. . . . I wrote the note with reluctance and only because I believe that the Society for Psychical Research is doing much to injure psychology. The authority of Professor James is such that he involves other students of psychology in his opinions unless they protest. We all acknowledge his leadership, but we cannot follow him into the quagmires.[22]

Cattell thus appears to acknowledge James's preeminence as a famous personality, but he goes to great lengths to disparage the scientific basis of James's claims to psychology, particularly after 1890.

Hugo Münsterberg

Hugo Münsterberg, German-born Harvard professor, distinguished student of Wundt, and later pioneer in applied psychology,[23] was the man who, by his very presence at the helm of the Harvard Psychological Laboratory, perhaps only inadvertently at first, played the largest role in convincing others that James had abandoned psychology after 1890.

Münsterberg was a thoroughgoing romantic idealist of the Teutonic stripe, who believed in a rigid social order in which each person had their place and should be grateful to fulfill their destiny in that station. Similarly, within the life of the mind, all thought for Münsterberg was organized into fixed categories that were absolute in terms of their reality and their relation to one another.

The question is, then, why William James even brought Münsterberg to Harvard at all. There are several reasons.

First, I think that James brought him because he wanted to maintain Harvard's status as a first-rate university, and this meant someone besides James had to indoctrinate graduate students into the details of laboratory methods, which, by the mid-1890s, were dominated by German procedures, problems, and apparatus. James could do laboratory work, but he never made it a compulsive habit. "I, at the age of 50," he wrote, wooing Münsterberg, "disliking laboratory work naturally, and accustomed to teach philosophy at large, altho I *could, tant bien que mal,* make the laboratory run, yet am certainly not the kind of stuff to make a first-rate director thereof."[24]

Second, James did not exactly abandon psychology, nor did he abandon the laboratory. He kept his title of Professor of Psychology from 1889 to 1898, during which time he not only continued to teach philosophy, general psychology, and experimental psychopathology, but he also supervised students in the laboratory, such as Gertrude Stein and Boris Sidis, both of whom worked on experimental problems of the subconscious.[25]

Third, and perhaps most important, Münsterberg must have had a definite place in James's ideal agenda for psychology. James conceived of psychology as a natural science, but one that was person-centered.[26] In James's view, the basic data of the discipline was raw human experience. Laboratory science helped us with precise methods of verifying certain phenomena, but as it then existed, its methods were so limited as to reveal little but the most insignificant aspects of our experience. What James called "functional psychology" demanded that psychologists attend as much to the practical consequences of their research as to the basic conceptualization of it.

In this vein, Münsterberg must have been attractive to James for several reasons. Foremost, he had been a student under Wundt at Leipzig, but soon surpassed his teacher in reputation as an empirical scientist in Europe. His coming to Harvard was thus something of a coup for the Jamesean camp. His philosophy was action oriented, which supported James's own investigations into ideo-motor activity. Münsterberg's dissertation on the will, after all, had shown he was no mere reflex psychologist. Moreover, Münsterberg not only held the Ph.D., but also the M.D., which meant to James that laboratory methods might be balanced with clinical, applied, and experiential concerns. Münsterberg thus seemed the ideal figure to bridge James's own interests between scientific and philosophic empiricism.

But as we know, the attempt failed. Münsterberg came to Harvard to represent experimental psychology, but he soon abandoned experimentation without ever abandoning the idea that German experimental laboratory psychology was superior to American—and therefore Jamesean—definitions of the discipline. When Münsterberg turned to applied psychology, it was James's functionalism gone awry. Münsterberg proceeded to superimpose the rigid dictates of his own intellectual categories onto art, industrial efficiency, jurisprudence, and the social order. He railed against psychopathologists such as Prince, Janet, and Sidis, who he believed espoused that hypothetical nonentity they called the subconscious. In his own text *Psychotherapy* (1909), Münsterberg uncompromisingly redefined psychotherapeutics only in terms of physiology and outwardly observable behavior.[27]

Most problematic, however, was his break with James over psychical research. Their relationship had begun in the late 1880s most cordially, but soured beginning in the late 1890s over a succession of incidents. The most blatant to draw James's ire was an article that Münsterberg had published in the *Atlantic Monthly* during 1899 on "Psychology and Mysticism." There, he divided the world into interior and exterior realities. The interior was the idiosyncratic world of the mystic. Such a world was not a part of public discourse and therefore not amenable to being reduced to the causal laws of science. In the outer was psychology, allied with the other natural sciences. Münsterberg readily admitted that science was based on an artificially constructed representation of the world, but this is precisely what led to the rules of logic and the laws of causality. Mystical phenomena could not be dealt with by psychology unless they were transformed into some framework, such as the mechanical or the physiological, in which logic and causality could be invoked: "So long as we consider spiritualism only from the point of view of its agreement with the system of scientific psychology, the discussion may be extremely short, for one sweeping word is sufficient. There are no subtle discriminations necessary, as in the other fields: the psychologist rejects everything without exception."[28]

Münsterberg firmly believed that people who thought the dead had spoken to them or who had seen the departed were suffering from illusions and hallucinations. Religious ecstasy was an example of the psychopathic temperament. Mrs. Piper was a paid hysteric. The psychical researchers, with their mathematical probabilities of occurrences of telepathy, were no different than the neo-Platonist mystic contemplating the Absolute.

A scientist, in other words, would be less than a man to give up his first principles. When it comes to mediums and incarnations, "The scientist does not admit a compromise: with regard to this he flatly denies the possibility." As a scientist, Münsterberg asserted, the psychologist "had a right," and even a duty, to reject these claims.

In a letter to a friend, James said that he had become so flustered at such continued attacks on psychical research that he intended to decline all further a priori discussion of the question and "so leave M's rot lying in the gutter to decay with similar garbage."[29] When Münsterberg sought James's aid against criticism by Schiller the same year, James wrote back, "Your mysticism article, to speak with perfect candor, seems to me a monumentally foolish performance . . . and I think it was a great compliment that he [F.C.S. Schiller] should have discussed your paper at all."[30]

Another episode that galled James was the International Congress of Arts and Sciences, held in St. Louis in 1904. The Congress was the brainchild of a consortium of American university presidents who believed that American higher education had progressed to the point of such sophistication that it could afford to consort with the finest European scholars in a grand exposition of all knowledge. Münsterberg, appointed one of the organizers, was responsible for the conceptualization of all the intellectual fields of knowledge. He accomplished this task according to the dictates of his own set of categories, moving James to remark, "To me the whole Münsterbergian Circus seems a case of the pure love of schematization running mad."

To demonstrate the point, Münsterberg arranged for several presentations in psychology, including C. Loyd Morgan, Robert Yerkes, and others. Pierre Janet and Morton Prince lectured on psychopathology, but they were relegated to a minor session entitled "Applied Psychology." Münsterberg had seen to it that the Germans constituted 30 percent of the delegates, and received due recognition for their superiority. One of those holding the "right view" was Titchener, who was given the limelight and who faithfully declared from this high vantage point that

German experimental psychophysics was the only legitimate foundation on which to base a scientific psychology.

Münsterberg also fell out again with James in 1909 over the visit to Harvard of the Italian psychic, Eusapia Palladino. Mme Palladino came to accept a challenge from Münsterberg, who planned to subject her seances to rigorous scientific scrutiny. He even managed to get his body pressed next to hers during a seance, and this, with the help of some of his students, led to the exposure of her tricks. As one author has put it, Münsterberg thought her a threat to the foundations of experimental psychology because she was so popular. Thus his ability to publicly discredit her, he fervently believed, was a blow for science. James was also suspicious that she might be a fraud, but believed Münsterberg was acting like a "buffoon" who practiced a "shallow dogmatism, which . . . is in no way more scientific than that of mystical superstition."[31]

James, who died a year later, did not get to see the finale of Münsterberg's pathetic career. In the end, Münsterberg proved himself to be a disgrace to Harvard. For instance, he became embroiled in a number of public controversies involving expert testimony at several nationally known trials, some of which he had invited himself into. His pronouncements as a Harvard professor were prominently quoted in the newspapers, which prompted a warning response from President Eliot.

The most devastating of his activities, however, involved his work for the German government. When he came to Harvard in 1892 he delayed adopting American citizenship because he was to stay only for a two-year trial period. Even after he returned permanently to Harvard, he never renounced his German citizenship. Then, in the early 1900s, as relations between Germany and America became more strained, Münsterberg became a vocal spokesman for improved ties, working openly as an adviser to the German government on American cultural affairs. This time the Harvard Corporation became directly involved and in 1908 Eliot had to force Münsterberg to confine himself to professional academic activities and to leave politics alone. By 1914, Münsterberg openly called for the defeat of the Allied powers and the spiritual triumph of Germany, prompting public outrage and calls for his immediate dismissal. Eliot, who had been receiving secret letters from Münsterberg, urged him to see a physician for what he could only describe as "grave hallucinations." Eventually, it was believed that Münsterberg may have actually been a secret agent working in the service of Kaiser Wilhelm.[32]

Nevertheless, even after his break with James in 1900, Münsterberg continued to wield enormous power over experimental psychology at Harvard. He supervised most of the Ph.D.s who graduated in psychology; he ran the laboratory; he helped solidify the introduction of experimental techniques from psychology into clinical psychiatry; he brought in his own choice, a German psychiatrist, to teach abnormal psychology;[33] and, after James's death, he turned away the spiritualists when they tried to give several million dollars to endow a chair in psychical research at the university (because, Münsterberg said, he did not want the psychical researchers to have that much power).[34] And when he taught James to the undergraduates at Harvard, he taught him only as a philosopher.[35] His supervision of doctoral dissertations for nearly a quarter of a century bears this out. All dissertations under his direction were based strictly on experimental laboratory methods.

Thus, when Münsterberg took over experimental psychology in 1892, he began to lay down a line of influence that marks psychology at Harvard to this day, and the psychology of William James ended up having little place in it. If anything, James is embraced as a great son of Harvard and as a hero of the older intellectual community at large, while most young psychology students barely know his name, usually confusing it with that of his more well-known brother, Henry. At the same time, Jamesean psychology continued to be pummeled from without, in a relentless onslaught led by another Wundtian graduate who was in many ways even more successful in redefining psychology as a laboratory science than Münsterberg.

EDWARD BRADFORD TITCHENER

E. B. Titchener, English born, Oxford educated, received his Ph.D. under Wundt in 1892 and, once installed at Cornell University in Ithaca, New York, proceeded to establish himself as the most zealous disciple of the Leipzig School in the United States. His agenda, it soon became apparent, was nothing less than to become the American Wundt. To do this, he carried the German laboratory ideal as his banner and launched a militaristic program of investigation designed to produce a complete system of psychology free of philosophical postulates and based solely on experimental evidence.[36]

But as numerous scholars have recently pointed out, he was not so much a student *of* Wundt, as much as he was his most enthusiastic *interpreter*.[37] Like Wundt's American students, Titchener ignored Wundt's voluntaristic psychology, which spanned problems ranging from physiology and cognition to society and culture, and focused instead on Wundt's experimental work. The result was a structuralist psychology based solely on reaction-time studies and the controlled introspective analysis of consciousness by trained observers in the laboratory.

The period of the 1890s was one of preparation for Titchener, as he began to attract students, publish in the literature, and write his first textbooks, anticipating his later more accelerated experimental and publishing agenda. And to establish himself, he had to first address the reigning Jamesean functionalist paradigm that dominated psychology. It was therefore almost inevitable that James and Titchener would meet in print in a head-on collision. Naturally, the issue was over psychical research.

The controversy between James and Titchener began in 1898, but actually had its origin two years earlier, when James first reviewed Hansen and Lehmann's *Ueber unwillkürliches Flüstern* and then followed with a series of additional comments. Hansen and Lehmann were concerned with a series of experiments that had been carried out by Professor and Mrs. Sidgwick of the Society for Psychical Research in England. The experiments concerned the transference of numbers from the mind of a Mr. Smith to two young men who had been hypnotized by him. Mr. S. randomly selected slips of two-digit numbers from a bag, while the subjects called out whatever numbers appeared in their field of vision. The subjects' correct responses were greater than chance occurrence. In a series of 354 trials, for instance, both digits were named correctly seventy-nine times instead of the probable number of four or five.

Hansen and Lehmann sought to replicate the Sidgwick experiments and to prove that the agent's inward articulation of the numbers guessed was probably heard hyperesthetically by the hypnotized subjects. When they repeated the experiments so that the subjects could actually hear the agent's suppressed whispering, not only the success but also the mistakes resembled the outcome of the Sidgwick studies, "and from such like effects they think that we ought to infer like causes."[38]

Both James and Sidgwick followed separately with a detailed analysis of the Hansen and Lehmann study and concluded that "their experiments do not show positive evidence for whispering as the source of the English results."[39] Thinking the matter over and done with, James then turned to other pursuits.

Then in the December 23 issue of *Science* for 1898, Titchener reported on a study he had undertaken called "The Feeling of Being Stared At." He was interested in testing "a superstition which has deep and widespread roots in the popular consciousness."[40] After a number of his own experiments, he explained the popular belief that "one may make a person look round by staring at the back of his head, by the fact that many persons are nervous when others are behind them, and, involuntarily looking round at intervals to reassure themselves, meet our eyes if we are making the experiment."[41]

To further justify this explanation, Titchener proclaimed, "No scientific-minded psychologist believes in telepathy." To disprove it, he said, "benefits real science one hundred fold." He then cited the report of Lehmann and Hansen, which "has probably done more for scientific psychology than could have been accomplished by any aloofness, how-ever authoritative."[42]

James immediately replied in a letter to the editor of *Science* (who was, of course, Cattell) on December 23, 1898, saying that, if Titchener had actually read both James and Sidgwick's replies to Hansen and Lehmann, he could not possibly take a document seriously which had already been exploded. He also chided Titchener for his paternalism.

Titchener replied on January 6, 1899, that he saw James and Sidgwick handling the fuse, but as yet Titchener had heard no detonation.

James gave a rejoinder in April, after he had heard from Professor Lehmann himself. Lehmann believed beyond a doubt that James and Sidgwick's analysis had demolished his own argument. James could only conclude that "Professor Titchener, meanwhile, still hugging the ex-ploded document, wanders what he calls 'the straight scientific path,' having it apparently all to himself. May the consciousness of his fidelity to correct scientific principles console him in some degree both for his deafness and for his isolation."[43]

Titchener replied on May 12, 1899. Even if Lehmann's experiments were exploded, they still represented a brilliant contribution to science. James's claim, on the other hand, that telepathy must therefore explain the original Sidgwick results was unfounded. If this is what James calls real science, Titchener said, he "prefers the isolation."

James followed with his last letter, dated May 26, 1899: "Why Professor Titchener should have taken an essay which he now admits to have com-pletely failed even to make probable its point, as an example of the 'bril-liant work' which 'scientific psychology' can do in the way of destroying the telepathic superstition, may be left to be fathomed by readers with more understanding of the ways of 'Science' than I possess."[44] James then pointed out two glaring inaccuracies in Titchener's description of the experimental situation, that Titchener claimed Lehmann was the first to consider telepathic whispering, and that he was also the first to introduce number habits. James ended by pleading that "even in anti-telepathic Science accuracy of representation is required, and I am pleading not for telepathy, but only for accuracy."[45]

On June 2, 1899, Titchener published his last rejoinder. "When a sci-entific discussion degenerates into protest and imputation of motive, it is time for the discussion to stop." Nevertheless, he could not resist hav-ing the last word. As his parting shot, he tried to refute James's two points on the basis of semantics, but he came off as inarticulate and ended inconclusively.[46]

Titchener proved to be a formidable opponent of Jamesean psychol-ogy for several reasons. First, he solidified his position at Cornell as dictatorial commander of the German view in America. He assigned his graduate students dissertation projects commensurate with his own views on what a systematic psychology should look like, while he took the role of public interpreter, textbook writer, and reviewer, addressing other professionals in psychology.

From this vantage point, he led the conceptual attack that clearly differentiated structural from functional psychology. As the younger generation of psychologists, like James Angell, took up the Jamesean position, while James himself turned to other matters, Titchener poured on the steam himself and rolled over the opposition through what has been called his methodological period (1899–1907).[47] After all, he had the legitimacy of the other natural laboratory sciences to fall back on, as well as the German ideal of graduate specialization, which was after 1900 the adored model of American higher education.

Epistemologically, Titchener has been identified as a follower of Machian positivism.[48] He believed that only the scientific method can lead to knowledge and that the facts of science must come from empirical laboratory investigation. To this he added the primacy of sensations as the basic building blocks of higher mental life, and he argued for the complete divorce of psychology from philosophy. Furthermore, he, like Mach, believed in the essential identity of all science; he paid scant attention to the Darwinian hypothesis, and he had no theory of the self. In the end, there was no adapting subject at the center of his system, but only "scientism," the pursuit of science, for its own sake. He had no use for the concept of the will, and he proved a radical materialist when he attempted to remove meaning from the kinds of phenomena to be explained by psychology.

Naturally, Titchenerian structuralism had close affinities with Watsonian behaviorism. Titchener and Watson were friends, and as Titchener progressively mauled Jamesean psychology in the name of pure science, Watson waited in the wings to take up the positivist banner in force after an exhausted Titchener began slowly to bow out after 1915 and the debates over structuralism versus functionalism had faded from the scene.[49]

Chapter Seven

JAMES'S REJOINDER: A CRITIQUE
OF EXPERIMENTALISM
IN PSYCHOLOGY

Le coeur a ses raisons, que la raison ne connaît pas.
—Pascal

JAMES CALLED the attitude he was attacking by many names: agnostic positivism, radical materialism, mechanical rationalism, a viscious intellectualism. It was the penchant to treat the world and everything in it as objects, all knowable and under the control of the rational mind. It was certainly a reasonable idea, but it had become reified by its adherents to the status of a cult, because they proclaimed it to be the only legitimate way to gain knowledge in modern life. Against it, James launched a new empiricism based on the facts of experience, shifting mental states, and the stream of consciousness. Theirs was a world that was purely rational, contained, impersonal, mechanical, and closed. His was personal, alive, overflowing, novel, and open.

The technical metaphysics that William James evolved to renovate this positivistic attitude had three parts: pragmatism, the philosophy for which he is best known; pluralism, its corollary; and radical empiricism, the formal core of his vision, which, unfortunately, he left the most undeveloped. James based his philosophy on the assumption that every explanation about reality is itself undergirded by a metaphysical system, whether overtly stated or simply implied. Even in the most airtight system, James had said, "the juices of metaphysical assumptions leak in at every joint." Positivistic science was a case in point. Positivism was not some ideal attainment of absolute truth, completely free of philosophic bias. Rather, it operated according to a set of implicit presuppositions like those of any other philosophy. Its uniqueness rests in the fact that, among other things, it promotes a metaphysics of physicalism. It is a philosophy about the relationship between consciousness and the material world that excludes all explanations not cast in rational-empirical terms. The basis for its success is that positivistic science approximately models material reality in such a way that material reality conforms to causal predictions about it most of the time.

The Birth of Radical Empiricism

Radical empiricism, on the other hand, is a metaphysics of experience.[1] It is like any other form of empiricism, in that it admits data from the senses, so that it includes within its purview the experience of the physical world. But it also encompasses the broad spectrum of inner realities articulated within the subjective life of the person. Empiricism in this sense becomes radical *when it refuses to admit into its constructions any element that is not directly experienced, nor exclude from them any element that is directly experienced.*[2] It deals both with reality and how we take it. Thus, within the entire range of human experience, all claims are a potential topic of scientific investigation, although not all may be ultimately verified by having a direct effect on the physical world.

Radical empiricism is also ultimately pluralistic. There can be many ways of taking reality. One person's phenomenological description may differ in large ways from another. In fact, the appreciation of individuality is a hallmark of the radically empirical point of view. As James once said, there is very little difference between people, but what difference there is, is very important. He constantly struggled with the problem of how two minds can know the same thing, however, realizing the accepted view that each individual creates his or her own analogue of outward reality, which everyone infers is at least approximately like everyone else's. But unanimity is never permanent. Experience is in a constant state of flux. What was fixed today will be moving tomorrow. Radical empiricism thus admits no single fact or theory as explaining the whole (although monism always can be one of a pluralist's options).

Radical empiricism is also pragmatic. There must be some sorting mechanism which differentiates and weighs the value of a variety of experiences, and this standard in the radically empirical view is always the outcome. That is, the reconciliation of all ultimate truth claims must be in the actual arena of living. The testing ground for all ideation is lived experience. Beliefs are proven or disproven by their effects. At the same time, such effects infer belief. Acts are motivated by ideas, even if not consciously realized. Acts can never be the sole determinant, however. Rather, both ideas and their consequences must constitute our perception of the whole.

This also means that radically different truth claims which appear to be in conflict with each other may find consensual validation by the commonality of their effects. A behavioral scientist says that a person does a good deed because he is driven by evolutionary and biological motives for self-preservation, thus contributing to the survival of the species. The Christian does the same good deed because he believes he will receive a favorable judgment in God's eyes in the life to come. A Buddhist may also do the same good deed because he thinks that selflessness burns out the seeds of past karma. Here, three different reasons lead to the same good deed. Beliefs are thus true for the person who holds them, and although dissimilar beliefs may be of different origins, they may lead to similar ends.

PSYCHOLOGY AS A NATURAL SCIENCE

Although the doctrine of radical empiricism had its most public introduction by that name in the preface to his *Will to Believe* (1897), James had begun broadcasting its outlines even before then. Lines of it appeared in germinal form in essays written before 1890, and numerous scholars see it in *The Principles*, but as a metaphysics not quite yet born. In 1892 James admits as much in his article, "A Plea for Psychology as a Natural Science."[3] This was his response to George Trumbull Ladd's then recent attack on the new vogue of cerebralism in psychology, in which Ladd had used James's *Principles* as a primary example. In his reply, James made plain that he did not clearly say in 1890 that psychology indeed *was* a natural science or in any way an exact science at all: "Psychology . . . is today hardly more than what physics was before Galileo, what chemistry was before Lavoisier. It is a mass of phenomenal description, gossip, and myth, including, however, real material enough to justify one in the hope that with judgement and good-will on the part of those interested, its study may be so organized even now as to become worthy of the name of natural science at no very distant day."[4] He then made his oft-quoted statement: "I wished, by treating Psychology *like* a natural science, to help her become one."[5]

His discussion led to the lines demarcating science from abstract philosophy. He reiterated his assertion that any new science had to renounce ultimate questions in the beginning of its endeavors and stick to the study of mental life within the context of natural history. The aim, he said, as in any science, is prediction and control. He then gave his interpretation of this approach for psychology:

> We live surrounded by an enormous body of persons who are most definitely interested in the control of states of mind, and incessantly crave for a sort of psychological science which will teach them how to *act*. What every educator, every jail-warden, every doctor, every clergyman, every asylum superintendent, asks of psychology is practical rules. Such men care little or nothing about the ultimate philosophic grounds of mental phenomena, but they do care immensely about improving ideas, dispositions, and conduct of the particular individuals in their charge.[6]

He divided the study of psychology into the philosophers, on the one hand, and the "biologists, doctors, and psychical researchers," on the other, each having entirely legitimate business to transact with psychology. He argued for the immediate superiority of the empiricists, "of the men of facts, of the laboratory workers and biologists."[7] Psychology, he said, should deal with the "facts of experience," by which he meant "mental states." Yet he said, "Not that today we *have* a 'science' of the correlation of mental states with brain states; but that the ascertainment of the laws of such correlation forms the *program* of a science well limited and defined."[8] He further clarified:

> We never ought to doubt that Humanity will continue to produce all the types of thinkers which she needs. I myself do not doubt of the "final perseverance" or success of the philosophers. Nevertheless, if the hard alternative were to arise of a choice between 'theories' and 'facts' in psychology, between a merely rational and a merely practical science of mind, I do not see how any man could hesitate in his decision. The kind of psychology which could cure a case of melancholy, or charm a chronic insane delusion away, ought certainly to be preferred to the most seraphic insight into the nature of the soul. And that is the sort of psychology which the men who care little or nothing for ultimate rationality, the biologists, nerve-doctors, and psychical researchers, namely, are surely tending, whether we help them or not, to bring about.[9]

James's use of the phrase "biologists, nerve doctors, and psychical researchers" is central to his argument, for he at once classes the three types under the same scientific and empirical mode of investigation. Between them, they cover the range of human experience, from the pathologic to the transcendent, but within a scientific context, as *judged by their results*. To the extent that his definition of legitimate science differs markedly from what academic laboratory psychology became shows that James, when he made this statement in 1892, was already heading toward radical empiricism, although not yet outwardly advocating a psychology of the subconscious.

1892: *PSYCHOLOGY: BRIEFER COURSE*

In *Psychology: Briefer Course* (1892), his abridgement of *The Principles*, James continued to express the evolution of his ideas about the metaphysical basis of psychology as a scientific discipline. In this regard, no more masterful account of the important differences between *The Principles* and the *Briefer Course* has yet appeared to best that of the historian of science Michael Sokal.[10] Yet certain emendations to Sokal's discussion might still be made in light of the present discussion.

Sokal points out that in his *Principles*, James defined psychology as "the Science of Mental Life," while in *Briefer Course* he defined it as "the description and explanation of states of consciousness as such." Sokal interprets the definition in *Briefer Course* as an abandonment of James's previous, more scientific emphasis and a reversion to the assumptions of the moral philosophers, largely in response to Ladd's criticism of James's failure to fully acknowledge the persistent philosophical foundation of psychology. While Sokal and I are in agreement that James appears to be making an important change in his 1892 revision, I interpret James's change in definition as a vast improvement over his too general description in *The Principles*. The new statement is entirely commensurate with his growing doubts about the efficacy of his previously stated positivist program. The question is, what would a science of psychology beyond that defined by positivist epistemology look like?

My primary reason for believing that James was still talking science and not reverting back to abstract philosophy is his use of the phrase "states of consciousness," which expresses the progressive unfolding of his theory that consciousness is not just the perception of objects. It was, rather, a plurality of successive fields, he said, which he based on evidence from hypnosis, crystal gazing, and automatic writing in the psychological laboratory. The field metaphor allowed him to break away from implying that everyday waking consciousness was always exclusively cognitive, rational, and connected through the senses to objects in the external material world. In James's view, the apparatus of perceiving, registering, and reacting might still be fully operative, but the ground or context at any given moment was in a constant state of flux. Not only did the stream flow onward, but what constantly changed was also the tone, the atmosphere, or the backdrop provided by shifting states. At the same time, James was also implying that positivism itself is a philosophy, albeit a narrow one. He firmly believed that the legitimacy of psychology as a science was not compromised simply because one abandons a narrow metaphysics for a wider one, if that is what the facts of experience require.

Probably the most significant example that signals the direction of James's new thinking, as Sokal also points out, is the omission in the *Briefer Course* of one of the five characteristics of what James now calls "the stream of consciousness" (in *The Principles*, he had referred to it only as "the stream of thought and feeling"). In 1890, James had said that the five characteristics were (1) "Every thought tends to be part of a personal consciousness"; (2) "Within each personal consciousness thought is always changing"; (3) "Within each personal consciousness thought is sensibly continuous"; (4) "It always appears to deal with objects independent of itself"; (5) "It is interested in some parts of these objects to the exclusion of others, and welcomes or rejects—*chooses* from among them, in a word, all the while." By 1892, he had retained all but one. By then, he had come to doubt that "consciousness always appears to deal with objects independent of itself."

This change of mind, James would later reveal, was due in large part to his continued investigations into the subliminal consciousness. In mediumistic trances, in certain instances of both psychopathology as well as transcendence, consciousness turns inward and takes for its object its own processes. Once the person had witnessed this internal phenomenon, there is a case to be made for the claim that all future distinctions between self and the external world are then called into question. The absolute and unquestioned certainty that there is only waking consciousness attached to external phenomena is shattered by the constant possibility of self-observation, by the intense experience of one's own personality as a witness to the object, not simply the object reified because of ignorance about its deep interconnections to our internal processes of perception. This was the germ of his idea that within the experience of each person, there is no object without consciousness. He had advanced his thinking a few steps, but a more forthright statement was to come in the form of his presidential address to the American Psychological Association in December 1894.

James's Presidential Address
to the APA

Originally delivered as "The Knowing of Things Together" and published under the alternate title "The Tigers in India," James used the occasion of his presidential address to the professional psychologists of the United States as the platform to state openly the unequivocal dependence of science on metaphysics, a position he had earlier appeared to deny in *The Principles*.

He began by taking up the question of the synthetic unity of consciousness. "Knowing" is the first problem, defining "things" another, and accounting for the experience of their unity yet another, he said.

In the first case, he presented his well-known distinction between knowledge about versus acquaintance with. Knowing about is representative knowledge. "The Tigers in India" calls forth an image in our minds without our having any direct contact with the reality of the phenomena. While it is true that we must have some direct experience at some point in some way with tigers and with India in order to know the meaning of the two ideas together, we certainly do not need to directly confront a tiger in India to know the words' referent. Nevertheless, we know that the phrase does refer to some reality in human experience.

Acquaintance with, on the other hand, is direct knowledge, immediately experienced and intuitively known. There is no presence in absence, no pointing to something else, only the bare relation between my consciousness and the thing as directly apprehended in itself. Standing in India, there is only myself and the tiger.

At the intersection of these two ways of knowing is James's struggle. There is immediate experience and our categories about it, both of which must converge in the present moment. But the present moment, he points out, is a convenient fiction, since nothing remains stable. Thus we can only speak of the passing moment as the only thing that ever concretely was or is or shall be. In the ever-changing present, there is a sense of the past and a portent of the future. Within this minimal pulse of experience we must find an explanation for how we experience things as a unity.

James's strategy was then somewhat tentative. He provided no final answer, but rather reviewed the various explanations that had been put forth to account for the unity of experience—physiological, psychological, animistic, and transcendental. In this vein, he used the majority of his speech to discuss theories of attention, reminiscence, synergy, and theories relating to self and to other objects, to the individual soul, and to the World Soul.

He then said: "You will agree with me that I have brought no new insight to the subject, and that I have only gossiped to while away this unlucky presidential hour to which the constellations doomed me at my birth. But since gossip we have had to have, let me make the hour more gossipy still by saying a final word about the position taken up in my own *Principles of Psychology.*"[11] He wanted to take up the subject, he said, because in 1890 he had plainly stated that in order for psychology to be considered as a natural science, it should clearly abandon all attempts to ascertain how we come to know things together. States of consciousness, which depend on brain states, are the only vehicle of knowledge we need to suppose. Now, by 1894, he showed a complete change of mind. Thus, he announced: "My intention was a good one, and a natural science infinitely more complete than the psychologies we now possess could be written without abandoning its terms. Like all authors, I have, therefore, been surprised that this child of my genius should not be more admired by others—should, in fact, have been generally either misunderstood or despised. But do not fear that on this occasion I am either going to defend or to re-explain the bantling. I am going to make things more harmonious by simply giving it up."[12]

He proceeded to explain that since publishing his book he had reached the conclusion "that no conventional restrictions *can* keep metaphysical and so-called epistemological inquiries out of the psychology-books." The chief reasons he gave were on the basis of his study of psychopathology: "I see, moreover, better now than then, that my proposal to designate mental states merely by their cognitive function leads to a somewhat strained way of talking about dreams and reveries, and to quite an unnatural way of talking of some emotional states."[13] He then states a correction:

> I am willing, consequently, henceforward, that mental contents should be called complex, just as their objects are, and this even in psychology. Not because their parts are separable, as parts of objects are; not because they have an eternal or quasi-eternal individual existence, like the parts of objects; for the various 'fields' of which they are parts are integers, existentially, and their parts only live as long as *they* live. Still, *in* them, we can call parts, parts.—But when, without circumlocution or disguise, I thus come over to your views, I insist that those of you who applaud me (if any such there be) should recognize the obligations which the new agreement imposes on yourselves. Not till you have dropped the old phrases, so absurd or so empty, . . . not till you have in your turn succeeded in some such long inquiry into conditions as the one I have just failed in; not till you have laid bare more of the nature of that altogether unique kind of complexity in unity which mental states involve; not till then, I say, will psychology reach any real benefit from the conciliatory spirit of which I have done what I can to set an example.[14]

If there is no science free of metaphysics, then the compromise must be to acknowledge that empirical research is more complex than a simplistic objective-subject dichotomy would presuppose. The complexity of mental states means that it is to the phenomenology of the science-making process itself that we must look to see the metaphysics at work. Scientists have, in fact, an obligation to acknowledge this state of affairs, if research is to go on. Only then, James believed, can psychology evolve into a first-rate science.

JAMES'S PRESIDENTIAL ADDRESS BEFORE THE PSYCHICAL RESEARCHERS

Emboldened by the emergence of his new metaphysics and heartened from the reception of his work at least by certain of his colleagues, within the year James again advanced his conception of scientific psychology. If we acknowledge the reality of the subconscious and can identify its pathological characteristics, then, from the standpoint of experience, we must also include the possibility of the supernormal. Within us, in other words, we have undeveloped capacities higher and more refined than those normally at work in waking material reality. He made these pronouncements in England in his presidential address before the Society for Psychical Research in early 1896.[15]

Reviewing first the early history of the Society, James noted that its members had started with high hopes that the hypnotic field would yield an important harvest, but this wave had neigh well subsided. Similarly, experimental thought transference seemed it would yield rich results in the early years, but this was a prophecy unfulfilled. While there was as yet no definitive proof, there remained a mass of convincing evidence. Certain definite advances could be claimed, however, as in the outcome of the census on hallucinations, and in the investigations of Miss X and Mrs. Piper and the extraordinary case of Stainton Moses.[16]

James then presented arguments for a mediumistic psychology based on the reality of the supernormal. The skeptics claimed that such phenomena simply do not occur in Nature, when in reality a close study of Nature provides just such examples. Moreover, the attempt of these skeptics to draw disparate facts from the various sciences and weave them together into a whole belies the fact that science as yet contains no such unity. On the basis of these weak arguments, James claimed, the positivists had quite used up their presumptive privileges in trying to discount psychical research by innuendo, simply because "no decisive thunderbolt of fact to clear the baffling darkness" had yet been presented.

Believing that such a thunderbolt had, in fact, been delivered, it was here that James presented his claim for the white crow:

> If you will let me use the language of the professional-logic shop, a universal proposition can be made untrue by a particular instance. If you wish to upset the law that all crows are black, you mustn't seek to show that no crows are; it is enough that you prove one single crow to be white. My own white crow is Mrs. Piper. In the trances of this medium, I cannot resist the conviction that knowledge appears which she has never gained by the ordinary use of her eyes and ears and wits. What the source of this knowledge may be I know not, and have not the glimmer of an explanatory suggestion to make; but from admitting the fact of such knowledge I can see no escape. So when I turn to the rest of our evidence, ghosts and all, I cannot carry with me the negative bias of the rigorously scientific mind, with its presumption as to what the true order of nature ought to be. I feel as if, though the evidence be flimsy in spots, it may nevertheless collectively carry heavy weight. The rigorously scientific mind may in truth easily over reach itself. Science means first of all a certain dispassionate method. To suppose that it means a certain set of results that one should pin one's faith upon and hug forever, is sadly to mistake its genius, and degrades the scientific body to the status of a sect.[17]

He then followed with references to ten cases of physical medium-ship which he believed to be convincing.[18] "We do not know where all this comes from," he said, therefore "we must accustom ourselves more and more to playing the role of a meteorological bureau." If the facts are true, we must first observe them before we can hope to fathom their cause.

He then took up what he called a "general reflection . . . relative to the influence of psychical research upon our attitude towards human history." Reiterating his former point, he said:

> Science taken in its essence should stand only for a method and not for any special beliefs, yet as habitually taken by its votaries, Science has come to be identified with a certain fixed general belief, the belief that the deeper order of Nature is mechanical exclusively, and that non-mechanical categories are irrational ways of conceiving and explaining even such a thing as human life. Now this mechanical rationalism, as one may call it, makes, if it becomes one's only way of thinking, a violent breach with the ways of thinking that have until our own time played the greatest part in human history. Religious thinking, ethical thinking, poetical thinking, teleological, emotional, sentimental thinking, what one might call the personal view of life to distinguish it from the impersonal and mechanical, and the romantic view of life to distinguish it from the rationalistic view, have been and even still are, outside of well-drilled scientific circles, the dominant forms of thought. But for mechanical rationalism, personality is an insubstantial illusion; the chronic belief of mankind that events may happen for the sake of their personal significance is an abomination; and the notions of our grandfathers about oracles and omens, divinations and apparitions, miraculous changes of heart and wonders worked by inspired persons, answers to prayer and providential leadings, are a fabric absolutely baseless, a mass of sheer *un*truth.[19]

Granted, he said, we must check the excess of the personal and romantic view with impersonal rationalism. "Our debt to Science is literally boundless, and our gratitude for what is positive in her teachings must be correspondingly immense." But the work of the Society in the previous dozen years has shown us conclusively that "the verdict of pure insanity, or gratuitous preference for error, of superstition without an excuse, which the Scientists of our day are led by their intellectual training to pronounce upon the entire thought of the past, is a most shallow verdict." The perspective of the unique person cannot be ignored, for "the great strength of the personal and romantic viewpoint is that it is fed by the facts of experience, whatever the ulterior interpretation of those facts may prove to be."

He then sought to tease out the question further by saying that narrative facts of experience have three things in common that the rationalists abhor: they are capricious, discontinuous, and not easily controlled; they require peculiar persons for their production; and their significance seems to be wholly for personal life. And as hard as it may be for the radical materialists to imagine, for those people who live in the narrative mode, science had become a cultural institution of reproach:

> The spirit and principles of Science are mere affairs of method; there is nothing in them that need hinder Science from dealing successfully with a world in which personal forces are a starting-point of new effects. The only form of [a] thing that we directly encounter, the only experience that we concretely have, is our own personal life. The only complete category of our thinking, our professors of philosophy tell us, is the category of personality, every other category being one of the abstract elements of that. And this systematic denial on Science's part of personality as a condition of events, this rigorous belief that in its own essential and innermost nature our world is a strictly impersonal world, may, conceivably, as the whirligig of time goes round, prove to be the very defect that our descendants will be most surprised at in our own boasted Science, the omission that to their eyes will most tend to make *it* look perspectiveless and short.[20]

Personality, in other words, is always a factor in the conduct of any kind of science and it becomes all the more important to account for the closer the scientific observer gets to the phenomena of consciousness.

THE WILL TO BELIEVE

But the text in which James first gave the name radical empiricism as best reflecting this new and burgeoning philosophical attitude was *The Will to Believe* (1897).[21] There he explained: "I say 'empiricism,' because it is contented to regard its most assured conclusions concerning matters of fact as hypotheses liable to modification in the course of future experience; and I say 'radical,' because it treats the doctrine of monism itself as an hypothesis, and, unlike so much of the half-way empiricism that is currently under the name of positivism or agnosticism or scientific naturalism, it does not dogmatically affirm monism as something with which all experience has got to square."[22]

The work was a pastiche of papers already published. The first four essays, which were the most important for articulating his emerging position, he presented as a defense of religious belief. His centerpiece was the lead essay, "The Will to Believe," which argued for the lawfulness of voluntarily adopted faith.[23] All antinomies exist *in potentia*. What becomes reality is that in which we invest our energy. Thus, he tried to show that since absolute objective certitude is unattainable, scientific objectivity is not a law but an attitude, subject to the vicissitudes of any system claiming infallibility in a fallible world. To expose this view, he asked: "Why do so few 'scientists' even look at the evidence for telepathy, so called? Because they think, as a leading biologist, now dead, once said to me, that even if such a thing were true, scientists ought to band together to keep it suppressed and concealed. It would undo the uniformity of Nature and all sorts of other things without which scientists cannot carry on their pursuits."[24]

What the biologist's comment meant to James was that our passionate nature must always be the deciding ground when two propositions cannot be resolved on strictly intellectual terms. As for objectification gone awry, he said: "When, indeed, one remembers that the most striking practical application to life of the doctrine of objective certitude has been the conscientious labors of the Holy Office of the Inquisition, one feels less tempted than ever to lend the doctrine a respectful ear."[25]

Reasonable men and women temper their standards to experience, but scientism goes too far:

> The most useful investigator, because the most sensitive observer, is always he whose eager interest on one side of the question is balanced by an equally keen nervousness lest he become deceived. Science has organized this nervousness into a regular *technique*, her so-called method of verification; and she has fallen so deeply in love with the method that one may even say she has ceased to care for truth by itself at all. It is only truth as technically verified that interests her. The truth of truths might come in merely affirmative form, and she would decline to touch it. . . . Human passions, however, are stronger than technical rules. "*Le coeur a ses raisons*," as Pascal says, "*que la raison ne connaît pas.*"[26]

Faith, organized around specific beliefs and feelings, James said, is not only what drives us, but what binds us together socially:

> A social organism of any sort whatever, large or small, is what it is because each member proceeds to his own duty with a trust that the other members will simultaneously do theirs. Wherever a desired result is achieved by the co-operation of many independent persons, its existence as a fact is a pure consequence of the precursive faith in one another of those immediately concerned. A government, an army, a commercial system, a ship, a college, an athletic team, all exist on this condition, without which not only is nothing achieved, but nothing is ever attempted. A whole train of passengers

(individually brave enough) will be looted by a few highwaymen, simply because the latter can count on one another, while each passenger fears that if he makes a movement of resistance, he will be shot before anyone else backs him up. If we believed that the whole car-full would rise at once with us, we should each severally rise, and train-robbing would never be attempted. There are, then, cases where a fact cannot come at all unless a preliminary faith exists in its coming. And where faith in a fact can help create the fact, that would be an insane logic which should say that faith running ahead of scientific evidence is the 'lowest kind of immorality' into which a thinking being can fall. Yet such is the logic by which our scientific absolutists pretend to regulate our lives![27]

Risk, uncertainty, chance were his focus. Here lies all the universe before us, he said, and what do we do? We attempt to confine it all inside one of our theories: "There is included in human nature an in-grained naturalism and materialism of mind which can only admit facts that are actually tangible. Of this sort of mind the entity called 'sci-ence' is the idol. Fondness for the word 'scientist' is one of the notes by which you may know its votaries; and its short way of killing any opin-ion that it disbelieves in is to call it 'unscientific.' "[28] He was, neverthe-less, sure that "whatever else may be certain, this at least is certain,—that the world of our present natural knowledge *is* enveloped in a larger world of *some* sort of whose residual properties we at present can frame no positive idea."[29]

The scientific attitude of agnostic positivism will almost always admit this principle theoretically in the most cordial terms, but it insists that we must not turn it to any practical use: "We have no right, this doctrine tells us, to dream dreams, or suppose anything about the unseen part of the universe, merely because to do so may be for what we are pleased to call our highest interests. We must always wait for sensible evidence for our beliefs; and where such evidence is inaccessible we must frame no hy-potheses whatever."[30] Such certitude can never be in reality, however, for "belief and doubt are living attitudes, and involve conduct on our part," he said. "That our whole physical life may lie soaking in a spiritual atmo-sphere, a dimension of being that we at present have no organ for appre-hending," he continued," is vividly suggested to us by the analogy of the life of our domestic animals."[31] In the same way that they look up to us ignorant of our higher motives, we may be witness to what is beyond our own human ken. As they do, we must live by faith, for "it is only by risking our persons from one hour to another that we live at all."

But in contrast to this vital kind of life, "Certain of our positivists keep chiming to us that, amid the wreck of every other god and idol, one

divinity still stands upright,—that his name is Scientific Truth, and that
he has but one commandment, but that one supreme saying, *Thou shalt
not be a theist,* for that would be to satisfy thy subjective propensities, and
the satisfaction of those is intellectual damnation."[32] What all these positivist types fail to realize is that you cannot postpone deciding until all
the evidence is in, or until there is absolute proof one way or the other,
for in most things this will never happen. Instead, we help to create what
is to come by our present investments: "While the future is uncertain,
whatever it will be it is decided in the *here* and *now*."

We can see plainly that James is heading toward his thesis in *The Varieties,*
that the primacy of inner life at its farthest reaches, to its deepest depths
and grandest heights, once experienced, must take precedence over the
mere logical ordering of sense data.

His intellectual path in psychology was not exactly straight, however.
By the late 1890s, his reputation as a psychologist was international and
still quite strong, despite the gradual eroding influence of the laboratory-oriented materialists who were busy redefining the day-to-day evolution of psychology as a new scientific discipline in their own terms. Then
in 1898, after he first enunciated his version of Peirce's pragmatism to a
packed audience at Berkeley, James soon attracted the attention of an
international audience of philosophers, including John Dewey in America, F.C.S. Schiller in England, Giovanni Papini in Italy, and Bergson in
France. Flournoy in Geneva, James's close compatriot in the development of a mediumistic psychology, also joined the pragmatist circle.
Both a psychologist and philosopher, himself, Flournoy would remain
James's link to what both of them referred to as "functional psychology,"
meaning a psychology of consciousness that had direct relevance to
human experience—the only true psychology worthy of the name, James
had once said to him.

The same year that he launched his pragmatism, James requested of
the Harvard Corporation that his title of Professor of Psychology, which
he had held since 1889, be changed back to Professor of Philosophy. It
was clear, if he ideally had gotten his way, that he intended to devote his
time to the technical elaboration of radical empiricism. But the Gifford
Lectures and recurring health problems stood in has path, and, with the
exception of a few philosophical skirmishes, during this period—at least
to 1902—his psychology of religion held the day.

He did manage to produce two major pieces (and six minor ones) on
radical empiricism in 1904, however, before he was carried away by the
floodwaters of the pragmatist movement.[33] The first was "Does Consciousness Exist?" and the other was "A World of Pure Experience."[34]

Both have been judged as foundation stones to a technical philosophy which one biographer has aptly called an unfinished arch, because six years later James died before he could articulate the full details of his metaphysical system.[35]

DOES CONSCIOUSNESS EXIST?

Like his theory of the emotions that preceded it, James's new view on consciousness created a shock wave. All rational thinkers, of course, believed that consciousness exists because they experience it. James's tack, however, was to deny it outright: "For twenty years past I have mistrusted 'consciousness' as an entity; for seven or eight years past I have suggested its non-existence to my students, and tried to give them its pragmatic equivalent in realities of experience. It seems to me that the hour is ripe for it to be openly and universally discarded."[36] This was no mere literary device; rather, it expressed the core of his thought. The natural tendency of the rational mind is to compartmentalize reality into categories, and in order to counter this tendency, James was intent on admitting into the philosophic discussion precisely those aspects of experience that were noncognitive. Throughout the literature of both psychology and philosophy, consciousness had been hypostatized into a category. Along with the other faculties of instinct, feeling, thought, and memory, human beings, it was said, also had consciousness. It was this *tendency* toward reification that had to be abandoned:

> To deny plumply that "consciousness" exists seems so absurd on the face of it—for undeniably "thoughts" do exist—that I fear some readers will follow me no farther. Let me then immediately explain that I mean only to deny that the word stands for an entity, but to insist most emphatically that it does stand for a function. There is, I mean, no aboriginal stuff or quality of being, contrasted with that of which material objects are made, out of which our thoughts of them are made; but there is a function in experience which thoughts perform, and for the performance of which this quality of being is invoked. That function is *knowing*.[37]

The idea of consciousness is meant to express not only the fact that things are, but also that they are reported and get known, he said. His thesis was that there is only one primal stuff of the world, "pure experience." Knowing, then, "can easily be explained as a particular sort of relation towards one another into which portions of pure experience may enter. The relation itself is a part of pure experience; one of its 'terms' becomes the subject or bearer of the knowledge, the knower, the other becomes the object known."[38] He appended a footnote to the word "knower," reminding the reader that in his *Psychology* back in

1890 he had tried to show that we need no knower other than the "passing thought." In the present context, that idea still held. Here, also, is another indication that he thus meant to square his metaphysics of radical empiricism with his earlier scientific agenda for psychology.

His main point, however, was to debunk the position of the neo-Kantians, who presumed that the world is a dualism between consciousness and its object. Experience, James countered, has no such inner duplicity. The separation of it by way of subject and object comes not by a process of subtraction but by one of addition. It was a totality to begin with, but rationality reflecting upon it creates different categories. Despite the categories, however, we do not have a real separation between subject and object. Rather, in the context of the whole, we have subject-and-object, which must be taken together: "The instant field of the present is at all times what I call the 'pure' experience. It is either virtually or potentially either object or subject as yet. For the time being, it is plain, unqualified actuality or existence, a simple *that*."[39] To differentiate subject from object, as the psychologists always did, was to cognize the whole twice, from two different vantage points, once as we objectively perceive the object and again as we subjectively experience it.

In his essay, "A World of Pure Experience," published the same year, James reiterated the meaning of radical empiricism and further argued for his doctrine of relations. By this he meant that "the relations that connect experiences must themselves be experienced relations, and any kind of relation experienced must be accounted as 'real' as anything else in the system."

The common doctrine in science asserted that mental life was built upon the association of ideas. James countered by saying that the relations between ideas were also an integral part of experience: "Life is in the transitions as much as in the terms connected; often, indeed, it seems to be there more emphatically, as if our spurts and sallies forward were the real firing-line of the battle, were like the thin line of flame advancing across the dry autumnal field which the farmer proceeds to burn."[40] In this context, he took up the problem of co-conscious transitions, "by which one experience passes into another when both belong to the same self."[41] Here he referred to the experience of continuity "within each of our personal histories, subject, object, interest, and purpose," harking back to his chapters on the "Stream of Thought" and "The Self" in *The Principles*. To this earlier discussion he added that change itself is one of the things we immediately experience. There is continuity from moment to moment, which we feel just as palpably as the experience of separation and discontinuity. Union to be real must also mean the reality of disunion.

RADICAL EMPIRICISM FOR PSYCHOLOGISTS

There are two other works worth mentioning that are considered minor by historians and philosophers but which underscore the point I have been trying to make, that radical empiricism was a metaphysics originally directed toward psychology. One is James's presidential address before the American Psychological Association in 1904 on "The Experience of Activity," delivered at a joint meeting with the newly formed American Philosophical Association.[42] The other is the only address James ever stood up and gave in French, "The Notion of Consciousness," delivered before the International Congress of Psychology, held in Rome in 1905.[43]

Put simply, "The Experience of Activity" was James's chance to show psychologists how radical empiricism could be applied to understanding a burning topic in psychology at the time—activity, the sense of change, or the feeling that motion went on against some form of resistance. The literature at the time was a jumble, with some theorists asking, "Do we have perceptions of it? What are these perceptions like, and when do we have them?" Others asked, "Is it an empirical fact, and if so how do we frame it as an idea?" Still others were asking, "When do we know it? By our feelings alone or through some other source of information?" The introspectionists claimed that the experience of activity could be understood by analyzing our feelings about it into its elemental sensations. Others in the experimentalist community maintained that subjective reports were of no consequence. Scientific understanding was arrived at by external measurement of the active organism. The philosophers, meanwhile, analyzed the concept in the abstract, as a metaphysical entity without reference to concrete persons.

Meanwhile, the radical empiricist, according to James, tried to see activity in its context: the pragmatic method, he maintained, starts from the postulate that there is no difference of truth that doesn't make a difference of fact somewhere; and it seeks to determine the meaning of all differences of opinion by making the discussion hinge as soon as possible upon some practical issue. The principle of pure experience is also a methodological postulate. Nothing shall be admitted as fact, it says, except what can be experienced at some definite time by some experiment; and for every feature of fact ever so experienced, a definite place must be found somewhere in the final system of reality. In other words: Everything real must be experienceable somewhere, and every kind of thing experienced must somewhere be real (p. 81).

He then referred to the works of Ladd, Stout, Bradley, Titchener, Shand, Ward, Loveday, Lipps, and Bergson as only some of the writers struggling in different ways and from different vantage points with the question of complex activity. "Is it purely mental?" "Is it physical?" "Can we really study it in discrete bits?" "Is it a fact or an artifact of experience?" and so on. His point appeared to be the reconciliation of these various claims within the wider domain of lived experience.

Moreover, he cautioned against omitting the experiencing person at the center of the equation. The individualized self (the only thing that should be properly so called, in James's opinion) was always a part of the content of the experienced world. The experienced world always comes to us in the form of a state of consciousness experienced with our body as its center. Nevertheless, our experiences are always but a portion of a wider world, "one link in the vast chain of processes out of which history is made." We think we are only drinking a glass of alcohol, but we do not see the end of the chain, that we are really creating the liver cirrhosis that will end our days.

Whether we ascribe activity to external forces, to the succession of thoughts, or to some chemical action in the body, the question for research is what practical difference will a particular explanantion make. This is the larger question of why we do scientific research in the first place. "The worth and interest of the world consists not in its elements, be these elements things, or be they the conjunctions of things; it exists rather in the dramatic outcome of the whole process" (p. 94). He then concluded by reminding his audience about the enduring but almost always hidden assumption behind their work: "To live our lives better is the true reason we wish to know the element of things," a fact, he said, which makes all psychologists pragmatists in the end.

The lecture on "The Notion of Consciousness" served a completely different purpose. It was a spur-of-the-moment, largely unplanned, and wholly spontaneous rendering of "Does Consciousness Exist?" delivered in forty minutes to an international audience. James had not even planned to go to the Fifth International Congress of Psychology, but changed his mind at the last minute. He shared a stateroom on the way over with the psychologist E. B. Holt for two weeks and toured Greece before arriving at the Congress in Rome by the end of April 1905. While he was registering, the woman at the desk went into a swoon upon hearing his name, saying that he was the talk of all Italy. Professor Santi De-Sanctis was summoned and, after having the same reaction, impressed upon James the necessity of speaking to the Congress, especially because several of the planned speakers on the program, such as Flournoy, had not been able to come. James acquiesced, wrote at a fever pitch for two days, and then delivered his remarks in French, finding that it was even easier than English, probably because his vocabulary was so much more limited. A lively discussion followed. Janet, who was in the audience, declared it stupendous, and Flournoy printed it in his journal, the *Archives de Psychologie*, eight weeks later.

The essence of James's talk was that reality and our sensations of it are identical. We speak of a separation, but this is a practical kind of dualism only. "Thought and actuality are made of one and the same stuff, the stuff of experience in general."

He ran out of time at the end and thus, to our own eventual benefit, was forced to summarize his views, which he cast into six theses. According to the position of radical empiricism:

1. Consciousness as it is ordinarily understood does not exist, any more than does Matter. . . .
2. What does exist is the susceptibility possessed by the parts of experience to be reported or known.
3. This susceptibility is explained by the fact that certain experiences can lead some to others by means of distinctly characterized intermediary experiences, in such a fashion that some play the role of known things, the others that of knowing subjects.
4. These two roles can be intelligently defined without departing from the web of experience and without reference to transcendental entities.
5. The attributes subjective and objective, represented and representative, thing and thought convey a practical distinction that is important, but they are of a functional and not an ontological order—that is, useful but not real as absolutes.
6. Finally, these opposites are not heterogeneous but made of the same stuff, which cannot be defined but only experienced.

I dwell on these passages deliberately to suggest the philosophical tone that James had taken after 1902. His subject matter was still the problem of consciousness, and the activities of psychologists still continued to figure into his narrative, but indirectly now, as long as his attention was distracted toward metaphysics and epistemology.

Radical empiricism was, nevertheless, *psychological*; that is to say, it placed immediate experience at the center of everything we have to say about the universe. Consciousness, therefore, knower-and-known, subject-and-object, person-and-world, formed the basis of all science and all knowledge-getting. Potisitivistic science had to conform as much to the dictates of such a psychology, as psychology was trying to conform to such a science.

PRAGMATISM

If radical empiricism was William James's psychology of immediate experience, then pragmatism was his philosophy of personality. True, pragmatism, the idea that beliefs are tested by their consequences, was remembered chiefly as a philosophical movement; but within James's own cosmology, I suggest that he also meant it to serve as the philosophical justification for a psychology that held the person as central to its scientific concerns. Jamesean pragmatism granted not only validity but sovereignty to the way an individual uniquely sees the world. It was a justification for why we live a life of values. It was a statement on how acts are always motivated by beliefs. It was a way of evaluating truth claims on the basis of their outcome. Finally, it was the basis of James's social philosophy. In it he saw a way of reconciling conflicting assertions about the nature of reality, hence, not only adumbrating disagreements, but also defining, in the social fabric of things, how individuals who are endowed with consciousness are connected to one another.

He made his most definitive statement as a series of public lectures before the Lowell Institute in Boston during November and December 1906, published the following year as *Pragmatism: A New Name for Some Old Ways of Thinking* (1907), to international acclaim. In this work he began with a rough typology by dividing the world into the rationalists, who base their conclusions on a predefined set of principles, and the empiricists, who define reality through the facts of experience. The first he called the tender-minded, the intellectuals, the idealists, and the optimists—religious types who believe in free will and dogmatic monism. The second are the tough-minded, those who live by obeying their sensations. They are the materialists and the pessimists among us, the irreligious and fatalistic. They are the skeptics who see a pluralistic rather than a monistic pattern to the universe.

The two parts, James said, appear hopelessly separated: "You find empiricism with inhumanism and irreligion; or else you find a rationalistic philosophy that indeed may call itself religious, but that keeps out of all definite touch with concrete facts and joys and sorrows."[44] He proposed the "oddly named thing pragmatism" as a philosophy that could both remain religious and at the same time preserve the richest intimacy with facts.

He then launched into a formal definition of the term: "To attain perfect clearness in our thoughts of an object . . . , we need only consider what conceivable effects of a practical kind the object may involve—what sensations we are to expect from it, and what reactions we must prepare. Our conception of these effects, whether immediate or remote, is then for us the whole of our conception of the object, so far as that conception has positive significance at all."[45] By this he meant two things; that the truth or falsity of any given individual's beliefs are tested by their effects, and that seemingly incompatible belief systems between individuals can be reconciled by comparing similarity of outcome.

Pragmatism, first of all, James said, according to its originator, Charles Sanders Peirce, maintains that our beliefs are really rules for action.[46] We act according to what we believe to be true about the world. Thus, our behavior is a product of inward values and attitudes.

This also means that beliefs can be tested by their consequences. That is, one way to test the truth of a belief system is to subject it to the criteria of outcome. If the outcome of what we believe is good and helps us to live, then we tend to remain committed to those beliefs that inspired the action. If the outcome is poor and our life is miserable, then we might examine our beliefs with an eye toward changing them, which will, in turn, be reflected in the way we act.

Second, pragmatism always establishes the criteria of practical consequences as the standard for judging the truth of any matter, when seemingly incompatible viewpoints are in disagreement. The rule is that in a conflict between seemingly opposite views, one traces each position out to its practical effect. If the outcome or benefit is approximately the same, then for all practical purposes the opposing views are identical.

The pragmatic maxim is understood, James said, by repeated applications to concrete incidences. These he provided in abundance, including a discussion of the meaning of substance, the problem of design in nature, the issue of determinism versus free will, and the old argument about whether or not the universe is run by matter or spirit. He appeared at once to be striking a melioristic chord between the opposing views of rationalism and empiricism, and at the same time making the case that each view has its field of application. Pragmatism alone is the only philosophy that can read an optimistic message into the nihilism of the materialists. Yet, one gets the sense he also is saying that in a positivistic, materialist, and overrationalized world, the subjective still counts for something extremely important, if we can show that it has specific and positive effects on people's lives. Pragmatism equally abjures absolute monism as well as absolute pluralism. "On principle," James said, "we cannot reject any hypothesis if consequences useful to life flow from it."[47]

Pragmatism, he further said, is an attitude, not a final solution. It simply means that the practical cash-value must be extracted out of every idea and set to work within the stream of our experience. "*Theories thus become instruments, not answers to enigmas, in which we can rest.*"[48] We are left not with a final answer, but with an attitude of orientation, with "*the attitude of looking away from first things, principles, 'categories,' supposed necessities; and of looking towards last things, fruits, consequences, facts.*"[49] Pragmatism

> represents a perfectly familiar attitude in philosophy, the empiricist attitude, but it represents it . . . both in a more radical and in a less objectionable form than it has ever yet assumed. A pragmatist turns his back resolutely and once and for all upon a lot of inveterate habits dear to pro-

fessional philosophers. He turns away from abstraction and insufficiency, from verbal solutions, from bad *a priori* reasons, from fixed principles, closed systems, and pretended absolutes and origins. He turns toward concreteness and adequacy, toward facts, toward action and toward power. That means the empiricist temperament regnant and the rationalist temper sincerely given up. It means the open air and possibilities of nature, as against dogma, artificiality, and the pretense of finality in truth.[50]

All our theories are instrumental, are mental modes of adaptation to reality, rather than revelations or gnostic answers to some divinely instituted world-enigma: *"For rationalism reality is ready-made and complete from all eternity, while for pragmatism it is still in the making, and awaits part of its complexion from the future."*[51] The rationalists proclaim that somewhere there is an already-made deluxe edition, surrounded by various incomplete and somehow more corrupt editions, which are finite and full of false readings. To them, pragmatism is a trunk without a tag, a dog without a collar. The pragmatist advocates a universe unfinished and growing in all sorts of places, especially where thinking beings are at work. Pessimists believe the world cannot be saved, optimists believe that it *must*, while pragmatists believe in the *possibility* that it could. Truth is always provisional.

Truth, James said, is the verification of an idea by the efficacious connection with other ideas: "When a moment in our experience, of any kind whatever, inspires us with a thought that is true, this means that sooner or later we dip by that thought's guidance into the particulars of experience again and make advantageous connection with them." "True ideas are those that we can assimilate, validate, corroborate, and verify. False ideas are those we cannot."[52] Truth is not a stagnant property, "Truth *happens* to an idea. It *becomes* true, is *made* true by events."[53]

Should the pragmatist view prevail, he further said, the result would be quite monumental for the present state of the disciplines. Ultra-rationalist types would be frozen out. Science and metaphysics would come closer together. A whole new way of thinking would come about that honored experience over intellectual abstraction and authoritarianism: "One misunderstanding of pragmatism is to identify it with positivistic tough-mindedness, to suppose that it scorns every rationalistic notion as so much jabber and gesticulation, that it loves intellectual anarchy as such and prefers a sort of wolf-world absolutely unpent and wild and without a master or a collar to any philosophic classroom whatsoever."[54] Rather, pragmatism centers on the person, believing that the human factor has to be accounted for in every definition of reality. Essentially, this was a statement about individual consciousness, for no definition of

reality, James said, is complete without considering the flux of our sensations, the relations between sensations and the apparent copies of reality
in our minds, and the previous truths of which every new inquiry takes
account. Pragmatism thus argues for a piecemeal supernaturalism in
which each individual must play a part:

> Take the hypothesis seriously and as a live one. Suppose that the world's
> author put the case to you before creation, saying: "I am going to make a
> world not certain to be saved, a world the perfection of which shall be con-
> ditional merely, the condition being that each several agent does his own
> 'level best.' I offer you the chance of taking part in such a world. Its safety,
> you see, is unwarranted. It is a real adventure, with real danger, yet it may
> win through. It is a social scheme of cooperative work genuinely to be done.
> Will you join the procession? Will you trust yourself and trust the other
> agents enough to face the risk?"[55]

But the transformation in thinking to which James is referring involves
not simply the addition of another category to the pantheon of rational
distinctions about reality. It involves the realization that separate realities
exist within radically different epistemological realms of human discourse. The rational mind must reconcile itself to the fact that there is
no one single grand truth, but as many truths as there are individuals
who hold them, an idea that James called "noetic pluralism."

PLURALISM

If radical empiricism was James's metaphysical call for a psychology of
immediate experience, and pragmatism his philosophy of personality,
then pluralism, from a psychological standpoint, was his justification for
a psychology of individual differences. Pluralism, to be noetic, implies,
first of all, that within personality there is a concatenation of states of
consciousness, each with their own knowledge center. A plurality of
states hidden away in the background from waking consciousness is the
norm. Meanwhile, single personalities exist as a democratic conjunction,
each one, to the degree that they accept their social responsibility to do
so, a unity-in-the-making.

This pluralistic way of taking reality is probably the most adaptive way
to regard the world and not that far off from the outlook of the majority.
In this way, most members of modern society are already Jamesean pragmatists, because a noetic pluralism enables them to avoid both the crude
nihilism of the scientific materialists as well as the fore-ordained Absolute of religious dogma. Thus James maintained: "A world imperfectly
unified still, and perhaps always to remain so, must be sincerely entertained. This latter is pluralism's doctrine."

The philosophical problem that plagued James, however, was the pro-
verbial one, namely, the relation of the one to the many.[56] If consciousness was an ultimate plurality of states, then what was the religious experience of unity? If simple states did not compound into more complex
ones, then what was the ontological relation of the lower to the higher,
of the parts to the whole? How can the individuality of specific entities be
preserved when they identify with their reference group? James realized
all too well that there was no logical way to work these problems out, for
every time the dichotomy was invoked each part automatically became
mutually exclusive, and the intellectual attempt to resolve them became
either an unsolvable conundrum or a mere semantic game that proposed a conceptual integration which had no relation to real life.

BERGSON, AND THE *ELAN VITAL*

James found a particularly thrilling answer to his problem in the work of
the French philosopher Henri Bergson. In his Hibbert Lectures at Oxford in 1908, later published as *A Pluralistic Universe* (1909), James devoted an entire chapter to Bergson's ideas. From this précis, we know
that James received corroboration not only for numerous psychological
conceptions, such as the stream of consciousness, but also his larger
metaphysics of radical empiricism.

Bergson advocated an intuitive and experiential philosophy that set a
major challenge for the intellectual categories of the analytic philosophers. Reality is a whole that flows, he said. All the analytic philosophers
did was to cut up reality into categories and then to construct theories
that were logically consistent with the pieces they started with. These
exercises were divorced from what happens in real life. Life does not sit
there in static form, but rather courses through us in dynamic pulses as
the *élan vital*: "Consciousness is this vital element that is at the origin of
life. Consciousness, which is a *need of creation*, is made manifest to itself
only when creation is possible. It lies dormant when life is condemned to
automatism; it wakens as soon as the possibility of choice is restored."[57]

Consciousness for Bergson corresponded exactly to the living being's
power of choice. It is coextensive with the fringes of possible action that
surround the real action; it is synonymous with invention and freedom,
the rising above the purely mechanistic and deterministic life of inor-
ganic matter and single organic reflex. "It is as if a vague and formless
being, whom we may call, as one will, man *or* superman, had sought to
realize himself, and had succeeded only by abandoning a part of himself
on the way."[58]

James found in these ideas an affirmation that intellectualism had to
be abandoned. The logical dichotomy between inner and outer was not

absolutely given, but was an invention of consciousness and, further, there was no law which emphatically states that the only way we can know reality is through conceptualization. Quite to the point, James believed that another more viable and potentially superior alternative was "a 'living contemplation or sympathetic acquaintance' with things."[59]

James had written to Bergson, "I think that the indispensable hypothesis in a philosophy of pure experience is that of many kinds of other experiences than ours, that the question of co-conscious/conscious synthesis (its conditions, etc.) becomes a most urgent question."[60] Bergson replied:

> I believe that on many essential points I could join you, but perhaps I would not go quite so far as you do in the way of "radical empiricism." The principal differences bears probably again (I am not wholly sure) in the role of the unconscious. I cannot avoid making a very large place for the unconscious, not only in the realm of psychology but also in the universe in general, the existence of unperceived matter seeming to me to be of the same *genre* as a psychological state which is not conscious. The existence of a reality outside of all actual consciousness is something intimately mingled with the conscious life, "interwoven with it," and not "underlying it" as substantialism would have it. But it is possible that even on this point I am nearer to you than I imagine.[61]

In his preface to the French translation of James's *Pragmatism,* Bergson wrote that, according to James, "we bathe in an atmosphere traversed by spiritual currents. Many resist, but others open themselves wide and thus allow themselves to be influenced by these wide beneficent breezes."[62]

Emphasizing the pluralistic nature of knowing, Bergson said:

> For James evolution meant the creation of what is true for man. Reality flows, we flow with it; and we call true any affirmation which, in guiding us through moving reality, gives us a grip upon it and places us under more favorable conditions for acting. While for other more traditional doctrines a new truth is a discovery, for James it was an invention. Truth, according to pragmatism, has come little by little into being, thanks to the individual contributions of a great number of inventors. Truth, as Kant says, may depend upon the general structure of the human mind, but James adds that the structure of the human mind is the effect of the free initiative of a certain number of individual minds.[63]

Eulogizing James, Bergson concluded: "No one loved truth with a more ardent love, no one sought it with greater passion. James was stirred by an immense unrest and went from science, from anatomy and physiology to psychology, and from psychology to philosophy, tense over great problems. All his life he observed, experimented, meditated. And, as if he had not done enough, he still dreamed, as he fell into his last slumber, of extraordinary experiments and superhuman efforts by which he could continue even beyond death to work with us for the greater good of science."[64]

FECHNER, ON AWAKENED CONSCIOUSNESS

In addition to Bergson, another figure in psychology of equal or exceeding influence on James in this last phase was Gustav Theodor Fechner, German physicist, aesthetician, and founder of modern psychophysics, whose cosmology was based on both mathematical thought and mystical revelation. James had not taken Fechner's psychophysics seriously in *The Principles* but rediscovered him in earnest after 1900. At that time, James read through Fechner's works and discovered a veritable spiritual psychology of consciousness that addressed the problem of the one in the many. While Fechner preached a doctrine of panpsychism, the inherent consciousness of matter, he also believed that "states of consciousness, so-called, can separate and combine themselves freely, and keep their own identity unchanged while forming parts of simultaneous fields of experience of wider scope."[65]James was so impressed that he penned an introduction to the English translation of Fechner's *Little Book on Life after Death* (1904), he devoted several articles to the interpretation of Fechner's works, and he included a chapter on him in *The Pluralistic Universe*.[66]

For Fechner, James said, the abstract lived in the concrete, and the original sin of both popular and scientific thinking was the habit of regarding the spiritual not as the rule, but as an exception in the midst of nature: "The hidden motive of all he did," James said, "was to bring what he called the daylight view of this world into even greater evidence, that daylight view being this, that the whole universe, in its spans and wavelengths, exclusions and envelopments, is everywhere alive and conscious."[67]

Fechner wrote, for instance, on the inner life of plants. Their consciousness, he said, may be of an entirely different quality than that of humans, commensurate exclusively with the type of organization they possess.

The earth, likewise, had a higher, more general conscious life than the merely human. The Earth-Soul, as Fechner called it, and all of the other planets, are in fact angels, intermediaries between God and humans. Passionately believing in the Earth-Soul, Fechner thought of the earth as a guardian angel of superior consciousness. We as persons are sense organs of the Earth-Soul and contribute what we can from our quarter, which ceases when we die. But our *effect* lives on as the immortal contribution of each unique being, influencing all others who survive us. Collectively as a species, if we are to evolve any higher, he said, we must come to terms with this Earth-Soul.[68]

Here we have the main theme of Fechner's thought, the awakening of the human being into a state of higher consciousness. Man has three lives, Fechner said. The first is in the womb. The baby exists in a watery medium, totally dependent on the mother and at the same time totally oblivious to the function of the physical body which is then forming. The physical body is actually the vehicle for the next life, which begins at the moment of birth—that is, consciousness-in-the-world. Human beings then function in material reality over the lifespan, completely oblivious of their ability to alter consciousness into a higher state. This is because, according to Fechner, present consciousness is the vehicle for a higher, spiritual life after death. Some persons can awaken to the higher function of consciousness while still in this life. These are our artists, our spiritual seekers, our intuitive types, those with great inspiration, and those who are inward and self-negating. They have a great tolerance for ambiguity and are capable of living simultaneously in multiple worlds. Yet these are precisely the types who are considered to be the most useless specimens of humanity by the more worldly savants of material culture. Higher consciousness, nevertheless, remains the ground of our very being.

BLOOD, THE PLURALISTIC MYSTIC

In a curious return to chemically induced states of mystical awareness, James, in the last year of his life, tried to bring before a wider public the works of Benjamin Paul Blood. Blood was a businessman from Amsterdam, New York, whose work, *The Anaesthetic Revelation* (1874), James had read at the beginning of his own career. The piece had fascinated him so weirdly that, he said, "I am conscious of its having been one of the stepping stones of my thinking ever since."[69] Blood was aphoristic and oracular, and James likened him at times to the glorious Emerson. He considered Blood a writer of rare quality, even though he had never published in any journal more sophisticated than the *Albany Times* or the *Utica Herald*.

The essence of Blood's philosophy was a pluralistic mysticism. Traditionally, the mystics declare themselves monists, because of the unity of their inner visions, but Blood's was the first account of a mystical philosophy that seemed to have a radically pluralistic sound. This tendency drew James to proclaim upon reading it that "I feel now as if my own pluralism were not without the kind of support which mystical corroboration may confer."[70]

Blood began an explanation of his thought by reverting to Hegelian dialectics. Being and non-being form an inseparable pair. Thereafter, in typical Hegelian fashion, the logic becomes circular—one cannot exist without the other, sameness and difference in one sense become the same, and so on. "Being and non-being have equal value and mainly are convertible in their terms."[71] Such dialectic monism is the only result.

But Blood also blasphemed the Kantian tradition by declaring: "Reason is neither the first nor the last word in this world."[72] The problem is that knower and known remain in apposition as long as they continue to be cast into objective categories. Immediate experience, which comes before intellectual categories, means freedom, which has no fertility and no reason for any special thing. For all of reason, the Mystery remains. Variety, not uniformity, is likely the key to progress. The genius of being is whimsical, not consistent. "Simply, we do not know."[73] Knowledge must be secondary and witness principal. "We have realized the highest divine thought of itself, and there is in it as much of wonder as of certainty; inevitable, and solitary and safe in one sense, but queer and cactus-like no less in another sense, it appeals unutterably to experience alone."[74]

The appeal here is not to our faculties of logic and preordained order but to our faculties of heroism and risk. There is no complete generalization, no total point of view, no all-pervasive unity. Making Blood's point his own, James ends this essay—the last he published before he died—by saying, "There is no conclusion. . . . There are no fortunes to be told, and there is no advice to be given.—Farewell."[75]

Chapter Eight

JAMES'S FINAL STATEMENT
TO PSYCHOLOGISTS

WHEN WE NOW look back over James's contribution to psychology after 1890, we see first that the dividing line is somewhat artificial. Not much occurs after that year that had not germinated earlier. Why, then, did he take up the positivist stance in the first place?

My answer has been that his definition of scientific psychology *evolved.* He began with a defense of consciousness in the context of Darwinian theory and progressed to a study of the mind-body problem within the context of physiological psychology. His main agenda was to seize the study of consciousness from the abstract philosophers and to appropriate it for the new science of psychology. At this point, he composed his *Principles,* which he based on a positivism ostensibly free of metaphysics. Yet even before he had completed his positivistic agenda, his encounter with the evidence for the subliminal, and for the reality of multiple states of consciousness, which had actually commenced in the late 1880s, led him to question the ability of any science to exist without presuming some kind of underlying body of metaphysical assumptions. The new evidence caused him to renovate his philosophy, at the same time that it justified the expansion of what could be included within the legitimate domain of his psychology. He was thus led more deeply into psychical research and to problems of psychopathology, to his lectures on "Exceptional Mental States," to *The Varieties,* and to the evolution of his metaphysics of radical empiricism. I have tried to indicate that, among other concerns, James intended for these developments, in turn, to have important philosophical implications for scientific psychology.

How, he was forced to ask, was the subconscious a naturalistic extension of his original claim that the thought is the thinker? He answered in two ways. First, the positivistic explanation works only by presuming that the condition of the observer is fixed and unitary, when in reality, not only its content but its very ground is always changing. At its farthest and deepest point, we simply cannot say what consciousness ultimately is. From this, he came to realize that the personal element and the subjective commitment to belief can never be eliminated completely from any discussion of objectivity. Second, by turning to the phenomenology of inner experience as an ultimately unknowable ground within which knowing of some kind still goes on, he came to the conclusion that *experience*—and not mental categories, nor overt actions, nor physical organs—should be the proper focus of scientific psychology.

An understanding of his change of view gives us room to interpret the two centers of gravity in James's *Principles*. It makes understandable his interest in the subliminal as an approach to psychopathology in his Exceptional Mental States Lectures of 1896. It supports his naturalistic theism, which recognized the transcendent quality of the mystical experience in *The Varieties*. Finally, it helps to explain James's attraction to the panpsychism of Fechner, the *élan vital* of Bergson, and the pluralistic mysticism of Blood at the end of his career.

The larger question also looms, however: Why might James's change of mind be so important for psychology? In the first place, he is describing a road that academic psychologists, by and large, have not taken. Behaviorism and psychophysics, adherents of which long ago rejected any philosophical claims on psychology, have persistently dominated the academic laboratory scene and only recently have been replaced by the cognitive sciences, which are only slightly more hospitable to acknowledging their own underlying metaphysics.

Meanwhile, personality, social, abnormal, and clinical psychologists, while still having to answer to it, have persistently resisted complete subjugation to the positivist and reductionistic paradigm. Not coincidentally, they also have drawn nutriment from the larger Jamesean vision of a functional psychology. But they have not had the impact on the philosophy of science that they might. Their voice has been small in comparison to the rhetoric of the experimentalists, partly because they have not carried the weight of the natural sciences with them in the twentieth century, like subdisciplines such as psychophysics, sensation and perception, or learning theory have. An interesting question is, what would psychology as a discipline be like if it had taken this other road?

Second, it may not come as a complete surprise to find that the psychology James envisioned actually does exists. But it has persistently come up throughout modern culture in places other than the universities. Instead, we see it in the clinical arena in a profusion of depth psychologies; we see it in existentialism and phenomenology; we see it in parapsychology and in the self-help movement (particularly throughout the history of groups such as Alcoholics Anonymous); it pervades the counterculture psychotherapies and the pastoral counseling movement. We even see it in the sheer diversity of programs within the annual meetings of the American Psychological Association. How truly functional, then, is university-based psychology? Does it produce a superior form of knowledge to these other cultural forms? Or is part of the human experience being disenfranchised by the fiat of administrators who categorize knowledge and by professionals who draw strict disciplinary boundaries? While these lines have perhaps been necessary to launch graduate education on a mass scale and to define the purview of psychology, even now, in their own domain, a major reorganization of traditional categories of knowledge is underway, fueled by the neuroscience revolution.

Third, James meant for his metaphysics of radical empiricism to serve a soteriologic function; that is, he intended not just to add to the cumulative knowledge base of a new science, but he fully intended to transform psychology into something ultimately different from what it had become. He meant it didactically as a periodic antidote—to instruct psychology on its shortcomings, to renovate what was outmoded, and to transform it into the new.

What, then, was his main message for psychologists? I believe that he had at least two. First, pointing the way toward modern depth psychology and personality theory, he enjoined psychologists to study within the stream of experience the rise and fall of the threshold of consciousness. Second, with regard to both theory and method, he preached tolerance and eclecticism in reconciling apparently incompatible views of the world.

His Depth Psychology

According to James, hovering beyond the penumbra of objects in the immediate focus of our attention are worlds of meaning. They are the springs of all thought, the motivators of all action. Meaning gets into the field of waking consciousness through the symbols of language and the concepts of abstract thought, warmed by emotion, and always being modified by incoming sensory data and the immediate physiological state of the organism. Yet, at the same time, we never see meaning; it is always only inferred by thought, word, and action. Whatever the systems of condensed experience are that lie beyond the margin, they are filtered out of waking awareness, otherwise the field would remain permanently flooded. Attention is, rather, almost always directed outward toward the external environment. Waking consciousness does not normally see into its own internal boundaries or into inner domains beyond itself, because there is a screen that separates waking consciousness from other states beyond the margin.

James believed that modern science had identified that barrier as the hypnagogic zone. The hypnagogic state was not only the twilight region between waking and sleeping, but also the region one passes through in the waking fugue, the so-called zone of forgetfulness separating one state of consciousness from another. Geniuses see these transitions in the waking state, as do the insane. Yogis see them as well in ecstatic trance. Here, coming up from below, impulses from within are translated into mental images, the transitional form of psychic energy before becoming cognitive abstract thought. Similarly, returning back into the depths, as hypnotic suggestion and falling asleep show, whenever there is a loosening of the bounds of waking consciousness, abstract thoughts become internal mental images.[1]

James identified the hypnagogic state as a physiological and mental reality, but he did not speculate on the content of mental imagery. F.W.H. Myers had broached the mythopoetic character of inner events, positing that there was something universal or highly energic about specific kinds of inner experience common to all people that could be conceptually analyzed. Janet had even alluded to the fact that the germ of the original trauma was hidden within the symbolic structure of the hysteric's symptoms. But James was not drawn to an analysis of the content of these inner images as Freud and Jung were later. He was satisfied to acknowledge that they occurred and had some important evolutionary function in the biological economy of the organism.

This physiological interest, however, extended in two directions. At one level of analysis, we find in various places (in *The Principles*, for instance) the attempt to use analogies of nerve functioning to explain the random associative processes in dreams and hallucinations. At another level of analysis (e.g., his Exceptional Mental States Lectures), James appears to be using the hypnagogic state as an explanatory mechanism in psychopathology to understand how physical trauma takes on psychological meaning, or conversely, how psychological trauma might be translated into physical symptoms.

At the same time, James recognized that some of the most intense inner imagery is associated with states of religious awareness. Mystics described diabolical images that caused them immense suffering, only to be followed by the most ecstatic and passionate visions of the Divine. Things that even ordinary people saw within could change them forever. In one instance, a hopeless drunkard suddenly gives up his habit. In another, a man who had lived a life of sin felt that he was forgiven and was able to start again. James well understood that certain kinds of numinous images had transforming power.

James's point was that if psychology truly wanted to influence character development, then it had to acknowledge that there was, in fact, a growth-oriented dimension within the normal personality to which one could make appeal and through which ideas could have an effect. The nature of this dimension, he said, was unfathomable. At its farthest reaches, we cannot say what it is; we can only say "it is *that*."

But the most important implication of James's thinking for the future of psychology, in my opinion, remains the problem of consciousness.[2] In a word, James could not see how the various sciences and all the systems of mathematical laws that allegedly govern our understanding of causality can have an existence independent of the human mind. The paradox is that we profess to know and control everything about the world of matter, but we know absolutely nothing about consciousness. In our quest for objectivity, we have been guilty in the past of denying that consciousness even exists.

James resolves the dualism of the mental and the physical by asserting no external world of objects can exist *except as a function of some consciousness.* This means that there can be no objective science without human consciousness to create it; no world of causal mathematical laws except insofar as they are a product of human thought. If true, then what contemporary definitions of objective science do is clearly to banish subjectivity by *holding the discussion of consciousness in abeyance.*[3] By so doing, they achieve a partial grasp of the physical dimensions of the world, but are denied access to the truly psychological aspects of human functioning.

For James, the essential problem of consciousness is that every time we attempt to study it, the phenomena under consideration become dissected and objectified through linguistic constructs and mental categories. We look to see if the subject is awake or asleep. We try to measure the difference. This way we grade consciousness into different levels. We articulate our theory to the world. Consciousness, then, becomes just another object in nature to be studied.

James's epistemology, however, posed a different approach for psychology; namely, that psychologists should focus on raw experience before the subject-object dichotomy is invoked. Traditionally, he maintained, experience is already reified into preestablished categories before psychology begins its work. In his time the categories were vision, taste, touch, smell, and feeling, grafted onto mental constructs such as sensation, emotion, perception, and cognition.[4] The self was a standard last chapter in the new psychology texts still influenced by the older moral philosophy, as if to say that adding up the categories produced the whole.

As the methods of studying the categories changed, some of these categories became more important than others according to the criteria of scientific precision.[5] What was originally called physiological psychology, meaning the study of the human organism within the natural sciences, became differentiated almost along ethnic lines into experimental psychology (the Germans), psychopathology (the French), and mental testing (the English). Eventually, the self was eliminated from the categories of experimentalism and pushed into allegedly less scientific fields that came to be called applied psychology.

Even as the concept of the person was being fast winnowed out of experimental psychology before 1900, James was calling for a reinstatement of the person at the center of the discipline. In essence, he was saying that if the field remains open, then any aspect of human experience is a potentially legitimate area of psychological inquiry. At the same time, central to his definition of psychology was that the individual—each human being in the singular—should be acknowledged as a potential essence extractor far superior to any method or machine made by man (or woman) for the same purpose. In a pluralistic world, exact scientific measurement could still remain part of the pantheon of ways of knowing available to human beings who pursue knowledge in its many forms. But it would properly become a tool of consciousness, instead of its *raison d'être*.[6]

For these reasons, James said, psychology would do well to study what Fechner called "the fall of the threshold" of normal waking awareness:

A movement of the threshold downwards will . . . bring a mass of subconscious memories, conceptions, emotional feelings, and perceptions of relation, etc., into view all at once; and that if this enlargement of the nimbus that surrounds the sensational present is vast enough, while no one of the items it contains attracts our attention singly, we shall have the conditions fulfilled for a kind of consciousness in all essential respects like that termed mystical. It will be transient, if the change in threshold is transient. It will be of reality, enlargement, and illumination, possibly rapturously so. It will be of unification, for the present coalesces in it with ranges of the remote quite out of reach under ordinary circumstances; and the sense of *relation* will be greatly enhanced. Its form will be intuitive and perceptual, not conceptual, for the remembered or conceived objects in the enlarged field are supposed not to attract the attention singly, but only to give the sense of a tremendous *muchness* suddenly revealed.[7]

He had elsewhere stated that psychopathology may be a restriction of the field or a dissociation of the field into many parts. Here, he believed that states of mystical intuition may be only very sudden and great extensions of the ordinary field of consciousness.

Thus, we see the renewed importance of James's call in *The Varieties* for a cross-cultural study of the subliminal. How individuals in different cultures comprehend what they consider to be the ultimate ground of their existence, James believed, is for psychology best reflected in accounts of immediate experience rather than in a comparison of the texts, schools of thought, or ecclesiastical history of different traditions. Indeed, an adequate comprehension of human nature may depend more on such an endeavor than the present views we hold of world cultures that rely exclusively on quantitative, economic, political, and historical forms of knowledge. The task of constructing such a comparative psychology of inner experience, however, has yet to be undertaken.

These interests were reflected in James's encounter with Freud and his followers at the Clark Conference in 1909. James was present for only a single day (at the fortuitous moment of the famous Clark photograph). At that time, he accompanied Freud on a walk, and in the midst of their stroll James clutched at his heart with an attack of angina. He insisted that Freud continue on, and Freud—physician and neurologist—did so, leaving the ailing James to his own devices. Freud later wrote of the episode, describing it in pathetic terms, but lauding James for his personal courage in the face of terminal illness.[8]

For his part, James listened patiently to Freud's account of psychoanalysis and then afterwards gave his opinion. He wrote to Mary Calkins, suspecting Freud to be "a regular halluciné." To Theodore Flournoy he confided that he thought Freud a man possessed by "fixed ideas." James could make nothing of the dream theories, and he thought that Freud's attack on the American religious psychotherapies was misplaced. Nevertheless, he hoped that "Freud and his pupils will push their ideas to their utmost limits, so that we may learn what they are. They can't fail to throw light on human nature."[9]

At the end of the conference, according to his own uncorroborated self-report, Ernest Jones maintained that James threw an arm around his shoulder and proclaimed, "The future of psychology belongs to your work."[10] Jones, of course, assumed James had meant that the future of psychology lay in Jones's own personal contributions to psychoanalysis. Some later interpreters at least allow that James was forecasting the potential future of the psychoanalytic movement, while others have even changed the story, claiming that James threw his arm around Freud and made the utterance. Additional evidence, however, suggests that James had something altogether different on his mind when he made that statement to James.

The thread has to be picked up back in the 1870s, when James first became enamored with the writings of the New York neurologist George Miller Beard. Beard had made an extensive study of trance consciousness and the larger problem of man's involuntary life. James supported Beard in his work, hoping that he would write the magnum opus on the unconscious. But Beard died prematurely of tuberculosis in 1882 before he could compose such a work.

Just about that time, James became involved with the activities of the Society for Psychical Research in England, and by 1885 had embraced F.W.H. Myers's conception of the subliminal consciousness. Myers had begun to frame his important formulations in a series of essays in the

Society's *Proceedings* throughout the 1880s, meanwhile working diligently on what James believed was the hoped-for volume on subliminal consciousness. But Myers got sidetracked on the question of life-after-death, dallied around for another eleven years, and finally died in 1901 without completing the book. His *Human Personality and the Survival of Bodily Death*, published posthumously in 1903 by Myers's wife and son, was but a pale reflection of the force and power exhibited by the original essays, in which Myers had only developed his doctrine piecemeal.

Then, between 1889 and 1904, we know that James had put his hopes behind the work of Pierre Janet. Janet's *Psychological Automatism*, which appeared in 1889, seemed to corroborate the work of the British psychical researchers on the phenomenon of suggestion from a distance, at the same time that it extended considerably the French model of dissociation. By 1894, with the publication of his medical dissertation, *The Mental State of Hystericals*, Janet had become widely recognized as Charcot's successor and the leading exponent of the psychogenic hypothesis—that traumatic psychological events could be transmuted into physical symptoms. By 1905, however, Janet had politically severed most of his connections to the psychical researchers and defined the subconscious in terms of a more rationalist epistemology.

Meanwhile, James had never ceased investigating plausible approaches that might lead to a scientific understanding of inner experience. In 1904 James, in fact, said the same thing to a Buddhist meditation teacher that he later had allegedly said to Jones in 1909. On that earlier occasion James heard the Theravada monk, Anagarika Dharmapala, lecture at Harvard on the major concepts of Buddhism. This must have included the Buddhist conception of personality as an ephemeral heap or conglomeration of conditions; the idea of *anatta*, that in all existence there is no evidence for a permanent, enduring underlying self; and that liberation meant the transformation of consciousness. Consciousness was liberated from its enslavement in the normal everyday waking state of passion and released into the freedom in *nirvana*, a process that takes place through intensive exploration of normally unconscious states using meditation. Afterwards, James rose and proclaimed to the audience, "This is the psychology everybody will be studying twenty-five years from now."[11] Obviously, in all these cases, it was to a larger dynamic psychology of the subconscious that James was referring.

Transmarginal consciousness was the name James gave to this domain of wider experience to which he believed psychologists should be looking more and more. He was aware, however, that the ordinary psychologist disposes of such phenomena under the conveniently "scientific" title of *petit mal*, if not "bosh" or rubbish." But since we know so little of the noetic quality of such states, he said presciently in 1910, we must develop a more sympathetic attitude and patiently continue to collect the facts for a long time to come. For he said, "We shall not *understand* these alterations of consciousness either in this generation or the next."[12]

In sum, he was not referring specifically to Jones or to psychoanalysis, but to *all* attempts at understanding the twilight region of human nature. This, he suggested, should be the future direction of psychology.

His Eclecticism

If James is known for anything in American thought, he is remembered for his cosmopolitan outlook and his great catholicity of spirit. Broad-minded in the extreme and knowledgeable in a number of fields at once, he would always rather strike up a conversation with someone very different from himself, so that a lively exchange might take place, rather than surround himself with like-minded thinkers who were all in such agreement that they had nothing new to talk about.

Thus, it is little wonder that his final message to psychologists should be to keep an open mind. But mainstream academic psychology paid little heed to his injunction, even though radical empiricism leaves the field open for communication between a wide range of specialties. In this regard, it may seem trite to assume that psychologists should be in communication with the arts and humanities as well with as the natural and social sciences, but academic and scientific psychology have largely insulated themselves within a set of epistemological presuppositions that actually forbids psychologists from engaging in interdisciplinary cross-fertilization with the humanities, except along only very narrow lines.

Jamesean psychology defined its purview as both an art and a science. James believed that objective laboratory methods could interface with the natural sciences, while a direct engagement with the phenomenology of the subjective would open up a dialogue with religion, history, philosophy, literature, and the fine arts. Psychology could yet renew this dialogue in ways that are now being little cultivated.

That such a dialogue, since James's time, might already be going on is a foregone conclusion. But for the past fifty years it has been woefully one-sided. Psychological interpretation of the modern novel takes place in English departments, but is not a legitimate area of study in academic psychology. Psychology of religion is alive and well, but chiefly among the theologians and scholars of religion. Clinical psychology is most often found confined to medicine and psychiatry, especially in universities where experimental laboratory procedures and their attendant methodological constraints have a stranglehold on academic departments of psychology. Psychology, in short, has been immeasurably diminished by a massive program of denial and disenfranchisement of most aspects of the human spirit.[13]

A simple truth about the present is that we are missing the essence of a psychology of adult development, of consciousness, of spiritual experience, and of religion. James saw that we needed a broader and more expansive psychology than that emerging even in his own time and he seems to have marched in a straight line through *The Principles* to *The Varieties* in a valiant attempt to get one going.

Psychologists, however, were barely able to heed his call while he was alive and found it completely impossible to do so after he died. Nevertheless, a certain unity in spirit is what he tried to achieve. That he did not completely succeed is attested to by an episode that occurred at the end of his life, which drew most of the major figures from the psychology of the day into both heated conflict and near-resolution. I refer to James's role in the aborted plans to hold the Seventh International Congress of Psychology in the United States during 1913. The story, which has been so well told in detail by the historian of psychology Rand Evans, need only be summarized here.[14]

The 1913 Congress was first proposed at the Fifth International Congress in Rome in 1905. We have already said that James was present at that meeting and attracted much attention with his lecture, "La Notion de conscience," which he delivered in French.[15] There, according to Evans, "some Americans pushed the idea of an American congress" (could James have avoided being a part of that effort?), and the organizational body appears to have approved in principle. At the following congress, held in Geneva in 1909, a petition for an American congress, to be held in 1913, was put forward by Morton Prince. Although it was not a formal invitation and was not sponsored by any university, the lure of the New World won out over the other proposals. James Mark Baldwin of Johns Hopkins, who was present, was named *President effectif*, and William James of Harvard, who was not present and without his permission, became the *President d'honneur*.

Baldwin immediately appointed an official congress bureau. For vice presidents he chose Titchener of Cornell and C. A. Strong of Columbia (a former student of James), and as secretary, E. C. Sanford of Clark.[16] Sanford declined immediately when he heard that he had been drafted, and the young J. B. Watson, who had just started teaching at Hopkins, was assigned instead. Several demanded that James McKeen Cattell of Columbia be drafted, but Baldwin resisted. He had been enmeshed in a running feud with Cattell ever since the two had launched the *Psycholog-ical Review* in 1894, and by 1909 their relationship, as characterized by Evans, was one of "bitterness to the point of malice."[17]

The first suggestion was to hold a split meeting, one on Boston and the other in New York. Münsterberg, writing to Cattell on August 9, 1909, had heard a rumor to the effect that Boston had definitely com-mitted, and he immediately concluded that Baldwin was up to some scheme to commit Harvard without permission, "all in order to play the president here without having any responsibility of the prepara-tions."[18] After complaining that the summer heat would be unbearable in Boston, that the place would be deserted, and that none of the Euro-peans would show up anyway, Münsterberg said: "I suppose that Bald-win forced Morton Prince to give an invitation and by skillfully bringing in James as honorary president, the congress probably conceived that it did the correct thing by Harvard, not knowing that James has taken no interest in actual Harvard psychology for many years" (meaning "James had taken no interest in Münsterberg's definition of psychology for many years").[19]

Cattell remained uncommitted as long as Baldwin appeared to be in charge. Meanwhile, Münsterberg found out that the rumor of the Bos-ton site was untrue. He threw his weight toward having the congress, said he would come, and was pleased that New York would host it. This left matters with Cattell at Columbia in New York.

Cattell, however, had moved from indifference to outright opposition. He had even approached the American Psychological Association to have the congress quashed.

Several events then conspired to fuel the passions of rival factions. Just at that time, Baldwin had been caught by the police in a brothel and was summarily dismissed from Hopkins. Titchener, meanwhile, one of the other vice presidents, had by then not only committed him-self to get involved, but appears to have had designs on Baldwin's presi-dency. Accordingly, Titchener wrote to Cattell. His hope was that Cattell would use the Baldwin incident, plus his desire not to get involved, to avoid taking up responsibility for the congress. Titchener's letter stated that he, Titchener, along with Watson, would go on, with Cattell or without him. Titchener also proposed that Baldwin be asked to resign the presidency and that G. Stanley Hall of Clark should be appointed in his place.

Cattell, however, had suddenly warmed to the congress as soon as it appeared that Baldwin was to be out of the picture and James was still to be involved. Meanwhile, Titchener had written to Baldwin, suggesting he resign. Under the circumstances, Baldwin agreed and, in turn, on

February 14, 1910, wrote to James, who was still honorary president, giving his resignation. Baldwin also wrote to W. B. Pillsbury, then president-elect of the American Psychological Association, requesting him to ask James to take over the active presidency. James, sensing that something like this might arise, had already written to Cattell saying he would absolutely decline. Honorary was fine, but acting meant work he simply could not do. James believed instead that the active presidency should reside with Cattell and Titchener.

Baldwin, meanwhile, had written to James expressing his preference for anybody except Cattell as the new president. Since both Baldwin and Pillsbury had left the decision to James, and seeing oppositon to Cattell arise, James wrote Cattell recommending Titchener as president. James wrote to Titchener the same day with the same news. Cattell, in turn, reacted by writing immediately to Titchener.

The content of Cattell's letter was shameless. He said Titchener was definitely not the right man to represent America, because he had for so long been opposed to the American Psychological Association (Titchener had originally been a charter member in 1892 but had dropped out immediately to form his own Experimentalist's Club). More to the point, Cattell said, Titchener was not an American (Titchener had never renounced his British citizenship). Furious, Titchener wrote to James declining the presidency and withdrawing from the activites of the congress altogether.

Numerous psychologists, among them J. B. Watson of Hopkins, H. C. Warren of Princeton, and Robert Yerkes, still at Harvard, wrote immediately to Titchener to get him to reconsider. Cattell, meanwhile, sensing the mounting opposition, visited William James at his home in Cambridge on March 12, 1910, and struck a deal. James wrote to Titchener proposing the following terms: James would remain honorary president with no duties; a large body of vice presidents would be appointed; J. B. Watson and A. H. Pierce would do all the work; and the APA and the Experimentalist's Club would agree on the final slate. James included a list of possible vice presidents, hoping that both Cattell and Titchener would add to the list. James's intention, it afterwards appeared, was that an active president be appointed at the very last minute, only after all the work of setting up the congress was complete. James ended with the supplication: ". . . and let us three be as harmonious as this pluralistic universe permits."[20]

Cattell also wrote Titchener. Without apologizing, he at least offered the olive branch by asking Titchener to accept James's proposal and return to the fold. For each of their own reasons, both Cattell and Titchener acceded to James's plan. Cattell agreed because he knew he could dominate any group of vice presidents. Titchener agreed because he thought he could be named the active president right away. Thus the war soon broke out again over which one would ascend to the active presidency.

Meanwhile, at meetings of both the APA and the Experimentalist's Club, the general consensus emerged that, with all the rancor, a congress should definitely not be held. Cattell, however, refused to put the matter down. For his trump card, he intended at all costs to have James accept the acting presidency. Immediately, letters and visitors bombarded James, who, on sabbatical from Harvard, had fled to Paris in a state of failing health. Finally, James capitulated. Writing a long letter to Watson on May 10, 1910, he proposed himself as president, Cattel and Titchener as vice presidents, and Watson as secretary. Watson agreed and the conference was again on.

James, meanwhile, could not forgo chastising Cattell a little. On May 21, 1910, James informed him: "If I can't preside when the time comes, I reserve the right to invite whomever I damn please to take the chair. Pray agree; and help to quench the inconceivable paltriness of spirit that seems to have shown its head for the first time in our American psychological world!"[21]

On the same day, James wrote to Titchener, asking him to return to the project. Although still extremely wary and forever at odds with Cattell from then on, Titchener agreed. Writing to Münsterberg on June 17, he said, "If James wants us we must all pitch in."[22] Titchener even rejoined the American Psychological Association after leaving it seventeen years earlier.

But the loose coalition was not to last. It all might have been integrated under James's aegis, even if only temporarily, but James died eight weeks later on August 26, 1910. The compromise unraveled and no international congress was held. World War One intervened, psychology fragmented in the Era of the Schools, and by the time a congress finally did convene in the United States in 1929, psychology was poised to enter a thirty-year period, which has come to be known as the Age of Theory, dominated by stimulus-response learning models, laboratory studies of the white rat, and the new determinism of the logical positivists.

Experimentalism, the very thing that James warned psychology to avoid, became even more pronounced after the 1930s. The trend was to last into the 1950s, when the first serious philosophical critiques of its shortcomings began to appear.[23] Since then, there has been a veritable groundswell of opinion and analysis of the metaphysical basis of psychology; phenomenologists, deconstructionists, critical thinkers, feminists, historians, and philosophers in the neurosciences, to name but a few, have been freely fielding their opinions.[24] Much of what is being said has confirmed James's point that the antidote to experimentalism is some form of epistemological pluralism, coupled with a focus on the primacy of immediate experience.[25]

Almost to a man and to a woman, however, these modern commentators have overlooked the sophistication of James's early work.[26] They had not realized that, far from abandoning psychology and ignoring its vast potential as a leading influence in any science of the future, James was, in fact, "the first to burst into that silent sea."

NOTES

PREFACE

1. E. I. Taylor, "Contemporary interest in classical Eastern psychology," in A. Paranjpe, D. Ho, and R. Rieber, eds., *Asian Contributions to Psychology* (New York: Praeger, 1988), pp. 79–122.

2. Professor Streng was himself a student of Mircea Eliade, Joseph Kitagawa, and Joachim Wach at the University of Chicago in the late 1950s and an interpreter of the ideas of Paul Tillich.

3. This was as close as the curriculum would allow me to come to my declared areas of concentration, Psychology of Religion and Asian Studies.

4. Secondary texts can be further differentiated by those commentators who have spent years poring over the primary documents versus those who come in and read the corpus in a single forced march or who only glance at segments of the collection. A category of tertiary texts, actually the bulk of the literature on James, is composed of commentators who rely almost solely on other commentators and have themselves never consulted the primary documents.

5. The interested reader can readily see this connection by examining the parallels between Mahayana Buddhist thought and James's metaphysics. See David Kalupahana, *Principles of Buddhist Psychology* (Albany: SUNY Press, 1987).

CHAPTER ONE
AN OUTLINE OF THE PROBLEM

1. The seminal text in this field remains Henri Ellenberger, *The Discovery of the Unconscious* (New York: Basic Books, 1970).

2. E. I. Taylor, "A metaphysical critique of expermentalism in psychology: Or 'Why G. Stanley Hall waited until William James was out of town to found the APA,'" in *Aspects of the History of Psychology in America, 1892–1992,* ed. Robert Reiber and Helmut Adler, *Annals of the New York Academy of Sciences,* 727 (1994), pp. 37–62.

3. According to E. G. Boring's interpretation of James, "The completion of the *Principles* marked for him the close of the domination of philosophical life by psychology. . . . He never ceased to be a psychologist but he grew away from psychology." E. G. Boring, *History of Experimental Psychology* (1929), p. 497. This was a clever way in which Boring was able to further establish the Titchenerian agenda by displacing James's psychology. The same idea has been recently expressed: "Whatever combination of factors that led to James's actions, he seems to have lost all interest in psychology after publication of *The Principles* and of *Psychology: Briefer Course* in 1892. In that year James turned over to Hugo Münsterberg the psychological laboratory, along with most of the teaching in psychology. By 1899, when his *Talks to Teachers on Psychology and to Students on Some of Life's*

Ideals was published, he appears to have said all he had to say about psychology." Rand Evans, Introduction, in F. Burkhardt, F. Bowers, and I. Skrupskelis, eds., *The Works of William James: The Principles of Psychology*, vol. 1 (Cambridge, Mass.: Harvard University Press, 1981), p. lxi. (Hereafter referred to as *Works*, followed by the appropriate title and citation.)

4. Dorothy Ross, "American psychology and psychoanalysis: William James and G. Stanley Hall," in J. M. Quen and E. T. Carlson, eds., *American Psychoanalysis: Origins and Development* (New York: Brunner/Mazel, 1975), pp. 38–51.

5. O. Marx, "American psychiatry without William James," *Bulletin of the History of Medicine*, 62:1 (1968), pp. 52–61.

6. M. Baum, "William James and psychical research," *Journal of Abnormal & Social Psychology*, 30 (1935), pp. 111–18; G. Murphy and R. O. Ballou, eds., *William James on Psychical Research* (New York: Viking Press, 1960).

7. G. Foster, "The psychotherapy of William James," *Psychoanalytic Review*, 32 (1943), pp. 300–18. H. D. Spoerl, "Abnormal and social psychology in the life and work of William James," *Journal of Abnormal and Social Psychology*, 37 (1942), pp. 3–19.

8. At least two senior theses at Harvard have dealt with these topics, both directly influenced by the work of the present author. See Cedric J. Priebe, "William James's application of Darwinian Theory to consciousness and the emotions in *The Principles of Psychology*" (1974), Harvard Archives: HU 92.84.712; Emily Cheh, "Psychical research, psychopathology, and William James: A synthesis for psychotherapy" (1991), Harvard Archives: HU 92.91.277. A reinterpretation of Henry James's ghost tales has also appeared, rejecting a psychoanalytic interpretation for that of James's definition of the subliminal, also based on the work of the present author. See Karen Halttunen, "Through the cracked and fragmented self: William James and the *Turn of the Screw*," *American Quarterly*, 40 (1988), p. 472.

9. J. C. Burnham, *Psychoanalysis and American Medicine, 1894–1918: Medicine, Science, and Culture. Psychological Issues*. Monograph 20:4 (1967); H. Ellenberger, *The Discovery of the Unconscious* (New York: Basic Books, 1970); N. G. Hale, *Freud in America: The Beginnings of Psychoanalysis in America, 1876–1917* (New York: Oxford University Press, 1971). See also Hale's *James Jackson Putnam and Psychoanalysis* (Cambridge, Mass.: Harvard University Press, 1971), and his *Morton Prince: Psychotherapy and Multiple Personality, Selected Essays* (Cambridge, Mass.: Harvard University Press, 1975).

10. N. Cameron, "William James and psychoanalysis," in M. C. Otto et al., *William James: The Man and the Thinker* (Madison: University of Wisconsin Press, 1942), pp. 53–84; and B. Ross, "William James: A prime mover of the psychoanalytic movement in America," in G. E. Gifford, ed., *Psychoanalysis, Psychotherapy, and the New England Medical Scene, 1894–1944* (New York: Science/History Publications, 1978), pp. 10–23.

11. S. Rosenzweig, "The Jameses' stream of consciousness," *Contemporary Psychology*, 3 (1959), pp. 250–57. Rosenzweig reexamines the origins of Freud's technique of free association in light of the Wilkinson material and James's various descriptions of the stream of consciousness. Historians of psychoanalysis assert that free association partly came from Galton and, if we believe Freud's

own claim, the satirist Ludwig Börne, who had published *The Art of Becoming an Original Writer in Three Days* in 1823. Rosenzweig, "Stream of Consciousness," p. 256.

12. Over the years, Perry had complete freedom to deal with the James material as he saw fit. When the James family library, containing several thousand volumes, was offered to Harvard in 1923, Perry and Benjamin Rand initially chose only fifty titles, mainly in classical Western philosophy, for the Library Treasure Room. Another thousand on religious autobiography, multiple personality, demon possession, psychopathology, and more would have been lost except for the tireless lobbying of the Yiddish psychologist, Abraham Roback, who made sure Harvard took these books as well. Also, during the several James family book sales, Perry allowed works by certain authors to be sold first, especially those whom he disliked or judged unimportant. James's copies of F.C.S. Schiller's work were disposed of early, for instance. Another clue we have to Perry's interpretation of psychology can be found in the last two chapters of his *Thought and Character of William James* (2 vols., Boston: Little, Brown, 1935; hereafter referred to as Perry, followed by the volume and page number). One gets the impression that Perry was under the sway of Freudian ideas about neurotic sublimation rampant in Boston during the 1930s when he concluded that James basically was a sick soul who lacked an adequate philosophy to live by and that James's work was somehow the product of his perverse genius. In the end, the best that Perry could muster was a catalog of James's morbid and benign traits.

Chapter Two
Consciousness

(*Note:* Originally presented to the annual meeting of the History of Science Society as part of a symposium on "The American Society for Psychical Research: Origin, Context, and Form," Gainesville, Florida, October 28, 1989.)

1. Boring states retrospectively in the unexpurgated version of his autobiography that he came to Harvard "with a mission" to live out Titchener's will. E. G. Boring, *A Psychologist at Large* (New York: Basic Books, 1961), pp. 33, 39, 41.

2. For this reason, I maintain that Wundt's laboratory in Leipzig was not really founded until 1950.

3. Even in his first edition, Boring maintained that, as a student, James went to study in Germany for "a year and a half." E. G. Boring, *A History of Experimental Psychology* (New York: Century, 1929), p. 496. Actually, James was there for a much shorter time, and then fled to France. He was no votary of the German tradition, as Boring's stretch of the point tries to imply. For James's attitude toward Wundt, see W. James, review of Wundt's *Grundzüge der physiologischen Psychologie*, in *North American Review*, 121 (1875), pp. 195–201; and W. James, "The importance to philosophy of the appointment of professors Wundt and Hitzig at Zurich," *Nation*, 20 (1875), pp. 377–78. For the larger picture of James's attitude toward French versus German culture, see W. James, review (unsigned) of E. Feydeau's *La Contesse de Chalis*, "The manners of the day in Paris," *Nation*, 6 (1868), pp. 73–74; James's comment in *Notes*, in which attention is drawn to *La critique philosophique*, in *Nation*, 16 (Feb. 6, 1873), p. 94; and James's notice (un-

signed) of F. Pappilon's *Nature and Life*, in *Nation*, 20 (1875), p. 429; a review (unsigned) on German pessimism, *Nation*, 21 (1875), p. 214. James could read, write, and speak several languages. He knew German, Italian, and some Portuguese, plus a smattering of Latin and Greek, but he knew far more French. He could even lecture in French, but not in German.

4. In the 1929 edition of his *History*, Boring gave James credit for his laboratory in 1875 as "anticipating" Wundt's laboratory four years later: "James's instruction at Harvard was very successful, and it was in conjunction with his course that he offered laboratory work in that early, informal, and unchristened psychological laboratory that antedated even Wundt's." E. G. Boring, *A History of Experimental Psychology* (New York: Century, 1929), pp. 318, 496. In the 1950 revision, Boring emphatically gave Wundt credit for founding the first lab, with extensive justification for his assertion. This caused him to say: "James' instruction at Harvard was very successful, and it was in connection with his course that he offered laboratory work in that early, informal, and unchristened psychological laboratory that was at least as early as Wundt's." E. G. Boring, *A History of Experimental Psychology* (New York: Appleton-Century-Crofts, 1950), p. 510.

5. Readers will certainly argue that there is much interaction between experimental laboratory work and the clinical delivery of patient care. But witness as a case in point the recent disaffection of 2000 experimentalists within the 75,000 member American Psychological Association, who in 1989 bolted to form their own independent group, The American Psychological Society, because they believed the APA was becoming too clinically oriented.

6. Ignace Skrupskelis, textual editor of the *Works of William James* project, evidently knew about these reviews before I discovered them independently in 1982 and before I communicated their whereabouts to Gerald Myers that same year.

7. W. James, review of T. H. Huxley's *Lectures on the Elements of Comparative Anatomy: On the Classification of Animals, and on the Vertebrate Skull*, in *North American Review*, 100 (1865), pp. 290–98; W. James, review of A. R. Wallace's *The Origin of Human Races and the Antiquity of Man Deduced from the Theory of Natural Selection*, in *North American Review*, 101 (1865), pp. 261–63.

8. E. I. Taylor, "William James on Darwin: An evolutionary theory of consciousness," *Annals of the New York Academy of Sciences*, 602 (1990), pp. 7–33.

9. P. Weiner, *Evolution and the Founders of Pragmatism* (Cambridge, Mass.: Harvard University Press, 1949).

10. Chauncey Wright, "The evolution of self-consciousness," in *Philosophical Discussions* (New York: Henry Holt, 1877), pp. 199ff.

11. James's relationship to Peirce is developed throughout R. B. Perry's *The Thought and Character of William James*, 2 vols. (Boston: Little, Brown, 1935), especially in vol. 2, chapters 45 and 46.

12. E. I. Taylor, "William James and C. S. Peirce," *Chrysalis* (Journal of the Swedenborg Foundation), 1:3 (1986), pp. 207–12. E. I. Taylor, "Ralph Waldo Emerson: The Swedenborgian and Transcendentalist connection," in R. Larsen, ed., *Emanuel Swedenborg; The Vision Continues* (300th anniversary volume) (New York: The Swedenborg Foundation, 1988), pp. 127–36. E. I. Taylor, "Some historic implications of Swedenborg's spiritual psychology," *Studia Swedenborgiana*, 4:4 (1984), pp. 5–38. E. I. Taylor, "Peirce and Swedenborg," *Studia Swedenbor-*

giana, 6:1 (1986), pp. 25–51. E. I. Taylor, "William James and C. S. Peirce: A Reappraisal," paper presented at the Charles S. Peirce Sesquicentennial Congress, Sever Hall, Harvard University, Sept. 12, 1989.

13. W. James, Medical School Notebook (1867–68). On deposit, Rare Books, Countway Library of Medicine, Harvard Medical School.

14. H. R. Tyler and K. L. Tyler, "Charles Edouard Brown-Sequard: Professor of physiology and pathology of the nervous system at Harvard Medical School," *Neurology*, 34:9 (1984), pp. 1231–36.

15. M. Foucault, *The Birth of the Clinic: An Archaeology of Medical Perception* (London: Tavistock Publications, Ltd., 1973).

16. E. H. Ackerknecht, *Medicine at the Paris Hospital, 1794–1848* (Baltimore: Johns Hopkins University Press, 1967), pp. 121–27; H. K. Beecher and M. D. Altschule, *Medicine at Harvard: The First Three Hundred Years* (Hanover, N.H.: University Press of New England, 1967), pp. 61–62; J. E. Lesch, *Science and Medicine in France: The Emergence of Experimental Physiology, 1790–1855* (Cambridge, Mass: Harvard University Press, 1984), pp. 197–224.

17. J. J. Putnam, "Contributions to the physiology of the cortex cerebrii," *Boston Medical and Surgical Journal*, July 16, 1874. Author's reprint. Putnam Papers, Rare Books, Countway Library, Harvard Medical School.

18. Meeting of the New York Society for Neurology and Electrology, January 18, 1875. *Medical Record*, 10 (1875), p. 132.

19. C. K. Mills, "Neurology in Philadelphia from 1874 to 1904," *Journal of Nervous and Mental Disease*, 31 (1904), pp. 353–67.

20. Saul Benison, A. Clifford Barger, and Elin Wolfe give important details of the early laboratory and the manufacture of apparatus, as well as the growth pains of physiology under Bowditch in *Walter Bradford Cannon: The Life and Times of a Young Scientist* (Cambridge, Mass.: Harvard University Press, 1987), pp. 90–94.

21. William James to James McKeen Cattell, January 15, 1902. Cattell Papers, Library of Congress.

22. W. James, "The sense of dizziness in deaf-mutes," *American Journal of Otology*, 4:239–54.

23. "The only *fact of nature* I ever predicted and verified, is that if you whirl a frog and stop him, he will point his nose in the direction you have whirled him!" James to Cattell, January 15, 1902.

24. The New York neurologist, George Miller Beard, wrote to James and confirmed his experiments by using the same kind of whirling chair, but on subjects who had been hypnotized and, through suggestion, were made completely deaf. Similarly, they, too, showed immunity from the feeling of dizziness. W. James, *Works: Essays in Psychology*, pp. 140–42.

25. W. James, "Reaction-time in the hypnotic trance," *Proceedings of the American Society for Psychical Research*, 1 (1887), pp. 246–48.

26. The subject was thought to be hysterical and therefore more highly suggestible to hypnotic influences than a normal person. G. S. Hall, "Reaction-time and attention in the hypnotic state," *Mind*, 8 (1883), pp. 170–82.

27. W. James, "The consciousness of lost limbs," *Proceedings of the American Society for Psychical Research*, 1 (1887), pp. 249–58.

28. W. James, "Notes on automatic writing," *Proceedings of the American Society for Psychical Research*, 1 (1889), pp. 548–64.

29. Much like writing down a dream in the middle of the night, only to awaken to find what one believes must have been written by someone else.

30. R. S. Harper, "The laboratory of William James," *Harvard Alumni Bulletin*, 52 (1949), p. 172.

31. R. S. Harper, "The first psychological laboratory," *Isis*, 41 (1950), pp. 158–61.

32. *Proceedings of the American Society for Psychical Research*, 3 (1887), p. 220.

33. W. James, "Report on the committee on mediumistic phenomena," *Proceedings of the American Society for Psychical Research*, 1 (1886), pp. 95–102.

34. E. I. Taylor, "Psychotherapy, Harvard, and the American Society for Psychical Research, 1884-1889," *Proceedings of the 28th Annual Convention of the Parapsychological Association*, Tufts University, Medford, Mass., Aug. 15, 1985, pp. 319–46.

35. E. I. Taylor, "On the first use of 'Psychoanalysis' at the Massachusetts General Hospital, 1903–1905," *Journal of the History of Medicine and Allied Sciences*, 43 (1988), pp. 447–71.

36. J. C. Burnham, *Psychoanalysis and American Medicine, 1894–1918: Medicine, Science, and Culture. Psychological Issues*, Monograph 20:4 (1967).

CHAPTER THREE
CONSCIOUSNESS AND THE SUBCONSCIOUS

1. Perry, II, p. 50.

2. John Dewey gave a parody of Sully's review by calling it "a good book, but too lively to make a good corpse, and every scientific book ought to be a corpse." Perry, II, p. 104.

3. W. James, *Principles of Psychology*, 2 vols. (New York: Henry Holt, 1890), I, pp. v–vi.

4. *Principles*, I, p. vi. Mill and Bain James would class as psychologists of the associationist school, while Royce would represent a Christian psychology of the spirit. It is fairly clear that James is not referring to occult spiritualists, but to the tradition of philosophic idealism in general.

5. Ibid.

6. James's near-suicidal crisis is described in James William Anderson, "'The worst kind of melancholy': William James in 1869," *Harvard Library Bulletin*, 30 (1982), pp. 369–86. The influence of Renouvier's work on James's recovery is described in Howard Feinstein, *Becoming William James* (Ithaca, N.Y.: Cornell University Press, 1984), pp. 307–12; and for Renouvier's influence on James's philosophy, see Perry, I, pp. 654–709.

7. Perry, I, p. 554.

8. Ibid., I, p. 503.

9. Ibid., I, p. 654.

10. Ibid., I, p. 613.

11. Ibid., I, p. 806.

12. Rand Evans, Introduction, in *Works: Principles of Psychology*, vol. 1, pp. xli–lxviii.

13. He included in this category the so-called Galtonian circulars, or questionnaires used by the English.

14. *Principles*, I, pp. 374fn, 401; II, 117, 130fn, 133fn.

15. In one place James mentions "mediumship rending the fabric of science in twain." *Principles*, II, p. 302fn. But in another he explains the mechanism of alleged telepathic powers in the willing game as muscle reading. *Principles*, II, p. 525.

16. Ibid., I, p. 66.

17. Ibid., I, p. 67.

18. Ibid., I, p. 138.

19. Ibid., I, p. 145.

20. Ibid., I, p. 304.

21. Ibid., I, p. 305. The final chapter is a discussion of psychogenesis, the origin of consciousness, and the effect of matter on mind.

22. Ibid., I, p. 24.

23. Ibid.

24. Ibid., I, p. 81.

25. Ibid., I, p. 107.

26. Ibid., I, p. 219.

27. Ibid., I, p. 220.

28. Ibid., I, p. 255.

29. Ibid., I, p. 276.

30. Ibid., I, p. 289.

31. Ibid., I, p. 182. James's answer was a definite yes, the unmediated correspondence *was* the simplest psychophysic formula, in order to avoid unsafe hypotheses.

32. Ibid., I, p. 370fn.

33. Ibid., I, p. 184.

34. While trying to define the word 'sensation,' James complains, "To the reader who is tired of so much *Erkenntnisstheorie* I can only say that I am so myself, but that it is indispensable, in the actual state of opinions about Sensation, to try to clear up just what the word means," i.e., some philosophical speculation can never be avoided, especially in the initial definition of terms. *Principles*, II, p. 9.

35. Ibid., II, p. 283.

36. James even delimits his view of the various metaphysical domains. His chapter on "The Perception of Reality" (21) contains a list of "different orders of reality," by which he means the world of sense, the world of science, the world of ideal relations, the various supernatural worlds, the various worlds of individual opinion, and the worlds of sheer madness. Ibid., II, pp. 292–93.

37. *Principles*, chapters 6 and 10. Gerald Myers has broached this comparison, but he did not analyze the significance of this discrepancy in *The Principles*, and he created more confusion by not realizing the difference between the unconscious and the subconscious in James. Myers mistakenly compares James to Freud, saying: "[James] believed in an unconscious, but one that is always per-

sonal and thus is unlike Freud's, for example." Gerald Myers, Introduction, in *Works: Principles of Psychology*, vol. 1 (1981), pp. xl, fn41(d).

38. In *The Will to Believe*, James referred to "Hartmann's wicked jack-of-all-trades, the unconscious" (New York: Longman's, 1897), p. 82.

39. *Principles*, I, p. 222.

40. Ibid., I, pp. 245–46.

41. Ibid., I, pp. 134–35.

42. Ibid., II, pp. 594–616; Harvard College Charging Records, 1889–96. Pusey Library, Harvard University Archives. His chapter on hypnotism, taken in conjunction with lists of books on the subject that we know he checked out of the Harvard College Library, and other evidence, shows that James was highly skilled in the induction of the hypnotic trance and exceptionally knowledgeable about current advances in the field. But this expertise did not appear to come about until the final years of composing *The Principles*.

43. Much debate went on after this finding concerning the subject's professed freedom of choice. The hypnotic evidence showed how acts could be predetermined without the knowledge of waking awareness.

CHAPTER FOUR
THE REALITY OF MULTIPLE STATES

1. In France, while Bernheim and the Nancy School came to dominate the French scene in the 1890s, the original center of the axis revolved around Charcot, Ribot, Richet, Binet, and Janet in Paris; August Forel and Theodore Flournoy in Switzerland; Myers, Gurney, Podmore, and others associated with the Society for Psychical Reserach in London; Van Roentergam and Van-Eeden in the Netherlands; and William James, Morton Prince, James Jackson Putnam, and others associated with the Boston School of Abnormal Psychology in America.

2. The other reason, of course, was that, off and on, James himself was seen as a patient by several of these mental healers.

3. W. James, "The hidden self," *Scribner's Magazine*, 7 (1890), pp. 361–73. Also reprinted in *Works: Essays in Psychology* (1983), pp. 247–68.

4. A. Binet, *On Double Consciousness* (Chicago: Open Court, 1889). Theta Wolf notes that this work was never published in French. T. H. Wolf, *Alfred Binet* (Chicago: University of Chicago Press, 1973), p. 351.

5. *Works: Essays in Psychology*, p. 250.

6. Ibid., pp. 256–57.

7. Ibid., p. 268.

8. W. James, "A record of observations of certain phenomena of trance," part 3, *Proceedings of the English Society for Psychical Research*, 6 (1890), pp. 651–59. Reprinted in *Works: Essays in Psychical Research*, pp. 79–88.

9. One possible exception is Justinius Kerner's *The Seeress of Prevorst: Being revelations concerning the inner-life of man and the interdiffusion of a world of spirits in the one we inhabit.*, trans. Mrs. Crowe (New York: Harper and Brothers, 1845).

10. W. James, "Report of the Committee on Mediumistic Phenomena," *Proceedings of the American Society for Psychical Research*, 1 (1886), pp. 95–102.

11. "Her condition in this semi-hypnosis is very different from her medium-trance. The latter is characterized by great muscular unrest, even her ears moving vigorously in a way impossible to her in her waking state. But in hypnosis her muscular relaxation and weakness are extreme." *Works: Essays in Psychical Research,* p. 82.

12. Ibid., pp. 83–84.

13. E. I. Taylor, "C. G. Jung and the Boston psychopathologists, 1902–1912," *Voices: The Art and Science of Psychotherapy,* vols. 3 and 4 (1985), pp. 131–44; and idem, "Jung in his intellectual context: The Swedenborgian connection," *Studia Swedenborgiana,* 7:2 (1991), pp. 47–69.

14. W. James, review of R. Hodgson's "A further record of observations of certain phenomena of trance," *Psychological Review,* 5 (1898), pp. 420–24. Reprinted in *Works: Essays in Psychical Research,* pp. 187–91.

15. Reprinted in ibid., pp. 187–88.

16. Ibid., p. 191.

17. Ibid.

18. Ibid., pp. 56–78.

19. Ibid., p. 56.

20. Ibid., p. 59.

21. Ibid.

22. Ibid., p. 75.

23. Ibid., p. 73.

24. B. Ross, "William James: A prime mover of the psychoanalytic movement in the United States," in G. E. Gifford, Jr., ed., *Psychoanalysis, Psychotherapy, and the New England Medical Scene, 1844–1944* (New York: Science/History Press, 1978), pp. 10–23. The claim is somewhat dubious, however. In 1887, the *American Journal of Insanity* had summarized Freud's defense of Charcot's views on hysteria before the doctors of Vienna, suggesting that Freud's psychological, rather than purely neurological, interests were already known to at least a select few of American readers. *American Journal of Insanity,* 43 (1887), p. 369.

25. Notice of Pierre Janet's *État Mental des Hystériques* and *L'Amnesie Continue,* J. Breuer and S. Freud's *Ueber den psychischen Mechanismus hysterischer Phänomene,* and L. E. Whipple's *Philosophy of Mental Healing,* in *Psychological Review,* 1 (1894), pp. 195–200. Reprinted in *Works: Essays, Comments, and Reviews* (1987), pp. 470–75.

26. *Works,* ibid., p. 470.

27. The method of distraction involved splitting the field of consciousness into two or more dissociated states. A person would read aloud from a book, for instance; meanwhile, someone else would engage the reader's attention in an animated conversation. Soon, parts of the conversation would intrude into the reading.

28. *Works: Essays, Comments, and Reviews,* p. 474.

29. H. Ellenberger, *Discovery of the Unconscious* (New York: Basic Books, 1970), pp. 406–7, for instance.

30. *Works: Essays, Comments, and Reviews,* p. 474.

31. W. James, letter on the Medical Registration Act, *Boston Evening Transcript,* March 24, 1894. Reprinted in *Works: Essays, Comments, and Reviews,* pp. 145–50.

32. *Works: Essays, Comments, and Reviews*, p. 148.

33. Ibid.

34. Ibid., p. 149.

35. This is not altogether true, since we know that after 1890 James had read and annotated books on the structure and function of the nervous system, underlining sections, for instance, that described new findings on the autonomic nervous system and the antigen-antibody response. Partial remains of the James Family Library, Rare Books, Harvard Medical Archives, Boston.

36. E. I. Taylor, "The case for a uniquely American Jamesean tradition in psychology," in Margaret E. Donnelly, ed., *APA Centennial Essays in Honor of James's Principles of Psychology* (Washington, D.C.: American Psychological Association Press, 1992).

37. W. James, "Person and personality," in C. K. Adams, ed., *Johnson's Universal Cyclopedia*, vol. 6 (New York: Appleton, 1897), pp. 538–40. First published in 1895. Reprinted in *Works: Essays in Psychology*, pp. 315–21. James's invitation to write the original entry came from the publishers through James Mark Baldwin. See *Works: Essays in Psychology*, p. 415.

38. Classical Eastern psychology is the name given to any psychological system embedded in the religious and philosophical texts from the classical periods of India, China, Tibet, Korea, and Japan, and which have a bearing on the way particular teachers, texts, or schools interpreted personality and consciousness. See E. I. Taylor, *An Annotated Bibliography in Classical Eastern Psychology* (Dallas, Texas: The Essene Press, 1973); E. I. Taylor, "Asian interpretations: Transcending the stream of consciousness," in K. Pope and J. Singer, eds., *The Stream of Consciousness: Scientific Investigations into the Flow of Human Experience* (New York: Plenum, 1978), pp. 31–54; and E. I. Taylor, "Contemporary interest in classical Eastern psychology," in A. Paranjpe, D. Ho, and R. Rieber, eds., *Asian Contributions to Psychology* (New York: Praeger, 1988), pp. 79–122.

39. E. I. Taylor, "Psychology of Religion and Asian Studies: The William James legacy," *Journal of Transpersonal Psychology*, 10:1 (1978), pp. 66–79.

40. Dale Riepe, "A note on William James and Indian philosophy," *Philosophy and Phenomenological Research*, 28 (1968), pp. 587–90.

41. The following is abstracted from Taylor, "Psychology of Religion and Asian Studies."

42. Kurt F. Leidecker, *Josiah Royce and Indian Thought* (New York: Kailas Press, 1931).

43. E. I. Taylor, "Swami Vivekananda and William James," *Prabuddha Bharata: Journal of the Ramakrishna Society, Calcutta*, 91 (Sept. 1986), pp. 374–85. Two pieces of archival evidence link James to Vivekananda. First, in his library, James had in pamphlet form a copy of Vivekananda's "The Atman," a lecture that the Swami had delivered to the Brooklyn Ethical Association in New York on Sunday, February 16, 1896. There are a number of marginal marks in the pamphlet that can be ascribed to James. Second is a letter in possession of Mrs. Marie Louise Burke from James to the Swami, dated March 28, 1896. James began by addressing Vivekananda as "Dear Master," and then proceeded to propose a meeting, suggesting as well a number of alternative times. Swami Nikhilananda calls James one of Vivekananda's disciples because of this incident. But, more likely this was

an honorific title that James bestowed upon Vivekananda as a gesture of respect and out of deference to public opinion.

44. The audience was probably small but appreciative. Evidence suggests that both James and Royce were present, along with several known graduate students. Boris Sidis and James Houghton Woods almost certainly attended. C. C. Everett, we know was there, as was Professor John Henry Wright, who had known Vivekananda since his first arrival in 1893. Hugo Münsterberg was not present, as he was still in Germany. C. H. Toy, founder of the History of Religions Club at Harvard, was undoubtedly present. We know for a fact that Charles Rockwell Lanman, Sanskrit scholar and editor of the Harvard Oriental Series, attended the lecture, and his diary for the period showed that he attended a reception that preceded the talk which was held at the home of Mrs. Olé Bull. Lanman Papers, Harvard University Archives, Pusey Library, Harvard University.

45. W. James, *Talks to Teachers on Psychology and to Students on Some of Life's Ideals* (New York: Henry Holt, 1899), pp. 74–75.

46. In a letter to Frances R. Morse, a longtime Cambridge friend, James had written from Scotland saying: "We had a splendid journey yesterday in an American (almost!) train, first class, and had the pleasure of some talk with our Cambridge neighbor, Mrs. Olé Bull, on her way to Norway to the unveiling of a monument to her husband. She was accompanied by an extraordinarily fine character and mind—odd way of expressing myself!—a young Englishwoman named Nobel, who has Hinduized herself (converted by Vivekananda to his philosophy) and lives now for the Hindu people. These free individuals who live their own life, no matter what domestic prejudices have to be snapped, are on the whole a refreshing sight to me, who can do nothing of the kind myself. And Miss Nobel is a most deliberate and balanced person—no frothy enthusiast in point of character, though I believe her philosophy to be more or less false [but] perhaps no more so than anyone else's." William James, *Letters*, vol. 2, ed. Henry James (Boston: Little, Brown, 1920), p. 144.

47. James wrote the preface in 1899, but it did not appear until later. See W. James, Preface to Wincenty Lutoslawski, *The World of Souls* (London: The Dial Press, 1924).

48. W. James, "The energies of men," *Philosophical Review*, 1, 16 (1907), pp. 1–22.

49. W. James, "The moral equivalent of war," *McClure's Magazine*, 35 (1910), pp. 463–68.

50. E. I. Taylor, *William James on Exceptional Mental States: Reconstruction of the 1896 Lowell Lectures* (New York: Scribner's Sons, 1982; U. Mass Press/Amherst, paperback, 1984). James first delivered the series under the title of "Recent Researches into Exceptional Mental Phenomena," January and February 1896, at the Brooklyn Institute of Arts and Sciences. See *Works: Manuscript Lectures*, pp. 516–17.

51. Ibid.

52. F.W.H. Myers, "The subliminal consciousness," *Journal of the English Society for Psychical Research*, 1 (1882), p. 301.

53. See J. Breuer and S. Freud, *Studien über Hysterie* (Leipzig and Vienna: Franz Deutick, 1895). James's copy, Houghton Library, Harvard University.

54. Whenever Freud was mentioned by members of the Boston School of Psychotherapy between 1894 and 1906, and these instances were several, it was always in terms of "Breuer and Freud," i.e., Freud was always considered the second author to Breuer. Freud was never mentioned alone, and their method was, on at least one occasion, referred to only as "Breuer's talk-cure." See E. I. Taylor, "James Jackson Putnam's fateful meeting with Freud: The 1909 Clark University Conference," *Voices: The Art and Science of Psychotherapy*, 21 (1985), pp. 78–89.

55. See James's two reviews of Nevius's *Demon Possession and Allied Themes*, in *Nation*, 61 (1895), p. 139; and *Psychological Review*, 2 (1895), pp. 529–31, and W. James, review of Gustave Lebon's *The Crowd: A Study of the Popular Mind*, in *Psychological Review*, 4 (1897), pp. 313–16.

56. W. James, review of Maudsley's *Responsibility in Insanity*, in *Atlantic Monthly*, 34 (1874), p. 365.

57. W. James, review of Wynter's *Borderlands of Insanity*, in *The Nation*, 21 (1875), p. 330.

58. Compare with W. James, "Degeneration and Genius," *Psychological Review*, 2 (1895), pp. 287–94; and E. I. Taylor, *William James on Exceptional Mental States* (1982), p. 204, fn5.

59. Ibid.

60. Walter B. Cannon, "The case method of teaching systematic medicine," *Boston Medical and Surgical Journal*, 142 (1900), pp. 31–36; and J. J. Putnam and G. A. Waterman, *Studies in Neurological Diagnosis* (Boston: Geo. Ellis, 1902).

61. Edward Cowles, Mimeographed Course Notes for Psychiatry, Rare Books, Countway Library of Medicine, Harvard Medical School, Boston.

62. J. Royce, "Some observations on the anomalies of self-consciousness," in *Studies in God and Evil: A Series of Essays upon the Problems of Philosophy and Life* (New York: D. Appleton, 1898).

63. R. C. Cabot, second annual report of the Social Service Department, 1906–1907. Annual Reports of the Massachusetts General Hospital, 1907, Harvard Medical Archives.

64. Thomas Upham taught a course in abnormal psychology at Bowdoin College that had been attended by Nathaniel Hawthorne when he was an undergraduate there in the 1820s. J. W. Fay, *American Psychology before William James* (New Brunswick, N.J.: Rutgers University Press, 1939).

65. H. Maudsley, *The Pathology of Mind* (London, 1879).

66. The system of the borrower entering information in the book was supplanted by the succession of idiosyncratic classification systems up to 1896, when the process of keeping handwritten charging records was abandoned altogether.

67. Dr. Thomas Cadwallader, Indiana University at Terre Haute, first brought the Charging Records to my attention, while Jennifer Zukowski and William Whalen on the staff of the Harvard Archives gave major assistance to us in reconstructing the history of the library classification systems.

68. The most frequently cited periodicals were *Pfluger's Archives*, *The Journal of Mental Science*, Wundt's *Philosophische Studien*, *Boston Medical and Surgical Journal*, and *Contemporary Review*.

69. Registrar's Returns, Harvard University Library, by permission.

70. J. R. Angell, Autobiography. In Carl Murchison, ed., *The History of Psychol-*

ogy in Autobiography, vol. 3 (Worcester, Mass.: Clark University Press, 1932), pp. 1–38. See also J. R. Angell, "William James," *Psychological Review*, 18 (1911), pp. 78–82.

71. F. P. Gay, *The Open Mind: Elmer Ernest Southard, 1876–1920* (New York: Normandie House, 1938).

72. G. E. Gifford, Jr., "George Arthur Waterman, 1872–1960, and Office Psychiatry," in G. E. Gifford, Jr., ed., *Psychoanalysis, Psychotherapy, and the New England Medical Scene, 1894–1944* (New York: Science/History Press, 1978), pp. 227–41.

73. Laurel Furumoto and Elizabeth Scarborough, *Untold Lives: The First Generation of American Women Psychologists* (New York: Columbia University Press, 1987).

74. Registrar's Returns, Harvard University Archives.

75. Allen B. Fleming, "Psychology, Medicine, and Religion: Early Twentieth-Century American Psychotherapy (1905–1909)," doctoral dissertation, Graduate School of Theology, Fuller Theological Seminary, 1989. Courtesy of the author and Hendrike Van de Kemp.

76. W. James, Preface to B. Sidis, *The Psychology of Suggestion* (New York: Appleton, 1898); and H. S. Linenthal, "Boris Sidis (Oct. 12, 1867–Oct. 24, 1923)," in *Dictionary of American Biography*, vol. 17.

77. R. B. Levinson, "Gertrude Stein, William James, and grammar," *American Journal of Psychology*, 54 (1941), pp. 124–28.

78. E. I. Taylor, "Transcending the Veil: William James, W.E.B. DuBois and the Afro-American religious tradition," the 1991 Wilfred Gould Rice Memorial Lecture on Psychology and Religion, delivered April 23, 1991, for the Swedenborg Society at Harvard University.

79. Harvard University Charging Records, Harvard University Archives.

80. W. James, "The physical basis of emotion," *Psychological Review*, 1 (1894), pp. 516–29.

81. Ralph Larrabee, Physiology Notebook, 1901–1902, HMS, on deposit, Rare Books, Harvard Medical Archives, Countway Library of Medicine, Boston. See also S. Benison, A. C. Barger, and E. Wolf, *Walter B. Cannon: The Life and Times of a Young Scientist* (Cambridge, Mass.: Harvard University Press, 1987).

82. See, for instance, Theodore Flournoy, *From India to the Planet Mars: A Case of Multiple Personality with Imaginary Languages*, with a new introduction by Sonu Shamdasani (Princeton: Princeton University Press, 1994).

83. E. I. Taylor, "The Boston School of Psychotherapy: Science, healing, and consciousness in 19th century New England." The 1982 Lowell Lectures. In preparation.

84. W. James, *Talks to Teachers on Psychology and to Students on Some of Life's Ideals* (New York: Henry Holt, 1899). Reprinted in *Works: Talks to Teachers on Psychology and to Students on Some of Life's Ideals* (1983).

85. *Works*, ibid., p. 15.

86. Dissociation was a term long used, at least from the 1850s, in chemistry to mean the separation of compound substances into their primary substances. Literary savants had already understood the psychological significance of the term: "Grief . . . does dissociate man, and sends him with beasts to the loneliness of the unpathed deserts." Owen Feltham, *Resolves*, II, xxxvi (London, 1661), p. 1710.

87. D. H. Tuke, "Dissociation," in *Dictionary of Psychological Medicine, Giving the definition, etymology, and synonyms of the terms used in medical psychology, with symptoms, treatment, and pathology of insanity and the law of lunacy in Great Britain and Ireland* (Philadelphia: Blakeston, 1892).

88. *Works: Essays in Psychical Research*, p. 192.

89. Ibid., p. 193.

90. Ibid., pp. 193–94.

91. Ibid., p. 194.

92. Ibid., p. 196.

93. Ibid.

94. Ibid., p. 197.

95. Ibid., p. 198.

96. Ibid. In other words, James recognized Myers, not Freud or Janet, as the pioneer of the subconscious who staked out the first scientific claim upon it.

97. Ibid., pp. 199, 200.

CHAPTER FIVE
MYSTICAL AWAKENING

1. G. Stanley Hall, *Jesus the Christ in the Light of Psychology*, 2 vols. (New York: Doubleday, 1917).

2. W. James, "Human immortality: Two supposed objections to the doctrine," in *Works: Essays in Religion and Morality* (1982), pp. 75–102.

3. *Works: Essays on Religion and Morality*, p. 96.

4. Ibid., p. 98.

5. Ibid., p. 76.

6. Ibid.

7. H. Van de Kemp, "Teaching psychology of religion in the seventies: Monopoly or cooperation?" *Teaching of Psychology*, 3, 1 (1976), pp. 15–18.

8. Perry, II, p. 337.

9. Ibid., p. 341.

10. W. James, *The Varieties of Religious Experience* (New York: Longmans, 1902), p. 2.

11. Ibid., p. 31.

12. Ibid., p. 74.

13. Ibid., pp. 97–101.

14. Ibid., p. 163.

15. Ibid., pp. 232–33.

16. Ibid., p. 242.

17. Ibid., p. 379.

18. Julius Seelye Bixler, *Religion in the Philosophy of William James* (Boston: Marshall Jones, 1926); Walter Houston Clark, *The Psychology of Religion* (New York: Macmillan, 1958); Henry S. Levinson, *The Religious Investigations of William James* (Chapel Hill: University of North Carolina Press, 1981).

19. E. I. Taylor, *William James on Exceptional Mental States* (New York: Scribner's Sons, 1982).

20. Walter Houston Clark, personal communication.

21. W. James, "Consciousness under nitrous oxide," *Psychological Review*, 5 (1898), pp. 194–96.

22. *Varieties*, p. 387.

23. Ibid., p. 388.

24. The following is taken from the Harvard College catalogs, 1896–1902.

25. James H. Woods, *The Value of Religious Facts* (New York: E. P. Dutton, 1899). James's copy in Phil 8602.13*, Houghton Library, Harvard University. See also Woods's *Practice and Science of Religion: A Study of Method in Comparative Religion* (New York: Longmans, 1906).

26. The students listed in this course were A. W. Birks, F. B. Boswell, A. W. Clark, P. Davis, A. L. Day, W. J. Dixon, H. W. Dresser, D. Drake, B. C. Ewer, R. S. Forbes, L. F. Hite, G. E. Hathaway, W. E. Hocking, G. Ireland, W. Lough, F. Manley, J. L. Mirriam, H. H. Saunderson, A. W. Towne, C. B. Van Wei, M. E. Ward, A. B. Whitney, H. B. Woolston, T. J. Browne. Registrar's Grade Returns for 1902, Harvard University Archives. By permission of the Harvard University Registrar.

27. William Ernest Hocking, "Psychology of Religion Notebook," Philosophy 6, Spring 1902. Hocking Papers, Houghton Library, Harvard University. By permission of Dr. Richard Hocking.

28. W. James, Summer School of Theology Lectures on "Intellect and Feeling in Religion" (1902), in *Works: Manuscript Lectures* (1988), pp. 83–99.

29. Announcement of the course of instruction for the Summer School of Theology Lectures for 1902 at Harvard Divinity School. Andover Harvard Library, Harvard Divinity School.

30. Without ever having read these references to James, Sigmund Koch, fifty years after *The Varieties of Religious Experience*, would adopt a similar nomenclature with not dissimilar meanings to explain his theory of extrinsic versus intrinsic motivation. S. Koch, "The allures of a meaning in modern psychology: An inquiry into the rift between psychology and the humanities," *Report No. 5* (La Jolla, Calif.: Western Behavioral Sciences Institute, 1961), pp. 1–56.

31. *Varieties*, pp. 483–84.

CHAPTER SIX
THE ANTI-JAMESIAN MOVEMENT

1. See W. James, "The Ph.D. octopus," *Harvard Monthly*, 36 (1903), pp. 1–9.

2. D. J. Kevles, J. L. Sturchio, and P. T. Carroll, "The sciences in America, circa 1880," *Science*, 209:4 (1980), pp. 27–32.

3. Yet, even with this emphasis, Professor Bert Moyer of Virginia Polytechnic University, in his biography of the American astronomer, Simon Newcomb, has shown that there was still a clear differentiation between what was said to educate the public about science in general, what the universities and government agencies were told in order to get science projects funded, and what the scientists actually discussed among themselves. Science was a fragile enterprise that had to be guided, protected, and molded in its national and international ascendancy.

Consistency was important for public purposes, while doubts about such problems as relevance and generalizability were kept to back-room conversations. A. E. Moyer, *A Scientist's Voice in American Culture: Simon Newcomb and the Rhetoric of Scientific Method* (Berkeley: University of California Press, 1992).

4. Murphy points out that there were numerous other centers of experimental psychology in Germany that owed nothing to Wundt's school, among them Lipps's studies on optical illusions, the separate work of Ebbinghaus and Müller on memory, Stumpf's experiments on the psychology of tones, and to some extent, Külpe's studies at Würzberg. G. Murphy, *Historical Introduction to Modern Psychology*, 2d ed. (New York: Harcourt Brace, 1949), p. 167.

5. J. Wharton Fay, *American Psychology before William James* (New Brunswick, N.J.: Rutgers University Press, 1939); M. G. Johnson and T. B. Henley, *Reflections on The Principles of Psychology: William James after a Century* (Hillsdale, N.J.: Lawrence Earlbaum, 1990).

6. Daniel W. Bjork, *William James: The Compromised Scientist* (New York: Columbia University Press, 1983), considers James's relation to Münsterberg, Cattell, and Titchener, but sees no Jamesean tradition emerging from their interaction.

7. The most complete biography of Hall to date is Dorothy Ross, *G. Stanley Hall: The Psychologist as Prophet*. See also E. I. Taylor, "An epistemological critique of experimentalism in psychology: Or, why G. Stanley Hall waited until William James was out of town to found the APA," *Annals of the New York Academy of Sciences* 727 (1994), pp. 37–61.

8. Thomas Cadwallader, "The historical roots of the American Psychological Association," in Rand B. Evans, V. S. Sexton, and T. C. Cadwallader, eds., *The American Psychological Association: An Historical Perspective* (Washington, D.C.: American Psychological Association Press, 1992).

9. Reprinted in *Works: Essays, Comments, and Reviews*, pp. 150–51. At the same time, James had written directly to Hall:

I have just received No. 1, of your new series of the A. J. of P. and no one can be gladder than I of the improvements that it promises or wish it more permanent prosperity. I am astonished however to find you asserting that the department of exp. psych. and the lab. at Harvard was founded under the influence of a Clark man. The only Clark man possible was Nichols who came after the lab. was founded. *You will of course rectify this error in your next number.* Another extraordinary bit of mistatement of fact is that the function of the publishing investigations in psycho-physics laboratories is not yet represented by any serial publication in English. Have you ever opened the Psychological Review? I think you owe *it* also an apology in your next number.

As an arm-chair professor, I frankly admit my general inferiority as a laboratory-teacher and investigator. But some little regard should be paid to the good will with which I have tried to force my nature, and to the actual things I have done. One of them for example was in directing you in experimental investigation, with very naive methods, it is true, but you may remember that there was no other place but Harvard where during those years you could get even that. I also remember giving a short course of psychological lectures at the Johns Hopkins years before you went there. They were exclusively experimental and I have been told, made an "epoch" there in determining opinion.

I will recognize how contemptible these beginnings were, and that you and your pupils have in these latter years left them far behind. But you are now professing to state history, beginnings are a part thereof, and should not be written down in inverted order. The statement that experimental psychology at Harvard came from Clark is simply ridiculous. In this world we all owe to each other. My debt to you and to Clark is great, and if only my own person was concerned, I should let you say what you like and not object, for the bystanders generally see truly. In this case, however, the mistake must concern the credit of my university, so I must insist on a correction in your next issue.

W. James to G. Stanley Hall, October 12, 1895, Cambridge, Mass., Hall Papers, Clark University Archives. Hall, of course, never printed any kind of correction.

10. J. M. Cattell, "Early psychological laboratories," *Science*, 67:1744 (1928), pp. 543–48. The issue of the first psychological laboratory recurs again and again and presentist historians are always prone to say two things at the same time: (1) that the issue over who founded the first lab is unimportant; and (2) that Wundt founded the first lab in Leipzig in 1879 and Hall the first lab in America in 1885. Clearly the question to ask in this case is not who founded the first lab, but why is the claim of firsts so important to the person making such a claim?

11. Gardner Murphy, *An Historical Introduction to Modern Psychology*, 2d ed. (New York: Harcourt, Brace, 1949), p. 168; Stewart H. Hulse and Burt Green, Jr., eds., *One Hundred Years of Psychological Research in America: G. Stanley Hall and the Johns Hopkins Tradition* (Baltimore: Johns Hopkins University Press, 1986).

12. G. S. Hall, "College instruction in philosophy," *The Nation*, 23 (1876), p. 180; and "Philosophy in the United States," *Mind*, 4 (1879), pp. 89–105.

13. G. S. Hall, *Founders of Modern Psychology* (New York: D. Appleton, 1912).

14. Murphy, *Historical Introduction*, p. 161, rev. ed.

15. For background on Cattell, see Michael M. Sokal, "The Education and Psychological Career of James McKeen Cattell, 1860–1904," Ph.D. diss., Case Western Reserve University, 1972; University Microfilms, #73–6341; and M. Sokal, ed., *An Education in Psychology: James McKeen Cattell's Journal and Letters from Germany and England, 1880–1888* (Cambridge, Mass.: MIT Press, 1981).

16. James was "'the sweetest, wisest soul of all my days and lands'; there is none like him, none, nor will be." J. M. Cattell, "The founding of the Association and of the Hopkins and Clark laboratories," *Psychological Review*, 50:1 (1943), p. 61.

17. J. M. Cattell, "Review of James's Presidential Address," *Psychological Review*, 3 (1896), pp. 582–83.

18. Reprinted in *Works: Essays in Psychical Research*, pp. 442–43.

19. Ibid., p. 184.

20. Ibid., p. 185.

21. Ibid.

22. Ibid., p. 186.

23. Margaret Münsterberg, *Hugo Münsterberg: His Life and Work* (New York: D. Appleton, 1922).

24. W. James to H. Münsterberg, Cambridge, Mass., February 21, 1892. Quoted in ibid., p. 33.

25. "I sympathize with you in re laboratorie. I am suffering similarly in Mberg's absence. A true nightmare"; James to Flournoy, Cambridge, November 8, 1895. "Last year was a year of hard work, and before the end of the term came, I was in a bad state of neurasthenic fatigue, but I got through it outwardly all right. I have definitely given up the laboratory, for which I am more and more unfit, and shall probably devote what little ability I may hereafter have to purely 'speculative' work"; James to Flournoy, Lake Geneva, Wisconsin, August 30, 1896. "*I* have got rid of the laboratory forever, and should resign my place immediately if they reimpose its duties upon me. The results that come from all this laboratory work seem to me to grow more and more disappointing and trivial. What is most needed is new ideas. For every man who has one of them one may find a hundred who are willing to drudge patiently at some unimportant experiment"; James to Flournoy, Cambridge, Mass., December 7, 1896. In R. C. Le Clair, *The Letters of William James and Theodore Flournoy* (Madison: University of Wisconsin Press, 1966).

26. My interpretation expands considerably the more limited but nevertheless excellent discussion presented by Matthew Hale, Jr., in his *Human Science and Social Order: Hugo Münsterberg and the Origins of Applied Psychology* (Philadelphia: Temple University Press, 1980), pp. 45–58.

27. Münsterberg, it will be recalled, did not attend the Clark University conference on that Friday in September 1909, when the well-known photo showing James, Jung, Freud, Hall, and others was taken.

28. H. Münsterberg, "Psychology and mysticism," *Atlantic Monthly* (1889), p. 75.

29. Quoted in Matthew Hale, Jr., *Human Science and Social Order: Hugo Münsterberg and the Origins of Applied Psychology* (Philadelphia: Temple University Press, 1980), p. 102.

30. Ibid.

31. Episode quoted in John Clendenning, *The Life and Thought of Josiah Royce* (Madison: University of Wisconsin Press, 1985), p. 340.

32. "Shortly before his death," wrote Stephen Royce, "my father [Josiah Royce] told me . . . that Münsterberg had been called in to the Wilhelmstrasse [presumably in 1910–11] and instructed to get into the limelight so that his name should be well-known when his propaganda should become necessary to the fatherland." In ibid., p. 388.

33. Edwin Katzenellenbogen, a psychiatrist from Danvers State Hospital who appears along with Freud, Jung, James, Titchener, and Hall in the famous Clark University photo, and who, after World War II, was convicted and sentenced for being a doctor in the Nazi death camps.

34. S. H. Mauskopf and M. R. McVaugh, *The Elusive Science: Origins of Experimental Psychical Research* (Baltimore: Johns Hopkins University Press, 1980), pp. 321–22, fn4.

35. P. W. Bridgeman, for instance, learned James's pragmatism from Royce and Münsterberg while mastering physics at Harvard. See A. E. Moyer, "P. W. Bridgeman's operational perspective on physics: Origins and development," *Studies in History and Philosophy of Science*, 22:2 (1991), pp. 237–56.

36. Ryan D. Tweny, "Programmatic research in experimental psychology: E. B. Titchener's laboratory investigations, 1891–1927," in M. G. Ash and W. R. Woodward, eds., *Psychology in Twentieth-Century Thought and Society* (New York: Cambridge University Press, 1987), pp. 35–57.

37. W. G. Bringmann and R. Tweny, eds., *Wundt Studies: A Centennial Collection* (Toronto: C. J. Hogrefe, 1980).

38. *Works: Essays in Psychical Research*, p. 169.

39. Ibid.

40. Ibid., p. 173.

41. Ibid.

42. Ibid., pp. 173–74.

43. Ibid., p. 175.

44. Ibid., p. 172. James thought of Titchener as "very energetic and reputed to be a great success as a teacher, but apparently not original in the way of ideas, and (although from Oxford) quite a barbarian in his scientific & literary manners, and quarrelsome in the extreme." W. James to Charles William Eliot, February 21, 1897. Eliot Papers, Pusey Library, Harvard University.

45. *Works: Essays in Psychical Research*, pp. 172–73.

46. Ibid. p. 177.

47. Titchner had written to Cattell: "James's influence both in philosophy & psychology appears to me to be getting positively unwholesome: his credulity and his appeals to emotion are surely the reverse of scientific. . . . even you, as younger, cannot stem the James tide." E. B. Titchener to J. M. Cattell, November 20, 1898. Cattell Papers, Library of Congress, Washington, D.C.

48. Ryan D. Tweny, "Programmatic research in experimental psychology: E. B. Titchener's laboratory investigations, 1891–1927," in M. G. Ash and W. R. Woodward, eds., *Psychology in Twentieth Century Thought and Society* (New York: Cambridge University Press, 1987), pp. 35–57.

49. Ibid., pp. 50–51. Tweny maintains that 1915 was the first year that Titchener's output was finally superseded by that of his students.

CHAPTER SEVEN
JAMES'S REJOINDER

1. On writing to the French philosopher, François Pillon, James said, "My philosophy is what I call radical empiricism, a pluralism, a 'tychism,' which represents order as being gradually won and always in the making. It is theistic, but not *essentially* so. It rejects all doctrines of the absolute. It is finitist; but it does not attribute to the question of the Infinite the great methodological importance which you and Renouvier attribute to it. I fear that you may find my system too *bottomless* and romantic. I am sure that, be it in the end judged true or false, it is essential to the evolution of clearness in philosophic thought that *someone* should defend a pluralistic empiricism radically." W. James, *Letters*, II, pp. 203–4.

2. W. James, "A world of pure experience," in *Works: Essays in Radical Empiricism*, p. 22.

3. Reprinted in *Works: Essays in Psychology*, pp. 270–77.

4. Ibid., p. 270.

5. Ibid.

6. Ibid., p. 272.

7. Ibid., p. 273.

8. Ibid., p. 275.

9. Ibid., p. 277.

10. M. Sokal, Introduction, in *Works: Psychology: Briefer Course* (1984), pp. xi–xli.

11. *Works: Essays in Philosophy*, p. 86.

12. Ibid., p. 88.

13. Ibid.

14. Ibid., pp. 88–89.

15. Reprinted in *Works: Essays in Psychical Research*, pp. 127–37. Read January 31, 1896, in Boston for the American branch, and (in James's absence) in London on the same day, and repeated again in New York on February 1.

16. Miss X, a well-known automatic writer, was Lucy Goodrich-Freer. Stainton Moses was a medium who had been investigated by F.W.H. Myers in England.

17. W. James, "Address of the President, delivered at the annual meeting of the Society for Psychical Research," January 31, 1896. Reprinted in *Works: Essays in Psychical Research*, pp. 131–32.

18. Ibid., p. 133.

19. Ibid., pp. 134–35.

20. Ibid., p. 137.

21. W. James, *The Will to Believe and Other Essays in Popular Philosophy* (New York: Longmans, Green, 1897).

22. Ibid., p. viii.

23. For the influence of the French philosopher Charles Renouvier on the evolution of James's thinking about the will to believe, see Perry, I, p. 654.

24. Ibid., p. 10.

25. Ibid., pp. 16–17.

26. Ibid., p. 21.

27. Ibid., pp. 24–25.

28. Ibid., p. 53.

29. Ibid., p. 54.

30. Ibid.

31. Ibid., p. 57.

32. Ibid., p. 131.

33. John McDermott gives the best history of radical empiricism from the standpoint of James's philosophy in his introduction to *The Works of William James: Essays in Radical Empiricism* (1976), pp. xi–xlviii. To this analysis, I have tried to add wherever James had aimed the discussion specifically at the emerging discipline of scientific psychology.

34. Both were reprinted posthumously with other related papers as *Essays in Radical Empiricism* (New York: Longmans, 1910).

35. Gay Wilson Allen, *William James: A Biography* (New York: Viking, 1967), p. 469. John McDermott deserves credit for pointing out to philosophers that the core of James's technical metaphysics was not pragmatism, but radical empiricism. See his introduction in J. J. McDermott, ed., *The Writings of William James: A Comprehensive Edition* (Chicago: University of Chicago Press, 1970).

36. *Works: Essays in Radical Empiricism*, p. 4.

37. Ibid.

38. Ibid., pp. 4–5.

39. Ibid., p. 13.

40. Ibid., p. 42.

41. Ibid., p. 25.

42. W. James, "The experience of activity," *Psychological Review*, 12 (1905), pp. 1–17. Reprinted in *Works: Essays in Radical Empiricism*, pp. 79–95.

43. W. James, "La notion de conscience," *Archives de Psychologie*, 5 (1905), pp. 1–12. Reprinted in *Works: Essays in Radical Empiricism*, pp. 105–117.

44. *Works: Essays in Radical Empiricism*, p. 20.

45. First enunciated by James in "Philosophical conceptions and practical results" (1898), and reproduced in *Works: Pragmatism* (1975), p. 29.

46. Charles Sanders Peirce, logician and philosopher, was the irascible, hot-headed son of Benjamin Peirce, professor of mathematics at Harvard. The influence of C. S. Peirce on James has been long established. See R. B. Perry, *The Thought and Character of William James* (Boston: Little, Brown, 1935), pp. 406–40; H. M. Kallen, remarks on R. B. Perry's portrait of William James, *The Philosophical Review*, 46, pp. 68–78; C. Morris, *The Pragmatic Movement in American Philosophy* (New York: Geo. Braziller, 1970); T. C. Cadwallader and J. V. Cadwallader, "America's first modern psychologist: William James or C. S. Peirce?" *Proceedings of the 80th Annual Convention of the American Psychological Association*, contributed papers to symposia, 7 (1972), pp. 773–74. James first befriended him in 1861, and Peirce then introduced James to the logic of the scientific method and to the German experimental laboratory tradition. By the early 1870s, Peirce and James were associated with the meetings of the Cambridge Metaphysical Club, out of which Peirce first enunciated his doctrine of pragmatism. In 1898, James then introduced Peirce's pragmatism to the Graduate Philosophical Union at Berkeley, after which, according to James's redefinition, pragmatism became the first uniquely American philosophy to have international consequences. Thereafter, James, feeling beholden to the destitute philosopher, garnered support for Peirce's upkeep from a pool of anonymous contributors. Despite this aid, Peirce, biting the hand that fed him, consistently disavowed any connection to James's views. The result was two major tributaries of American pragmatism. The first great river was the Jamesean, a philosophy of action in which truths are tested by their beliefs. The second, renamed *pragmaticism*, was the Peircean, a rule of logic in which the goodness of thought is rounded out by a consideration of its consequences. The Jamesean captured the popular imagi-

nation and influenced psychology, education, religion, political science, and philosophical humanism. The Peircean influenced modern technical philosophy, particularly the logic of relations and normative statistics.

47. *Pragmatism*, p. 273.

48. Ibid., p. 53.

49. Ibid., p. 55.

50. Ibid., p. 51.

51. Ibid., p. 257.

52. Ibid., p. 201.

53. James devoted an entire collection of papers to this problem, See his *The Meaning of Truth* (New York: Longmans, 1909).

54. *Pragmatism*, p. 267.

55. Ibid., pp. 290–91.

56. A central theme of James's *Some Problems of Philosophy* (New York: Longmans, 1911).

57. From H. Bergson, *L évolution créatrice* (Paris: Alcan, 1907). James's copy is WJ607.75.2, Houghton Library, Harvard University. Quoted in E. I. Taylor, "James on Darwin: An evolutionary theory of consciousness," in S. M. Pfafflin J. A. Sechzer, J. M. Fisch, and R. L. Thompson, eds., *Psychology: Perspectives and Practice, Annals of the New York Academy of Sciences*, 602 (1990), pp. 7–33.

58. Ibid.

59. Richard J. Bernstein, "Introduction," in *Works: A Pluralistic Universe*, p. xxiii.

60. Ibid., p. 22.

61. Ibid., pp. 22–23.

62. Ibid., pp. 24–25.

63. Ibid.

64. Ibid., p. 25.

65. Quoted in Richard J. Bernstein, "Introduction," in *Works: A Pluralistic Universe*, p. xx.

66. Ibid., pp. 63–82. See also E. I. Taylor, "Fechner's *Das Büchlein vom Leben nach dem Tode*: A reply to David Bakan," *Journal of Pastoral Counseling*, 27 (1992), pp. 44–51.

67. Ibid., p. 26.

68. Fechner's doctrine of the Earth-Soul was inspired by his reading of Swedenborg according to W. Bringmann, "Fechner and psychical research," in J. Brozek and H. Gundlach, eds., *G. T. Fechner and Psychology* (1988). Passauer Schriften zur Psychologiegeschichte (Institut für Geschichte der neueren Psychologie der Universität Passau. Leitung, W. Traxel, no. 6, Passavia Universitätsverlag), p. 245. For a useful statement on the relation between Fechner's panpsychism and his psychophysics, see Rudolf Arnheim, "The other Gustav Theodor Fechner," in S. Koch and D. Leary, eds., *A Century of Psychology as Science* (New York: McGraw-Hill, 1985), pp. 856–69.

69. W. James, "A pluralistic mystic," in *Memories and Studies* (New York: Longmans, Green, 1911), p. 273.

70. Ibid., p. 375.
71. Ibid., p. 91.
72. Ibid., pp. 392–93.
73. Ibid., p. 408.
74. Ibid., p. 409.
75. Ibid., p. 411.

CHAPTER EIGHT
JAMES'S FINAL STATEMENT TO PSYCHOLOGISTS

1. E. I. Taylor, "Psychological suspended animation: Heart rate, blood pressure, time-estimation, and introspective reports from an anechoic environment," Master of Arts thesis, Department of Psychology, Southern Methodist University, Dallas, Texas, 1973.

2. E. I. Taylor, "Some epistemological problems inherent in the scientific study of consciousness," paper presented at the Louisa Rhine Conference on Consciousness and Healing, Durham, N.C., November 10, 1991.

3. As a case study of this point, I hope to develop at a later time some of the implications of the neuroscience revolution for understanding the epistemological dilemma of modern scientific psychology, part of which I began in *Cyberphysiology: The Science of Consciousness* (Minneapolis: The Archaeus Project, 1989).

4. In our own time, they are sensation and perception, learning, motivation, developmental, abnormal, personality, social, and so on.

5. Danziger maintains that there were three general approaches to conducting experimental research: (1) where the psychologist in the role of the experimenter measured some aspect of the subject, usually in the laboratory; (2) where the experimenter also served as a subject who was a trained observer, so that the experimenters always studied themselves; and (3) where the psychologist studied the subject as a patient in a clinical setting. In each case, the point was to extract scientific information. K. Danziger, *Constructing the Subject: Historical Origins of Psychological Research* (Cambridge, Mass.: Cambridge University Press, 1990).

6. An example is the Aesthetics Research Project at Boston University, described in S. Koch, "An example of 1:1 qualitative research," paper presented at the annual meeting of the American Psychological Association, August 1991, San Francisco.

7. W. James, "A suggestion about mysticism," *Journal of Philosophy, Psychology, and Scientific Methods*, 7 (1910), pp. 85–92. Reprinted in W. James, *Memories and Studies* (New York: Longmans, 1920), p. 503.

8. S. Freud, "An autobiographical study," in *Standard Edition of the Complete Psychological Works of Sigmund Freud*, vol. 20, ed. J. Strachey (London: Hogarth Press, 1959), p. 52.

9. Quoted in Peter Gay, *Freud: A Life for Our Time* (New York: Norton, 1989).

10. Ernest Jones, *The Life and Work of Sigmund Freud*, vol. 2 (New York: Basic Books, 1955), p. 15.

11. Rick Fields, *How the Swans Came to the Lake* (Boulder: Shambhala, 1981), p. 135. I am indebted to Edward Podvol, director of the Maitri Project at the Naropa Institute, for bringing this episode to my attention. For a modern forecast, see E. I. Taylor, review of Peter Gay's *Freud: A Life for Our Time*, in *Commonweal*, March 21, 1989.

12. W. James, "A suggestion about mysticism," *Journal of Philosophy, Psychology, and Scientific Methods*, 7 (1910), p. 92.

13. A group of enlightened souls did attempt a rapprochement some decades ago when a blue ribbon panel was commissioned by President Nathan Marsh Pusey to evaluate the status and future prospects of psychology at Harvard. The result of that panel's investigation was *The Place of Psychology in an Ideal University*. Sagaciously, they suggested that every individual in any other discipline having anything to do with psychology as a subject area should have at least an adjunct appointment with the principle department of psychology in an ideally constituted university. Their recommendations were largely ignored. See Committee to Assess the Status of Psychology, etc., *The Place of Psychology in an Ideal University* (Cambridge, Mass.: Harvard University Press, 1946).

14. Rand Evans and F. J. Down Scott, "The 1913 International Congress of Psychology: The American congress that wasn't," *American Psychologist*, 33 (1978), pp. 711–23; Daniel Bjork, *The Compromised Scientist: William James in the Development of American Psychology* (New York: Columbia University Press, 1983), also recounts this episode, but makes a different point.

15. W. James, "La notion de conscience," *Archives de Psychologie*, 5 (1905), pp. 1–12.

16. Evans and Scott, "The 1913 Congress," p. 712.

17. Ibid.

18. Ibid.

19. Ibid.

20. Ibid., p. 715.

21. Ibid., p. 718.

22. Ibid.

23. Sigmund Koch, *Psychology: The Study of a Science* (New York: McGraw-Hill, 1959), vol. 3.

24. Abraham Maslow, *The Psychology of Science: A Reconnaissance* (Chicago: Regnary/Gateway, 1969); A. Giorgi, *Psychology as a Human Science: A Phenomenally Based Approach* (New York: Harper and Row, 1970); K. J. Gergen, "Social psychology as history," *Journal of Personality and Social Psychology*, 26 (1973), pp. 309–20; J. F. Rychlak, *The Psychology of Rigorous Humanism* (New York: Wiley, 1977); R. L. Rosnow, *Paradigms in Transition: The Methodology of Social Inquiry* (New York: Oxford University Press, 1981).

25. Peter T. Manicas and Paul F. Secord, "Implications for psychology of the new philosophy of science," *American Psychologist* (1983), pp. 399–413; James E. Faulconer and Richard N. Williams, "Temporality in human action: An alternative to positivism and historicism," *American Psychologist*, 40 (1985), pp. 1179–88; Karl H. Pribram, "The cognitive revolution and mind/brain issues," *American Psychologist*, 41 (1986), pp. 507–20.

26. Some exceptions are Amedeo Giorgi, "The implications of James's plea for psychology as a natural science," in M. G. Johnson and T. B. Henley, *Reflections on The Principles of Psychology: William James after a Century* (Hillsdale, N.J.: Lawrence Earlbaum, 1990), pp. 63–76; and David E. Leary, "Psyche's Muse: The role of metaphor in the history of psychology," in David E. Leary, ed., *Metaphors in the History of Psychology* (Cambridge, England: Cambridge University Press, 1990), pp. 19–21.

ANNOTATED BIBLIOGRAPHY

ALMOST EVERYONE of any stature in the academic discipline of psychology has had something to say about William James, whether their opinion has been historically informed or not. Each person, rather, tends to express the whole through his or her own little corner of the universe.

J. Wharton Fay, *American Psychology before William James* (New Brunswick: Rutgers University Press, 1969), for instance, is a charming look at psychology defined as an academic subject in the context of American moral philosophy and as a product of the European rationalist tradition before James led the way into the new science through physiological psychology. However, the work omits any reference to the burgeoning industry of folk psychology (phrenology, mesmerism, spiritual healing); the literary psychology of the transcendentalists, the medico-psychological movement—that is, the use of psychology by physicians such as George Miller Beard, or the development of practical psychology in the state normal schools. In contrast, R. Wozniak, *Mind and Body: Descartes to William James* (Bethesda, Md.: Joint publication of the National Library of Medicine and the American Psychological Association, 1992), which acknowledges these streams, maintains that all thought on the mind-body problem in Western philosophy and science converges by the late nineteenth century in James's work.

Meanwhile, the life of William James has been a subject of perpetual interest, although mostly by nonpsychologists. Although preceded by a chronological collection of correspondence, see Henry James Jr., ed., *The Letters of William James*, 2 vols. (Boston: Atlantic Monthly Press, 1920); the best biography, still unsurpassed, remains Ralph Barton Perry, *The Thought and Character of William James*, 2 vols. (Boston: Atlantic, Little Brown, 1935). Although Perry acknowledges James's interest in psychical research, he could not figure out where it fit in his own understanding of James's philosophy; he missed James's extensive influence on experimental psychopathology, and, in retrospect, probably under the influence of Freudian psychology in the 1930s, concluded that James was a sick soul who lacked an adequate philosophy to live by. Nevertheless, a lifework of depth and erudition by a man designated as his biographer while James was still alive, Perry's book still stands as definitive.

Various family studies have also been produced, including Hartley Gratten, *The Three Jameses: A Family of Minds* (New York: Longmans, Green, 1932), which is sympathetic to a missing link in James studies because it was written by a Swedenborgian; and F. O. Matheissen, *The James Family: Including Selections from the Writings of Henry James, Senior, William, Henry, and Alice James* (New York: Knopf, 1948), which is still one of the best group portraits, written by a Harvard man who was immersed in the James family milieu as it still existed in the 1940s. Howard Feinstein, *Becoming William James* (Ithaca, N.Y.: Cornell University Press), is a look at three generations of Jameses (William of Albany, Henry Sr., and William), up to 1880, from a family-systems approach. Written by a psychiatrist and trained psychoanalyst who also had a Ph.D. in history, the work remains remarkably clear of Freudian ideas except, appropriately, where the interpretation of James's art is involved. (Will there be a volume two?) Recently we have seen R.W.B. Lewis, *The Jameses: A Family Narrative* (New York: Farrar, Straus, and Giroux, 1991), which is lively and well written and unearths important new information on the genealogical background of the James family.

The first full chronological sequence of James's life was Gay Wilson Allen, *William James: A Biography* (New York: Viking, 1967). Still indispensable, it does not, however, deal in any in-depth way with the substance of James's ideas. Numerous works looking at James's thought have followed. One is Jacques Barzun, *A Stroll with William James* (New York: Harper and Row, 1983). On the order of a Great Books course in James's thought, this work is a tour of James's major writings by one of the senior deans of American letters who explores the many expressions of the artistic temperament in James's thought. The author correctly situates James's *Exceptional Mental States* as a transitional text between the *Principles of Psychology* (1890) and *The Varieties of Religious Experience* (1902).

There is also Gerald Myers, *William James: His Life and Thought* (New Haven: Yale University Press, 1986), a superb lifework by a follower of Wittgenstein and Russell who sought to situate James in relation to normative Western philosophy. Although not really a biography (the work is primarily organized around themes from James's *Principles of Psychology*), there are new biographical morsels for public consumption. The study is also not really a Jamesean text, since it was not the center of James's vision that the author was trying to catch but the puzzlement of analytic philosophers over where James might actually be coming from.

In my opinon, the primary philosophical frame of reference for understanding James (and one which has yet to be plumbed) begins with Swedenborg and Emerson, and then proceeds to Henry James, Sr., and on to Peirce. All else are secondary ecretions superimposed. See, for instance, E. I. Taylor, "Peirce and Swedenborg," *Studia Swedenborgiana*, 6:1 (1986), pp. 25–51; and E. I. Taylor, "Ralph Waldo Emerson: The Swedenborgian and Transcendentalist connection," in R. Larsen, ed., *Emanuel Swedenborg: The Vision Continues* (300th anniversary volume), pp. 127–36 (New York: The Swedenborg Foundation, 1988).

There are also the works by Daniel Bjork, *The Compromised Scientist* (New York: Columbia University Press, 1983); and *William James: The Center of His Vision* (New York: Columbia University Press, 1988), two excursions into the field of Jamesean thought by an American studies scholar who has also written a biography of B. F. Skinner. In *The Compromised Scientist*, Bjork has clutched the central problem of James's vocation—the struggle between the artistic and scientific sensibilities (the same theme is developed in greater detail by Feinstein in *Becoming William James*). In *William James: The Center of His Vision*, Bjork marches through a chronological sequence of James's unpublished manuscripts seeking the focal point of James's thought. He finds it in "the flux of experience," but takes it no farther.

More recently, a new study has tried to paint a completely different picture of James. Based upon only two letters James wrote to his much younger girlfriend, Pauline Goldmark; two or three books in his library; and one annotated volume which James got through his brother and read just once (written by an author who was probably a devotee of Henry James Sr.), William James is somewhat inappropriately cast into the backdrop of twentieth-century social revolutions and made out to be an anarchist in Deborah Coon, "Courtship with anarchy: The sociopolitical foundations of William James's pragmatism," Ph.D. diss., Harvard University.

In my opinion, a more appropriate context would have been the American utopian socialism of the 1840s, to which James was a direct heir through Henry James Sr. and Emerson. See E. I. Taylor, "Divine communities: The utopian experience in America," *Chrysalis* (Journal of the Swedenborg Foundation), 1:2 (1986), pp. 36–45; and E. I. Taylor, "The American Visionary Tradition," *Noetic Sciences Review*, Fall 1993 (Institute of Noetic Sciences, Sausalito, Calif.). And rather than deriving James's pragmatism from anarchist tendencies in the late 1890s, one might look further into the complex of relationships between Emerson, Henry James Sr., William James, C. S. Peirce, and Chauncey Wright in the 1860s. See E. I. Taylor, "William James and C. S. Peirce," *Chrysalis* (Journal of the Swedenborg Foundation), 1:3 (1986), pp. 207–12. Nevertheless, the work makes an extraordinarily important contribution toward analyzing some of James's activities with the international peace movement around 1900.

JAMES AND THE PSYCHOTHERAPEUTIC SCENE

There are at present a number of different works on the history of psychotherapy. They are all examples of how psychotherapy continues to have a problematic place in the history of psychology, in my opinion because psychotherapy is ubiquitous; that is, it cuts across many diverse disciplines and takes too many amorphous forms to be pinned down. More importantly, psychotherapy is problematic because the attempt to continually refine the definition of psychology as a reductionistic science remains in conflict with the epistemological assumptions underlying dynamic theories of the unconscious and conceptions of personality based on intuitive rather than logico-rational norms.

James's solution was to turn psychologists' attention toward experience in all its richness and away from only the rational products of a reductionistic science. The revolution was only partially successful, as two psychologies, the one experimental and laboratory oriented and the other social and experiential, clearly exist today, and while they often overlap, they remain at odds with each other. See S. Koch, "The nature and limits of psychological knowledge," *American Psychologist*, 36 (1981), pp. 257–69; and E. D. Cahan and S. H. White, "Proposals for a second psychology," *American Psychologist*, 47:2 (1992), pp. 222–35. The resulting conflict and frequent confusion of the two has created an incomplete picture of psychotherapy in the history of psychology.

Each work on the history of psychotherapy only seems to present a part of the larger history. A. Crabtree, *From Mesmer to Freud: Magnetic Sleep and the Roots of Psychological Healing* (New Haven: Yale University Press, 1993), gets at the historical source of psychotherapeutic healing through a chronology of authors, but it is not a systematic reconstruction, nor is it concerned with the problematic place of psychotherapy within both psychology and psychiatry. J. M. Reisman, *The Development of Clinical Psychology* (New York: Appleton-Century Crofts, 1966), is an important beginning to the history of clinical psychology, but again picks and chooses on the topic of psychotherapy, especially in the early period, where it jumps from Charcot to Freud, as if nothing happened in between. Donald Freidman, ed., *History of Psychotherapy: A Century of Change* (Washington, D.C.: American Psychological Association, 1992), is a good introduction, but is strongest in the period after World War Two and contains only imaginary and social deconstructionist accounts of American psychotherapy between 1880 and 1920. The most significant work to date on the history of psychotherapy has been Henri Ellenberger, *The Discovery of the Unconscious* (New York: Basic Books, 1970), which broke new ground because it was not exclusively Freudocentric and because it introduced a large mass of French sources normally unavailable to English-language readers. While this is the book that actually launched the new scholarship in alternative forms of depth psychology beyond Freud, it made little mention of the American psychotherapeutic scene between 1880 and 1920.

A work that emphasizes the contribution of Lightner Witmer, a student of Cattell and Wundt, to the founding of clinical psychology is P. McReynolds's, "Lightner Witmer: Little-known founder of clinical psychology," *American Psychologist*, 42 (1987), pp. 849–58. But because the history of clinical psychology remains incomplete, Witmer is still claimed as the "founder" of clinical psychology. This contention is consistent with the origin myth that if clinical psychology is scientific, it must have been derived from the type of scientific psychology founded in Leipzig in Wundt's laboratory in 1879. Witmer was extraordinarily hostile to depth psychology (that is, psychotherapy and dynamic theories of consciousness), so histories that claim him as the founder of clinical psychology conveniently omit reference to unconscious processes until the advent of Freud.

Meanwhile, no single general work yet exists on the Boston School of Psychotherapy or the place of William James in it. Indeed, Otto Marx's lament that James is missing from an account of the history of psychiatry is nearly true; see his "American psychiatry without William James," *Bulletin of the History of Medicine*, 42, pp. 52–61. John Burnham mentioned James and discussed the Boston School of Psychotherapy in *Psychoanalysis and American Medicine, 1894–1918: Medicine, Science, and Culture* (New York: International Universities Press, 1970), while Nathan G. Hale Jr. devotes fleeting sections to both James and the Boston School in *Freud and the Americans* (New York: Oxford, 1971). The closest treatment so far has been G. E. Gifford Jr., ed., *Psychoanalysis, Psychotherapy, and the New England Medical Scene, 1894–1944* (New York: Science/History Press, 1978). This work is a collection of papers from an important symposium held in 1976 at Harvard Medical School, which was innovative and before its time because it did not have an exclusively Freudian emphasis. A new monograph has also just appeared: Sanford G. Gifford, *The Emmanuel Movement and Medical Psychology in New England* (Boston: Countway Library of Medicine, 1995), which extends this non-Freudian picture.

The seminal lectures that launched the Boston School were James's unpublished Lowell Lectures of 1896. See E. I. Taylor, *William James on Exceptional Men-*

tal States (New York, Scribner's Sons, 1982). Forthcoming is a written version of Lowell Lectures originally delivered in 1982: E. I. Taylor, *The Boston School of Psychotherapy: Science, Healing, and Consciousness in Nineteenth-Century New England*, in preparation.

James's connections to the larger French, Swiss, English, and American psychotherapeutic alliance to which the Boston school was connected have to be pieced together from several places. For James's relation to Charcot's circle, see the letters between James and Theodule Ribot, which also reveal the earliest contact James had with Alfred Binet; James Papers, Houghton Library, Harvard University. For Janet's connections to James and the Boston scene, see Henri Ellenberger, "Pierre Janet and his American friends," in G. E. Gifford Jr., ed., *Psychoanalysis, Psychotherapy, and the New England Medical Scene, 1894–1944* (New York: Science/History Press, 1978), pp. 63–72. For James's connections to the English psychical researchers, see the letters between James and F.W.H. Myers, James Papers, Houghton Library, Harvard University, and the F.W.H. Myers Papers, Trinity College, Cambridge University, Cambridge, England. James's connections to the Swiss scene are revealed in his relationship with Theodore Flournoy; see R. C. Le Claire, ed., *The Letters of William James and Theodore Flournoy* (Madison: University of Wisconsin Press, 1966). Flournoy was one of the primary routes by which the Jamesean tradition influenced Edward Claparède and Jean Piaget, as well as Jung. For the connections between Jung and James, see E. I. Taylor, William James, and C. G. Jung, *Spring: Annual of Archetypal Psychology and Jungian Thought*, 39 (1980), pp. 157–69; E. I. Taylor, "C. G. Jung and the Boston psychopathologists, 1902–1912," *Voices: The Art and Science of Psychotherapy*, 21:3, 4 (1985), pp. 131–44; idem, "Jung in his intellectual context: The Swedenborgian connection," *Studia Swedenborgiana*, 7:2 (1991), pp. 47–69; and idem, "The new Jung scholarship," in a special forthcoming issue of *Psychoanalytic Review* (1996).

JAMES AND FREUD

Several comparisons have been made between James and Freud. Most of these, however, have been from what the Jung scholar Sonu Shamdasani has called a Freudocentric perspective. That is, in discussing any topic, several assumptions are presumed as given; namely, the pervasiveness of Freud's ideas throughout all departments of human thought, the absolutely affirmed status of psychoanalysis as a science, and the superiority of Freud's definition of the unconscious over all other conceptions of inner experience. In my own historical opinion, it was necessary for psychoanalysis to be established in this way in order for it to become the only depth psychology of the late nineteenth century to persist into the ultra-orthodox positivist era that followed.

Any mention of William James in a Freudian context would be secondary to this monolithic view. For such comments on James, see, for instance, David Shakow and David Rapaport, *The Influence of Freud on American Psychology*, in *Psychological Issues*, 4:1, Monograph 13 (New York: International Universities Press, 1964); Barbara Ross, "William James: A prime mover of the psychoanalytic movement in America," in G. E. Gifford, Jr., ed., *Psychoanalysis, Psychotherapy, and the New England Medical Scene, 1894–1944* (New York: Science/History Press, 1978); and Peter Gay, *A Godless Jew: Freud, Atheism, and the Making of Psychoanalysis* (New Haven: Yale University Press, 1987), pp. 21–24; Gerald Myers, *William James: His Life and Thought* (New Haven: Yale University Press, 1986), pp. 167–68. For a symposium held in 1990 at the annual meeting of the American Philosophical Society to celebrate the one hundredth anniversary of James's *Principles of Psychology*, see Gerald Myers, "James and Freud," *Journal of Philosophy*, 87:11 (1990), pp. 593–99.

In my own opinion, James and Freud come from two entirely different epistemological traditions and their conceptions of personality, consciousness, and psychotherapy cannot be compared until their respective historical frames of reference are reconstructed. In Freud's case this has been microanalyzed in excruciating detail (see, for instance, Gail Hornstein, "The return of the repressed: Psychology's problematic relations with psychoanalysis, 1909–1960," *American Psychologist*, 47:2 (1992), pp. 254–63). In James's case, facile overgeneralizations are made on incomplete evidence or by ignoring what evidence plainly exists.

Important misunderstandings occur, for instance, when referring to James, Janet, or F.W.H. Myers. The psychoanalytically oriented authors consistently use Freud's term and definition of the "unconscious," when the more historically accurate conception held by the French, Swiss, English, and American experimental psychopathologists was "the subconscious," or "co-consciousness." The difference is important because the conception in James and Putnam's hands contains the iconography of the transcendent, which Freud and his interpreters flatly denied as an integral part of human experience. Freud claimed that Putnam was dabbling in Protestant theology; see N. G. Hale, Jr., *James Jackson Putnam and Psychoanalysis* (Cambridge, Mass.: Harvard University Press, 1971), and later maintained that religion in all its forms was a form of neurosis (see Freud's *Civilization and Its Discontents* and *Moses and Monotheism*).

One of the most interesting and important, if idiosyncratic, statements on James and Freud has been made by Saul Rosenzweig, Morton Prince's last and Henry Murray's first student at the Harvard Psychological Clinic in 1930 and later founder of the field of Ideodynamics. See Saul Rosenzweig, *Freud, Jung, and Hall the King-Maker: The historic expedition to America (1909) with G. Stanley Hall as host and William James as guest. Including the complete correspondence of Sigmund Freud and G. Stanley Hall and a new translation of Freud's lectures at Clark University on the origin and development of psychoanalysis* (Seattle: Hogrefe and Huber, 1992). The work, which in many ways supersedes Erik Erikson's analysis of James in *Childhood and Society*, brings out much new evidence, only some of which was already known to James scholars. It presents a historical and psychoanalytically assisted intepretation of James's meeting with Freud, some of James's dreams which James himself later reported, and an in-depth analysis of James's amorous but platonic relationship with the much younger Pauline Goldmark. Rosenzweig correctly assesses the James-Myers-Janet connection; but he makes only one mention in a footnote of James's 1896 Lowell Lectures on experimental psychopathology, does not look into the documentation on the subconscious, and treats psychical research only in the context of James's relation to G. Stanley Hall, not in relation to James and his earlier role with the American Society for Psychical Research in launching experimental psychopathology and the so-called Boston School of Psychotherapy.

PSYCHOLOGISTS' REJECTION OF
JAMES AS A PSYCHOLOGIST

Psychologists' rejection of James as a psychologist probably began with comments made by James himself when, by the 1890s, he became too exasparated with addressing the specific encroachment of laboratory science and the trends toward narrowness and specialization and elected instead to turn his attention full time to critiquing the metaphysical foundations of such a mistaken enterprise and to articulating its appropriate correction. I have already indicated those who, of the most influential graduates from Wundt's laboratory in Leipzig who returned or emigrated to America to found university laboratories, fell into some controversy with James. Certainly the most openly vitriolic was Lightner Witmer; see Anon, "Is the psychology taught at Harvard a national peril?" *Current Literature*, 46 (1909), pp. 437–38; and L. Witmer, "Mental healing and the Emmanuel Movement," *Psychological Clinic*, 2 (1907), pp. 212–23, 239–50, 282–300.

Two historical texts that later perpetuated this view were Gardner Murphy, *An Historical Introduction to Modern Psychology* (New York: Harcourt, Brace and Co., 1929), and E. G. Boring, *The History of Experimental Psychology* (New York, 1929, and 2d ed., 1950). Boring's work was practically required memorization for all Ph.D.s graduating in psychology beginning in 1929, the year the book first came out, to 1969, the year Boring died.

And while he was still alive, where James himself was not attacked directly, what he represented was targeted instead—religious experience, psychic phenomena, the dynamic subconscious, and the philosophical assumptions of scientism in psychology.

For a contemporary assessment on one such subject, see Deborah Coon, "Testing the limits of sense and science: American experimental psychologists combat spiritualism, 1889–1920," *American Psychologist*, 47:2 (1992), pp. 143–51, which reviews the reductionist's critique of spiritualism, a debunking attitude that continues to the present and targets even those who attempt to study the phenomenon. The article makes no mention of dynamic theories of the subconscious, however; it talks about James but never gets into why he was interested in psychical research in the first place; it does not consider the problem of psychotherapy in psychology and its historical origins in psychical research; and it does not consult the historical literature on psychical research at the time, nor current historical research beyond the standard trade books in the parapsychological literature today, in order to make the case that the reductionists were justified in their rejection of the subject.

There is an important consequence from this analysis, however. Having rejected James's involvement in psychical research, having established laboratory measurement as the standard by which to judge whether or not psychology was a legitimate science, and having rejected dynamic theories of inner experience, it is easy to see how the growing number of academic psychologists could have overlooked the import of James's radical empiricism.

THE JAMESEAN TRADITION IN AMERICAN PSYCHOLOGY

Nevertheless, after James's death in 1910, numerous works appeared by his intellectual compatriots attempting to articulate the trajectory of his thought. Among them were Theodore Flournoy, "Radical empiricism," in T. Flournoy, *The Philosophy of William James* (orig. French ed., 1911) (New York: Henry Holt, 1917), pp. 68–69; Emil Boutroux, "Metaphysical views," in E. Boutroux, *William James* (New York: Longmans, Green, 1912); Horace Kallen, "Radical empiricism and the philosophic tradition," in H. Kallen, *William James and Henri Bergson* (Chicago: University of Chicago Press, 1914), pp. 1–30; Henri Bergson, "De la multiplicité des états de conscience: L'idée de durée," in Bergson, *Essai sur les données immédiates de la conscience* (Paris: Alcan, 1908), pp. 57–106; Henri Bergson, "On the pragmatism of William James: Truth and reality," in Bergson, *The Creative Mind* (Introduction to *Le Pragmatisme*, 1911), trans. Mabelle L. Addison (New York: Philosophical Library, 1946), pp. 248–60; William Ernest Hocking, "The elementary experience of other conscious being in its relations to the elementary experiences of physical and reflexive objects," Ph.D. diss., Harvard University, 1904, HU 90.589 (a thoroughly Jamesean and Roycean document that mentions neither one of them even once. Signed instead by Münsterberg, Palmer, and Santayana); J. Dewey, "The vanishing subject in the psychology of James," *Journal of Philosophy*, 37 (October 24, 1940), pp. 589–99; W. MacDougall, "The work of William James: II. As a psychologist," *Sociological Review*, 3 (1910), pp. 314–15, and others.

In 1908, Edwin Bissell Holt completed his manuscript for *The Concept of Consciousness* (London: George Allen and Co., 1914), in which he expressly stated that "the definition of consciousness in the following pages is in no small part inspired by the Radical Empiricism of Professor James; and is, I believe, throughout consonant with that view" (p. xiii). Holt then proceeds to a discussion of mathematical logic, ignoring any reference to a dynamic conception of the subconscious, or to James's urging of psychologists to study the fall of the threshold. The result is a text in which consciousness fulfills its promise, as the title implies, by ending up as the mere object of a preposition. Holt participated with Ralph Barton Perry and others in launching the New Realism (E. B. Holt, W. T. Marvin, W. P. Montague, R. B. Perry, W. B. Pitkin, and E. G. Spaulding, *The New Realism: Comparative Studies in Philosophy* [New York: Macmillan, 1912]), a philosophical movement refuting naive realism, dualism, and subjectivism, which began with James's radical empiricism but veered off in the direction of each author's respective interests. Holt later wrote *Animal Drive and the Learning Process: An Essay toward Radical Empiricism* (New York: Henry Holt, 1931), dedicated to Morton Prince and allegedly based on James's ideas, which by then in Holt's hands had become a justification for behaviorism.

James's influence on the personality-social psychologists of the 1930s and 40s, particularly Gordon Allport, Gardner Murphy, and Henry Murray, is assessed in E. I. Taylor, "The case for a uniquely American Jamesian tradition in psychology," in Margaret Donnelly, ed., *Reinterpreting the Legacy of William James* (APA Centennial William James Lectures) (Washington, D.C.: American Psychological Association, 1992), pp. 3–28. Compare this, however, with Daniel Robinson, "Is there a Jamesean tradition in psychology?" *American Psychologist*, 48:6 (1993), pp. 638–43, where the author claims that the Jamesean tradition is to be located in James's own skepticism toward theorizing, his commitment to pragmatism, and his attempt to ground psychology in experience, in whatever way it comes to us. The conclusion is that this is all so broad that no Jamesean "school" is thus possible. I would counter by saying that this does define a "school," largely made up of most psychologists; and that it is precisely this functional Jamesean tradition that defines the larger portion of American psychology.

For some contemporary statements on James within the psychology of religion, see Mark Stern, ed., "Fechner's *The Little Book on Life after Death*," including an introduction by William James with contemporary essays and commentaries by David Bakan, Eugene Taylor, Wolfgang Bringmann, and Stanley Krippner, special issue of *The Journal of Pastoral Counseling*, 27 (1992); G. William Barnard, "Exploring unseen worlds: William James and the philosophy of mysticism, University of Chicago diss., the Divinity School, 1994; Bennett Ramsey, *Submitting to Freedom: The Religious Vision of William James* (New York: Oxford University Press, 1995); and now Paul Croce, *The Eclipse of Certainty: Science and Religion in the Era of William James* (Chapel Hill: University of North Carolina Press, 1995).

The classic work in parapsychology remains G. Murphy and R. Ballou, *William James and Psychical Research* (New York: Viking, 1960); and for an assessment of the Jamesean line running into humanistic psychology, see E. I. Taylor, "William James and the humanistic tradition," *Journal of Humanistic Psychology*, 31:1 (1991), pp. 56–74, in which connections are drawn from James to modern-day parapsychology, contemporary interest in classical Eastern psychology, the existential-phenomenological movement, and humanistic psychology of the 1960s through the personality-social psychologies of the 1930s and 1940s.

JAMES AND EXISTENTIAL PHENOMENOLOGY

While experimental psychologists rejected James's metaphysics of radical empiricism as too philosophical and irrelevant for psychology as a developing science, his metaphysics addressing experimentalism was taken seriously by European existentialists and phenomenologists. Bergson was a main avenue of entry into French philosophy after 1900, leading to existentialists such as Sartre and French phenomenologists such as Merleau-Ponty. First Brentano and Stumpf, then William Ernest Hocking were the avenues by which Jamesean thought reached Husserl and hence influenced the German phenomenological tradition. These lines are only partially documented by the existentialist and phenomenological historians themselves, however.

Meanwhile, there is a case to be made for the interpretation that radical empiricism incubated in these essentially pessimistic, nonrational, and radically European traditions until the 1950s, when a series of historical events brought the era of Hullean behaviorism to a close and led to, among other developments, the humanistic revolution in American psychology. Existentialism and phenomenology then found their way into American psychology and psychiatry through the writings of Karl Jaspers, Ludwig Binswanger, Medard Boss, and Victor Frankl. A seminal text in this return was Rollo May, E. Angel, and H. Ellenberger, *Existence: A New Dimension of Psychology and Psychiatry* (New York: Basic Books). Meanwhile, May continued to represent William James's ideas to the burgeoning community of humanistic psychologists. Through the humanistic psychologists, the continental tradition of Satre, Merleau Ponty, Heidegger, Husserl, Uno Muno, e Gassett, Kierkegaard, and others became distinctly Americanized. One product of this assimilation was R. May, *Existential Psychology* (New York: Random House, 1961), a collection of invited papers by psychologists such as Carl Rogers and Gordon Allport on the existential and phenomenological aspects of the new psychology.

Meanwhile, James's work was experiencing a renaissance in existential and phenomenological circles in Europe and the United States: Aron Gurwitsch, "William James's theory of the transitive parts of the stream of consciousness," in A. Gurwitsch, ed., *Studies in Phenomenology and Psychology* (Evanston, Ill.: Northwestern University Press, 1966); John Wild, "William James and existential authenticity," *Journal of Existentialism*, 5 (1965), pp. 243–56; Joseph Cockelman, *Edmund Husserl's Phenomenological Psychology: A Historico-Critical Study* (Pittsburgh: Dusquesne University Press, 1967); Johannes Linschoten, *On the Way toward a Phenomenological Psychology: The Psychology of William James*, 1968, ed. Amedeo Giorgi, trans. from the Dutch (Utrecht, 1959); Bruce Wilshire, *William James and Phenomenology: A Study of the Principles of Psychology* (Bloomington: Indiana University Press, 1968); James M. Edie, "William James and the phenomenology of religious experience," in M. Novak, ed., *American Philosophy and the Future* (New York: Scribner's, 1968); and John Wild, *William James and Radical Empiricism* (Garden City, N.Y.: Doubleday, 1969), to name but a few.

James and Contemporary Psychology

While these developments were going on outside American academic psychology, many symposia on James have been held by academic psychologists throughout the decades. One such occurred in 1966, when a group within the American Psychological Association paid their tribute to James with presentations that were meant to honor the seventy-fifth anniversary of the APA. Four symposia were held, chaired, respectively, by R. B. MacLeod, Sigmund Koch, Richard L. Solomon, and David Shakow. David Kretch spoke on "Does Behavior Really Need a Brain? In Praise of William James: Some Historical Musings, Vain Lamentations, and a Sounding of Great Expectations," with responses by George Mandler and Peter Milner. Harry Harlow presented "William James and Instinct Theory," with responses by Sidney W. Bijou and Ogden Lindsley. Ernest Hilgard presented "Levels of Awareness: Second Thoughts on Some of William James' Ideas," with responses by Paul Bakan and Jerome L. Singer. Rollo May presented "William James's Humanism and the Problem of the Will," with responses by James F. T. Bugental, Nevitt Sanford, and Silvan Tomkins.

While the point was to honor both James and the APA in the spirit of fair play, the commentators were instructed to be as nasty as possible. For some this was difficult, for others easy. In fact, three of the respondents not included were unwilling to have their comments placed on record. The partial proceedings were subsequently published as Robert B. MacLeod, ed., *William James: Unfinished Business* (Washington, D.C.: APA, 1969).

THE COLLECTED WORKS PROJECT

During the 1970s and 1980s, the American Council of Learned Societies, in cooperation with the National Endowment for the Humanities, produced a definitive edition of the works of William James: F. Burkhardt, F. Bowers, and I. Skrupskelis, eds., *The Works of William James*, 17 vols. (Cambridge, Mass.: Harvard University Press, 1975–88). Because so much material continued to be unearthed, a chronological edition was deemed unfeasible. Therefore, the attempt was made to organize James's writings by field and then publish his individual works chronologically within each field. While the task was monumental, needed, and, finally, masterful in its completion, the final product had several problems. For instance, individual items cannot easily be located because there is no chronology of James's complete writings since publication of the *The Works*; there is no master index to the Harvard edition, nor are there even any volume numbers on the covers; and most of the smaller essays are mixed up under philosophy, psychology, and religion in ways that are arbitrary or that cut into the interdisciplinary character of James's thinking.

But all this is a minor inconvenience when compared to the ease of availability of James's writings that the set provides. The inconvenience is further adumbrated by reminding students of the old archival anecdote: When asked about assisting in the compilation of a concordance to the Bible, one religious scholar replied, "But why do you need a concordance if you've read it?"

The larger point is that the project was organized by philosophers and archivists, so that not only the order of texts, but the various introductions are all largely philosophical or archival. Only three psychologists contributed introductions, all absolutely worth reading. None of them were strictly so-called Jameseans, however, but rather Titchenerians, Cattelleans, and Germanic scholars in the history of psychology who valiantly attempted to represent James's point of view. The introductions in chronological order are as follows:

H. S. Thayer, introduction to *Pragmatism* (1975), pp. xi–xxxviii. Looks into the historical origins of pragmatism in James's writings before 1907, considers the intention and content of James's chapters and the response to the book once it was published, but remains thoroughly analytic and philosophical in its tone and orientation.

John J. McDermott, introduction to *Essays in Radical Empiricism* (1976), pp. xi–xlvii. Perhaps the most important and seminal of the introductions in the series, except that the author traces the history of James's doctrine of radical empiricism for philosophers, not with an eye toward reconstructing the doctrine as James orginally meant it for psychologists.

H. S. Thayer, Introduction to *The Meaning of Truth: A Sequel to Pragmatism*

(1975), pp. xi–xlvi, presents an analysis by a philosopher who deals only with James's pragmatism as a verification of truth claims and with James's arguments against absolute idealism.

Richard J. Bernstein, introduction to *A Pluralistic Universe* (1977), pp. v–xxix. Being the Hibbert Lectures, which James delivered at Oxford in 1908, the author notes that their content coincides with James's increasing preoccupation with metaphysical and epistemological questions at the end of his career, through which James wove a distinctly psychological content. Bernstein maintains that, while James had lectured on the nature of philosophic vision, later commentators were disappointed that he developed nothing *systematic*. (A *systematic* Jamesean, it seems to me, is possible, but something of an oxymoron.) James had preferred instead to outline the major defects of absolute idealism, the type of philosophy which in various forms continues to grip the center of Western thought to this day. Not unexpectedly, James comes across in this introduction, as in others, as primarily a philosopher.

John J. McDermott, introduction to *Essays in Philosophy* (1978), pp. xi–xxxv. Achieves the difficult task of summarizing the main themes of a polyglot of essays on approximately the subject of philosophy (as conceived by the editors, not James himself) which James published over a thirty-four-year period. As an indication of the arbitrariness of placement, James's presidential address to the American Psychological Association, delivered in 1894, is included here, for instance.

E. H. Madden, introduction to *The Will to Believe* (1979), pp. xi–xxxviii. States the main thread of this collection of essays that James penned during a seventeen-year period, emphasizing the impossibility of intellectual decisions that are devoid of volition and personal subjectivity and reiterating the unequivocal subordination of thought to emotion. Here, radical empiricism is finally named, although not extensively developed. Madden is skeptical, however, that James is really serious, claiming like so many other empiricists who follow the British tradition that he cannot see the relation between James's radical empricism in the "Will to Believe" and "Does Consciousness Exist?" Madden does well in interpreting the first four of James's essays on the question of belief when the evidence in support of a conclusion is indecisive; he fares about the same, discussing the essays that show how neither determinism nor indeterminism can be finally established on purely intellectual grounds; that moral judgments are derived from experience, not the other way around; and that Hegel's problem was that he lacked oxygen. But Madden had no idea what James was getting at with his interest in psychical research, believing that it held him back from developing his later philosophy of natural realism.

Peter Hare, introduction to *Some Problems in Philosophy* (1979), pp. xiii–xli, comments on the last book James was working on just weeks before he died, his unfinished arch, in the sense that it failed to carry the philosophical weight he had intended. Thus, this is a philosophical introduction to James's attempt at a systematic philosophy combining radical empiricism with pragmatism and pluralism.

Gerald E. Myers, "Introduction: The intellectual context," in *The Principles of Psychology*, vol. 1 (1981), pp. xi–xl. Analyzes James from the present reality that philosophy and psychology are now "legally and politically divorced," whereas James's thought, the author points out, epitomizes the ambivalent bonding of the two. The discussion proceeds along the assumption that the proper criteria for judging James's ideas are logic, proof, and consistency. The author notes the new interest in *The Principles* by the phenomenologists, but believes erroneously that "James' interest in abnormal psychology and in psychical research led him to a belief in the unconscious" (p. xl), since the unconscious is a distinctly Freudian and not a Jamesean term.

Rand B. Evans, "Introduction: The historical context," in *The Principles of Psychology*, vol. 1 (1981), pp. xli–lxvi. A rich and detailed essay in the history of psychology about William James, written by an experimentalist and a Titchenerian from those viewpoints.

John J. McDermott, introduction to *Essays in Religion and Morality* (1982), pp. xi–xxvii. A survey of essays James wrote on religious and religiously tinged subjects between 1884 and 1910, including a comparison of William with his father, Henry James, Sr., and the ways in which much of William's later work was a perpetual and unending answer to his father's religious metaphysics.

William Woodward, introduction to *Essays in Psychology* (1983), pp. xi–xxxix, acknowledges James's stronger emphasis on secondary personalities, hypnosis, and "saving sick souls," after 1890, and James's point of view as largely "functional" and "phenomenological." Then he did a good job of reviewing the essays, which in toto, as I have indicated, were writings that the editors, not James, grouped under the rubric of psychology. The general discussion of functionalism in psychology is an important one.

Gerald E. Myers, introduction to *Talks to Teachers on Psychology* (1983), pp. xi–xxvii. An informative historical essay by a philosopher on the content of *Talks to Teachers* and James's ideas concerning education. Slights the *Talks to Students on Some of Life's Ideals* (the second part of James's original title, omitted on the cover of the Harvard edition), despite the fact that James himself said the *Talks to Students* represented the central vision of his own worldview. Further, Myers skips two of the most important pieces, "On a certain blindness in human beings," and "What makes a life significant"; and with regard to what he does mention, he overemphasizes the usual list of suspects always mentioned as the sources of James's ideas without reference to the more likely historical sources unknown to the author (the obvious influence of Vivekananda on James's "Gospel of Relaxation," for instance).

Michael M. Sokal, introduction to *Psychology: Briefer Course* (1984), pp. xi–xli. Written by a historian of psychology and biographer of James McKeen Cattell, this is a lively introduction to the book in James's corpus held by all in lowest regard, but which probably made for James the most money as a college textbook because it was widely adopted for years after its first appearence.

John E. Smith, introduction to *The Varieties of Religious Experience* (1985), pp. xi–li. The author believes this was a book on religion rather than the psychology of religion, but acknowledges James's own comment that it was both psychology and metaphysics. Looks into James's own religious convictions, but sparingly, and with no mention of Swedenborg or the works of Henry James, Sr. The author does consider reception of *The Varieties* in terms of both praise and criticism and is prescient enough to see the connection between James and Jung, but gives no details, which are already a part of the published literature. He also has a section on James's ideas about subliminal consciousness and the influence of this idea on various themes in *The Varieties*, and ends with a note on the significance of James's analysis of religious experience, whether one agrees with it or not.

Robert McDermott, introduction to *Essays in Psychical Research* (1986), pp. xiii–xxxvi. Addresses James's intent to bear the tension between psychic phenomena, science, and religion, but gives no clue that, especially after 1890, a dynamic psychology of the subconscious was the focus of this concatenated union. Emphasizes the British Society for Psychical Research, yet omits any reference to the role James played for two decades in the American Society for Psychical Research. Gives a good account of the investigations with Mrs. Piper and of F.W.H. Myers's influence on James's thinking. Considers a few general philosophical implications but does not draw them out or link them to James's radical empiricism, and ends with a section on the general and permanently negative reception afforded investigators of the paranormal from James's time to the present.

I. Skrupskelis, introduction to *Manuscript Essays and Notes* (1988), pp. xiii–xlviii. Struggles once again with the problem of categorizing James's thought, opting in the end for the categories of philosophy, psychology, and religion, but again the grouping of manuscripts under these headings was not James's own. The editors' job is made even more difficult with these materials because, although approximately dated, they were unpublished, making James's intentions even less clear.

I. Skrupskelis, introduction to *Essays, Comments, and Reviews* (1987), pp. xx–xxxix. An essay on the route by which previously unknown writings by James were unearthed and the impact on scholarship of bibliographic gaps in the known James corpus, to which the present volume makes numerous new additions. The emphasis is primarily on what would interest philosophers.

I. Skrupskelis, introduction to *Manuscript Lectures* (1988), pp. xvii–lxiii. Starts with the relationship between William James and Charles William Eliot, two men whose careers were extensively intertwined, before turning to comments on James's teaching career at Harvard. Historically detailed, very full—one of the best introductions of the series.

JAMES'S *PRINCIPLES* AT ONE HUNDRED

Psychological Science

One of the many events celebrating the one hundredth anniversary publication of James's *Principles of Psychology* in 1990 was the May issue of *Psychological Science*, 1:3, journal of the American Psychological Society, at their core a group of some 2,000 academic psychologists who bolted from the 75,000-member American Psychological Association because of the growing power of clinical psychologists. Papers for the special issue of *Psychological Science* were invited to estimate James's importance and to report on the status of his ideas today in selected subject areas of the discipline.

The introduction (*Psychological Science*, 1:3 [May 1990], pp. 149–50) is by Professor William Estes (former editor of the journal and current resident of James's old house), who notes James's extensive influence on developments in cognitive psychology, but who invited his writers to review James for any actual principles in *The Principles*.

Gregory Kimble, author of "A search for principles in *Principles of Psychology*," pp. 151–55, is convinced that the discipline is nothing but the science of behavior and that after a century psychology has made only two contributions—the controlled experiment, and the mental test. He takes a stab at the task of analyzing James with reference to his own published standards *á la* content and methodology. In the end, he finds James's work "a compendium of speculation, with very few threads to tie materials together," containing no methodology to speak of. He was excited, however, about the numerous correspondences between James's insights and what we know today.

David LaBerg, who wrote on "Attention," pp. 156–62, did a retrospective survey of the literature on attention and found nothing startlingly new since James's original statements, but only further conceptual refinement and more exact laboratory measures. These include studies on selection and expectation, automatic processing, shifts in attention, and the relation of James's ideas to modern connectionism and to recent studies on brain localization.

William Dember, who wrote "William James on sensation and perception," pp. 163–66, tackled James by focusing primarily on James's chapter on "Discrimination and comparison." While James covered many topics still of interest today, Dember pointed out, perceptual psychologists do not cite him. This may be due to James's attitude toward classical psychophysical methods, in which James himself said that he found "the proper psychological outcome of that work [to be] just nothing." Nevertheless, Dember concludes on rereading James's S & P chapters that "they are filled with insights and examples both from real life and from the laboratory that at the very least can help students and researchers locate their narrow, parochial problems in a richer, broader psychological/philosophical context."

Raymond Nickerson, who authored "William James on reasoning," pp. 167–71, addressed James on reasoning, that is, the ability to deal with novel data, which separates human beings from the mere reproductive abilities of the beasts. Nickerson claimed that James's treatment of the subject, however, was not exhaustive, but selective. James failed to mention the relations between reason and language, or reason and thinking, and he omitted even mentioning deduction and induction. But, Nickerson pointed out, psychology has yet to improve upon James's accurate and widely referenced distinction between association by similarity and association by contiguity. The author then makes the shrewd observation that many psychologists claim originality for ideas that James had already written about one hundred years ago. This is because, quoting George Miller, that, while every psychologist has a copy of *The Principles* on the shelf, few have actually read the book from cover to cover. The work, Nickerson concludes, actually deserves to be read.

Richard Thompson, author of "The neurobiology of learning and memory," pp. 172–73, maintained, following Kretch, that James did much to set the stage for psychobiology. "Beyond insisting that brain structures and processes must be the basis of explanations of mental phenomena, [James] expressed ideas about brain localization and plasticity in neural networks that foreshadowed many aspects of current neurobiology of learning and even connectionist theory."

John Kihlstrom and Kevin McConkey, who wrote "William James and Hypnosis: A centennial reflection," pp. 174–77, reviewed the current status of James on hypnosis. While modern researchers will find much that is familiar in *The Principles*, they say, subsequent research since 1890 has shown that posthypnotic amnesia is suggested rather than spontaneous, and that hypnotized subjects show neither sensory hyperesthesia nor transcendence of their normal cognitive and motor abilities. James also ignored individual differences in hypnotic suggestibility. He did believe, however, that the suggestion theory of hypnosis was correct, "provided we grant the trance-state as its prerequisite." Here again, James scooped modern researchers, who remain split on this issue, probably because of their own narrow biases.

George Mandler, author of "William James and the construction of emotion," pp. 179–80, reviewed James on the emotions. James's controversial theory, that the physiological reverberations of immediate perception *were* the emotions, was flatly rejected at the time by Wundt, Sully, and others, later ignored by the behaviorists, then allegedly debunked by Cannon's neurohumoral theory. It has made a recent comeback, however, with the sudy of cognitive/visceral theories.

Hazel Markus, who wrote "On splitting the universe," pp. 181–85, concluded with an analysis of James on the self, probably the best paper of the collection. The self is not only central to James, but is probably central to all of psychology. Nevertheless, psychologists are still only allowed to study what they can measure, so they ignore this major orienting idea. Perhaps this is what James meant when he said that there is an inverse ratio between exactitude and relevance. A functional psychology of the self may yet have its day, however.

Professor Estes returned again for a postscript on p. 185, concluding that psychologists still have to figure out the goal of basic research; they must address the conundrum of applied scientific knowledge, since most research is relevant only to abstract theory, and they have to ascertain the relation between experimentation and scholarship, since this has not yet been established. Psychology, in other words, has not yet reached a stage where agreement on basic principles is possible.

In the present reviewer's opinion, this may be because, as James knew one hundred years ago and Sigmund Koch has recently affirmed, a single unified field may never occur, since psychology appears to be an inherently pluralistic enterprise spanning both the arts *and* the sciences.

Personality and Social Psychology Bulletin

Another event commemorating James's *Principles of Psychology* at 100 was a special issue of the *Personality and Social Psychology Bulletin*, 16:4 (1990).

J. T. Cacioppo, "The Centennary of William James's *Principles of Psychology*: From the chaos of mental life to the science of psychology." pp. 601–61, defines the parameters within which the rest of the articles will fall, namely, to address James's contemporary relevance to theory and methods in psychology, especially on topics related to personality and social functioning. James's conception of the self is worked over in the majority of the articles, including E. S. Knowles and

M. E. Sibikey, "Continuity and diversity in the stream of selves: Metaphorical resolutions of William James's one-in-many-selves paradox," pp. 676–787; M. J. Strube, "In search of self: Balancing the good and the true," pp. 699–704; R. A. Lamphere and M. R. Leary, "Private and public self-processes: A return to James's constituents of the self," pp. 717–25; A. H. Baumgardner, C. M. Kaufman, and J. A. Cranford, "To be noticed favorably: Links between private self and public self," pp. 705–16; S. E. Cross and H. R. Markus, "The willful self," pp. 726–42; and J. Suls and C. A. Marco, "William James, the self, and the selective industry of the mind," pp. 688–98. The Jamesean theory of the emotions is the next most frequently considered topic: J. Blascovitch, "Individual differences in physiological arousal and perception of arousal: Missing links in James's notion of arousal-based behaviors," pp. 665–75; C. E. Izard, "The substrates and functions of emotion feelings: William James and current emotion theory," pp. 626–35; J. D. Laird, "William James and the mechanisms of emotional experience," pp. 636–51. James on thinking and perceiving comes next: J. W. Pennebaker, J. A. Czajka, R. Cropanzano, B. C. Richards, S. Brumbelow, K. Ferrara, R. Thompson, and Toosje Thyssen, "Levels of thinking," pp. 743–57; J. A. Schellenberg, "William James and symbolic interactionism," pp. 769–73; and W. M. Winton, "Jamesean aspects of misattribution research," pp. 652–64. One article deals with motivation in the context of religious behavior; Daniel Bateson, "Good Samaritans—Or priests and Levites? Using William James as a guide in the study of religious prosocial motivation," pp. 758–68; while only one article starts to think globally about certain aspects of personality theory and epistemology: R. Buck, "William James, the nature of knowledge, and current issues in emotion, cognition, and communication," pp. 612–25.

American Journal of Psychology

As well, the *American Journal of Psychology*, 103:4, carried two articles: Rand Evans, "William James, *The Principles of Psychology*, and experimental psychology," pp. 433–47; and D. W. Massaro, "A century later: Reflections on *The Principles of Psychology* by William James and on the review by G. Stanley Hall," pp. 539–45.

Evans takes up two questions: First, why is William James remembered as the father of experimental psychology in America if he hated laboratory work so much and was so critical of the experimentalists' tradition? And second, what were some of the lines of influence that can be traced from *The Principles* up to today in experimental psychology? Evans believes (somewhat erroneously in my opinion) that "James's early education had contained very little science," and, without reference to the primary documents (James's studies using descriptive statistics, for instance) he relies too heavily on what other commentators such as Perry have said (they both thought that James's early training was merely biological and observational). Evans's article is, nevertheless, quite thoughtful from an experimentalists' perspective. He concludes, rightly, in my opinion, that "To the degree that he was more than a philosophical psychologist, James was closer to being a scientific psychologist in the broad meaning of that term, rather than an experimental psychologist" (p. 443). Evans also retraces his steps a little from his previous statement in his introduction in James's collected works by now saying that *The Principles* was not James's last word on psychology (referring now to James's later formulations of radical empiricism). He concludes by comparing James to the larger science of figures such as Darwin or Freud, rather than the tedious measurements of Cattell or Titchener, or modern laboratory researchers, and he holds the line on the still implied superiority of the experimentalists' position in psychology.

Massarro's introduction to the reprint of Hall's review of James's *Principles* (which first appeared in that same journal one hundred years earlier), is a delightful and not inaccurate statement on James by an experimentalist, although he believes James was a dualist (which is not exactly correct—James was probably a dualist only one day a month. A day later he may have sounded like a monist, but all the rest of the time he stuck to noetic pluralism).

William James after a Century

And another commemoration of *The Principles* was M. G. Johnson and T. B. Henley, eds., *Reflections on The Principles of Psychology: William James after a century*. With a foreword by Roger Brown (Hillsdale, N.J.: Lawrence Earlbaum, 1990).

In his foreword, Harvard psychologist Roger Brown begins by praising James's writing style, even elevating some of the chapters in *The Principles* to the level of the poetic. The remainder of the foreword is a discourse on Brown's study of the tip-of-the-tongue phenomenon, in the hope that James would have also acknowledged this as one of the "hard facts of psychology." Other chapters are as follows:

Rand B. Evans, "William James and his *Principles*," pp. 11–32. In a densely packed biographical statement, Evans reviews James's life up to the writing of *The Principles*, concluding that many of James's problems stemmed from a prolonged adolescence that lasted until he was in his late thirties.

E. I. Taylor, "New light on the origin of James's experimental psychology," pp. 33–62. Locates James's experimental method in the tradition of French experimental physiology and the French Experimental Psychology of the Subconscious, a fact that continues to be overlooked by psychologists who claim that James never did any experiments because he was not a Wundtian.

Amedeo Giorgi, "The implications of James's 'Plea for Psychology as a Natural Science,'" pp. 63–77. Reviews James's controversy with George T. Ladd over whether or not it was possible to have a psychology free of metaphysics. Giorgi then proceeds to define what such a psychology might look like from a phenomenological point of view, using the concepts of essence, intentionality, and the phenomenological reduction from Husserl.

Mary Henle, "William James and Gestalt psychology," pp. 77–100, makes an intellectual rather than historical comparison between James and Gestalt on the concepts of mechanism, atomism, associationism, organization, and convergences. Henle concludes that, with regard to the advances made by the Gestalt psychologists, James was a transitional figure who was constrained by the inherent limits of the physiology of his day.

David E. Leary, "William James on the self and personality: Clearing the ground for subsequent theorists, researchers, and practitioners," pp. 101–38, is a close analysis of James on the self and personality, especially during the last two decades of James's writing. Leary presciently cites Emerson's early influence and also mentions James's work on psychopathology during the 1890s. He also correctly cites the extensive influence of F.W.H. Myers, draws important inferences regarding James's subsequent impact on personality, abnormal, and social psychology, and includes some surprising references to James in authors such as Vygotsky.

John C. Malone, Jr., "William James and habit: A century later," pp. 139–66. *The Principles* contained nothing original, particularly the chapter on habit, a theme which, Malone feels, pervades almost every chapter in *The Principles*. Defined as the law of association by contiguity, Malone also finds the construct of habit in Watson and Thorndike, as well as in later learning theorists such as Hull, Guthrie, and Skinner. It is then only a short step to modern connectionist models and social cognitive theory. He concludes that if the first one hundred years show us anything, it is that psychology will likely still look the same in the year 2090.

Herbert F. Crovitz, "Association, cognition, and neural networks," pp. 167–82, also takes up the concept of association, which, the author maintains, rather than dying out, has experienced a new vogue with computer modeling of brain states, much to the chagrin of some cognitivists. The author's position is that the differences between associationist and cognitive theory rest in the investigation of two hypothesized brain systems: one for memory, and one for habit and learning.

Sohee Park and Stephen M. Kosslyn, "Imagination," pp. 183–96. Although it somewhat overblows James's learning experience in Germany, the article maintains that James's study of imagery in *The Principles* remains surprisingly modern. Imagery, the authors believe, is to be understood by studying how we conceptualize and the neural substrate of such activities, which is how James also approached the topic.

Irvin Rock, "A look back at William James's theory of perception," pp. 197–230. Agrees with other commentators that James's grasp of the field of perception was significant and that, despite more sophisticated brain chemistry, methods of measurement, and hundreds of thousands of man-hours of experiments, during the past one hundred years not much has been added.

Edward S. Reed, "Space perception and the Psychologists' Fallacy in James's *Principles*," pp. 231–48. Shows how James used the issue of our perception of space as a battleground to joust with the followers of Wundt and Helmholtz. For James, space was a sensation, full and rich with meaning as either a direct experience or as a sign of experiences we have had before. His opponents saw sensation as nothing more than meaningless fragments, a view that prevails to this day. They suffer, Reed believes, from what James called the Psychologists' Fallacy, confusing one's own state of mind for the reality under investigation. Gestalt psychologists, however, tended to agree with James, as did E. B. Holt and, more recently, James Gibson.

Ronald Baenninger, "Consciousness and comparative psychology," pp. 249–70. James did not attribute consciousness in the way humans experience it to lower animals; thus, he did not suffer from zoomorphism, the belief that knowledge about lower animals was directly translatable to humans, a tendency which took over learning theory in the half century that followed James's death. Probably to James's surprise if he were alive today, consciousness in lower animals is a new topic of interest, a phenomenon that, Baenninger hopes, may help to transform our understanding of consciousness generally.

Howard R. Pollio, "The stream of consciousness since James," pp. 271–94. Examines the stream of consciousness as understood by writers in experimental psychology, psychoanalysis, literature, and philosophy (especially Bergson and the phenomenologists), ending with a summary of the major metaphors used in its modern study. Concluding that it also implicates our conception of time and the self, the author sees more pervasive use of the metaphor as the consciousness revolution proceeds.

James Deese, "James on the will," pp. 295–310. Discusses the will, a construct widely used in the era of moral philosophy, even developed by James in the context of the new scientific psychology, but soon abandoned by behaviorists and psychophysicists alike, who thought it too philosophical. James's problem, the author concludes, was that he had to spend too much time defending himself against the German experimentalists and was therefore constrained to develop the concept in more creative ways that would have benefited psychology today.

The American Psychological Association

Also in 1990, the American Psychological Association, through its Division 1 (General Psychology), commissioned the New York psychologist, Margaret Donnelly, to launch a program of William James Lectures at the annual APA meeting in Boston. Two years later, to commemorate the one hundredth anniversary of the founding of the APA, the James Lectures, which had been given by twenty-seven contributors, were gathered together and published as M. Donnelly, ed., *Reinterpreting the Legacy of William James* (Washington, D.C. : American Psychological Association, 1992).

I will select only a few of the more cogent pieces for the present discussion. The volume opened with E. I. Taylor, "The case for a uniquely American Jamesean tradition in psychology," pp. 3–28. E. G. Boring's ambivalence for William James is documented, while Henry Murray, Gordon Allport, and Gardner Murphy are raised up as the new Jameseans who held out against the reductionism of psychophysics and the hypothetico-deductive paradigm of learning theorists in American academic psychology.

In D. A. Crosby and Wayne Viney, "Toward a psychology that is radically empirical: Recapturing the vision of William James," pp. 101–17, the authors raise the question of what a radically empirical psychology might look like. The first place they look is in various chapters of *The Principles*. Then, after considering James's formal statements on radical empiricism made after 1900, they go back and ask how James might have revised *The Principles* in light of his later thought. They do not, in this exercise, make any reference to James's seminal 1894 statement to the American Psychological Association or to his 1904 presidential address, and they consider none of the information James had available on abnormal psychology that would have significantly changed *The Principles* the way he had originally written it. Skrupskelis (1995; see below) has shown, however, that in the Italian translation of *The Principles* a decade later, James still stuck to the same guns—that every science needs to be positivistic in order to launch itself, despite its ultimate dependence on metaphysics.

G. Myers, "William James and Contemporary Psychology," pp. 49–64, is a comparison of James with the behaviorism of Skinner and the cognitive psychology of William Estes, with added excursions into modern cognitive science. In the end, Myers suspects James would be very sympathetic to Kurt Goedel's theorem, suggesting that even mathematicians know equations to be true that they cannot formally prove. The author "surmises" that James's spirit is shared by Merleau-Ponty, A. Gurwitsch, R. B. MacLeod, K. Pribram, R. May, J. J. Gibson, D. Shakow, Jerome Singer, Gordon Allport, Gardner Murphy, Abraham Maslow, Saul Rosenzweig, Tom Natsoulas, and Carl Rogers, among others (p. 56).

A. Giorgi, "A Phenomenological Reinterpretation of the Jamesean Schema for Psychology," pp. 119–36, poses what psychology would look like if it were completely ensconced in a phenomenological perspective. Psychology would be conceived as a non-natural science. Metaphysics would be avoided by practicing the phenomenological reduction. Our understanding of consciousness, Giorgi believes, is not necessarily dependent on the methods of the physical sciences. Intentionality, and not purposiveness, is the essence of consciousness. Psychology is a descriptive rather then an introspective science. The subjective domain of consciousness separates psychology from the other sciences and requires a different mode of access. Here, the mind becomes an object of its own observation, and the subjective phenomenology of the science-making process becomes obvious.

In this realm, Giorgi moves us away from the exclusive focus on the presuppositions of reductionistic natural science, but still stays within the Western rational overemphasis on analysis. He prepares us, however, without specifically stating such, for the epistemological leap into classical Asian psychology.

J. Schull, "Selection—James's principal principle," pp. 139–51, focuses on selection as James's key contribution to understanding the role of consciousness in biological evolution. The author claims that we are only now in a position to understand what James was getting at, and that his contributions are relevant to understanding neural cell assemblies, connectionism, the mind-body problem, and even the biological basis of religious experience.

William Woodward, "James's evolutionary epistemology: 'Necessary Truths and the Effects of Experience,'" pp. 81–95, claims William and Henry James for the German ontological tradition of hermeneutics, which would be an entirely new development in the German reception of James's work, since only the German phenomenologists appeared to take James seriously after his death. The analysis is a good one, however. For instance, according to Woodward, Richard Rorty sees James as a Kantian (R. Rorty, *Philosophy and the Mirror of Nature*. Princeton: Princeton University Press, 1979). James, of course, wasn't; he was a reader of Swedenborg, from whom Kant borrowed heavily. The correction to Rorty, Woodward points out, is in T. B. Carlson, "The pragmatic individual: From Kant to James," Ph.D. diss., Harvard University, 1990, which chastises Rorty for reading too much Kant into James and claims that Kant was instead proto-Jamesean.

James Averill, "William James's other theory of emotion," pp. 221–29, is a creative interpretation of the *Varieties*, suggesting that James actually had two theories of emotion, one before *The Principles* and one after. Although Averill omitted any reference to James's activities in the fields of psychical research and experimental psychopathology during this 1890s, his interpretation coincides completely with my view that James's change of mind about positivistic psychology also required a radical reinterpretation of emotional life. Averill deduces this from passages in *The Varieties* rather than from looking for any new evidence in the James corpus.

The new evidence shows that, while he continued to maintain a physiological frame of reference, James began to take seriously the psychogenic hypothesis with regard to the pathology of the emotions, and this led him after 1894 to a dynamic psychology of the subconscious in the vein of F.W.H. Myers, Pierre Janet, and Morton Prince, as well as Josef Breuer and his junior partner, Sigmund Freud. As I see it, this was the new psychology of the emotions that constituted the basis for James's cases in the 1896 Lowell Lectures on "Exceptional Mental States" and *The Varieties of Religious Experience* (1902).

Wayne Viney, "A study of emotion in the context of radical empiricism," pp. 243–50, deals with James's varying definition of emotions from the standpoint of James's own later philosophical works on radical empiricism. But the author omits any reference to James's important work on experimental psychopathology, and he omits the crucial role played by scientific data on the dynamic psychology of the emotions, which eventually formed the basis for James's shift from positivism to radical empiricism (after 1894 and before *The Varieties* in 1902).

Helmut Adler, "William James and Gustav Fechner: From rejection to elective affinity," pp. 253–61, reviews the paradox of James's rejection of Fechner's psychophysics while embracing his metaphysics. The piece accepts uncritically the distorted separation by modern commentators of Fechner's empirical and mathematical studies from his later philosophical writings (Fechner himself saw them as a whole piece). The author also believes James became enamored with Fechner's metaphysics only after abandoning psychology for philosophy, so that panpsychism and psychical research could be considered (an erroneous interpretation, in my opinion). While he acknowledged that James felt Fechner's daylight view of consciousness would yet have its day, Adler concludes that James's view was merely idiosyncratic and must be judged in historical context.

Donald Dewsbury, "William James and instinct theory revisited," pp. 263–91, is an important historical paper by a distinguished comparative animal psychologist. The work reviews James's theory of instincts and traces the impact of James's theories on E. L. Thorndike, William MacDougall, Harry Harlow, and on subsequent developments in social psychology and ethology. It also contains additional notes on the influence of James's ideas in education and psychoanalysis.

Daniel N. Robinson, "William James on mind and body," pp. 313–22, and Joseph F. Rychlak, "William James and the concept of free," pp. 323–38, both deal with James's conception of consciousness, but omit any reference to a dynamic interpretation of subconscious processes which appeared throughout

James's work. Paradoxically, they are joined by Gertrude Schmeidler, "William James: Pioneering ancestor of modern parapsychology," pp. 339–52, which takes up the question of James's interest in psychical research, but without referencing its important historical relation to the development of abnormal psychology.

History of the Human Sciences

More recently, a special issue of the British journal *History of the Human Sciences,* 8:1 (1995), was devoted to articles on William James, whose star, the editor believes, appears on the rise again. Paul Jerome Croce opens the issue with "William James's scientific education," pp. 9–27, where Croce focuses on James's early interpretation of Darwin and delves into the influence of C. S. Peirce. The discussion stops there, however. Croce does touch on James's physiological background, but he does not get at the source of James's experimental method, which focused on the French experimental physiology of Claude Bernard and Charles Edouard Brown Sequard (James's experimental attitude was further informed by the German physiological techniques of Ludwig and the views of Mynert and Benedict, both of which James got through Bowditch and Putnam; see E. I. Taylor, "New light on the origin of James's experimental psychology," in T. Henley and M. Johnson, eds., *Reflections on The Principles of Psychology: William James after a Century* [New York: Earlbaum, 1990], 33–62).

E. I. Taylor writes on "Radical empiricism and the new science of consciousness," pp. 47–60, which makes the case for James's relevance to new developments in the neurosciences.

Max Herzog follows with "William James and the development of phenomenological psychology in Europe," pp. 29–46. Herzog gives an altogether new and original interpretation of James's place in the history of phenomenology. Up to now, James has been considered a proto-phenomenologist, because he came before Husserl. Herzog shows, however, that phenomenology was already developing (James called it "phenomenalism") in the work of Brentano, Stumpf, Bergson, Avenarius, and Mach, before Husserl, and that "James responded to the work of these writers and formed on this basis a phenomenological unity. The place of honor as a founder of phenomenological psychology therefore belongs to James" (p. 30). Herzog further chronicles the reception of James's ideas in European phenomenological circles and describes the new renaissance of interest in James's phenomenology over Husserl's after being recently reintroduced to contemporary phenomenologists by Linschoten, Gurwitsch, and Giorgi. (There may be, however, a still unmined connection between James and Husserl through William Ernest Hocking. See E. I. Taylor, "William James and the humanistic tradition," *Journal of Humanistic Psychology,* 31:1 [1991]).

Edward Reed writes on "The psychologist's fallacy as a persistent framework in William James's psychological theorizing," pp. 61–72. Reed's analysis spans the period of what he believes to be James's three texts in psychology, proper: *The Principles* (1890), *Briefer Course* (1892), and *Talks to Teachers* (1899). While he supports the idea that James continued to write on psychology during the 1890s, he makes no references to James's work in experimental psychopathology, nor to psychical research. Consequently, he skips over the epistemological problem of the subconscious altogether, although trying to make a comprehensive statement. (See, however, E. I. Taylor, *William James on Exceptional Mental States: Reconstruction of the 1896 unpublished Lowell Lectures* [New York: Scribner's Sons, 1982]).

Ignas Skrupskelis follows with "James's conception of psychology as a natural science," pp. 73–89. In this essay, Skrupskelis examines the James corpus for those texts that shed light on what James said about the relation between psychology and metaphysics. He rightly acknowledges James's view that "the ordinary positivist has simply a bad metaphysics which he refuses to critique or discuss." But Skrupskelis "explains away," on rather thin grounds and without analyzing the piece in detail, James's 1894 statement in "The Knowing of Things Together," in which James disavows an exclusive focus on the positivist agenda for psychology. (For a more detailed look at this 1894 essay, see chapter 7 of the present volume.)

David Leary ends the special James issue with "William James, the psychologists' dilemma, and the historiography of psychology: Cautionary tales," pp. 91–105. Leary explores James's dilemma to construct either an objective science of the self or a psychology compatible with the self as subjectively experienced. He does so by showing how the psychology that James evolved is a vote for the idea that there is no such thing as disinterested knowledge. Leary therefore would be sympathetic to my thesis that James was creating a person-centered science. Leary is also one of the few psychologists who correctly places James in line with the transcendentalists as well as Darwin; he acknowledges the Jamesean debt in the work of Allport, Murray, Rogers, and Kelly; and outlines the relevance of James's ideas on the new self-psychology and on the burgeoning postpositivist philosophy of science.

PSYCHOLOGISTS' PERCEPTION OF JAMES

A case in point is Richard L. Gregory, "Editorial: Perceptions of William James—at the centenary of *The Principles of Psychology*, in *Perception*," 19 (1990), pp. 701–4. After some general biographical facts, the author declares emphatically, "Although James set up a laboratory at Harvard he did virtually no experimental work himself" (p. 701). The author sees James's pragmatism ("which held that meaning is use") as a forerunner of logical positivism (it was the forerunner of many strands of philosophy, most of which were hostile to the reductionism of the positivists); he believes that the James-Lange theory has been largely abandoned for modern theories of emotion as "brain-based" (which contradicts the opinion of other psychologists who have similarly commented on James's theory) and believes that James spoke across a range, from experience to behavior (James voted for experience, not experience and behavior, which is the compromising phrase psychologists today use in the new cognitive-behaviorist era). Finally, he largely confines his comments about James to just those sections of *The Principles* that deal with perception (generalizing from there to the rest of psychology).

A much more challenging piece can be found in Daniel N. Robinson's "Is there a Jamesean tradition in psychology?" *American Psychologist*, 48:6 (June 1993), pp. 638–43. Robinson's position is that, regardless of what James said, mainstream psychology has remained to this day largely positivistic and experimental. Psychology still lacks any sense of a personally identifiable human being at the center of what it studies. In this sense there is no trace of the "tradition" of William James. That tradition, according to Robinson, resides with James's own originality, so there cannot really be a Jamesean tradition in psychology, except where we find the impulse toward self-criticism. I demur, believing that the experimentalists' position that has gotten the upper hand since James's time does not really represent what the majority of psychologists actually do. What they do is, instead, thoroughly Jamesean in that it is pluralistic, pragmatic, eclectic, and not able to be unified under any one banner, let alone be principally informed by the experimentalists' methods (compare, for instance, what a college textbook says psychology is, with the annual program of the American Psychological Association).

Radical Empiricism for Psychologists

Arthur F. Bentley, in "The Jamesean datum," *Journal of Psychology*, 16 (July 1943), pp. 35–79, and "Truth, reality and behavioral fact," *Journal of Philosophy*, 40 (April 1943), pp. 169–87, is one of the first in the modern period to remind psychologists that radical empiricism and not pragmatism was the core of James's philosophy. The main voice today establishing that radical empiricism was the core of James's metaphysics has been John J. McDermott in his introduction to *The Writings of William James* (New York: Random House, 1967). The argument has been most cogently carried forward by McDermott's student, Charlene Haddock Seigfried, in *Chaos and Context: A Study in William James* (Athens: Ohio University Press, 1978), and *William James's Radical Reconstruction of Philosophy* (Albany: State University of New York Press, 1990). Beyond these works, the philosophical literature on James's radical empiricism is actually significant and growing. See, for instance, the collection of papers in M. H. DeArmey and S. Skousgaard, eds., *The Philosophical Psychology of William James* (Washington, D.C.: Center for Advanced Research in Phenomenology and University Press of America, 1986). The question is, to what extent do these philosophers have any impact on the epistemological foundations underlying the way psychology is conducted? The answer is that their impact is probably very small. However, great storms are often announced by a small breeze. More recently, in the contemporary literature the psychologist Wayne Viney has been reviewing the relevance of James's radical empiricism for the discipline of psychology (see above). And for an application of James's radical empiricism to some of the larger epistemological problems arising from the way we conduct science in the West, see Willis Harman and Jane Clark, eds., *New Metaphysical Foundations of Modern Science* (Sausalito, Calif.: Institute of Noetic Sciences, 1994).

Recently, David C. Lamberth presented a doctoral dissertation, "Squaring logic and life: Metaphysics, experience, and religion in William James's philosophical worldview," Department of Philosophy, Harvard University, 1994, which he followed with "James's *Varieties* reconsidered: Radical empiricism, the extramarginal and conversion," a paper presented at the thirty-seventh annual meeting of the American Academy of Religion. Eiljah Mirachnick, a graduate student at the University of California, Berkeley, is preparing a dissertation in the School of Architecture on the application of James's radical empiricism to a new understanding of space perception. See, for instance, Elijah Mirachnick, "Knowledge of body: Another picture of architects and design education," *Proceedings of the 83rd ACSA Annual Meeting* (Washington, D.C.: ACSA Press, 1995), pp. 12–18.

Perhaps an even more important development within the heart of the philosophy of science to question the presuppositions of the reductionistic platform has been recent discussion initiated among the Quinian logicians at the American Academy of Arts and Sciences by the Harvard philosopher Hilary Putnam. See, for instance, one of Putnam's statements on James (with Ruth Anna Putnam) but to a literary audience, in "William James's ideas," *Raritan*, 8:3 (Winter 1989), pp. 27–45; and Putnam's essay, "James's theory of perception," in James Conant, ed., *Realism with a Human Face: Hilary Putnam* (Cambridge, Mass.: Harvard University Press, 1990), pp. 232–51, which has important implications for reassessing the problem of representation—the idea that the brain merely models the world of objects, a conception which still dominates contemporary neuroscientific explanations of consciousness.

INTO NEUROSCIENCE

While various authors have remarked on the potential connections between James's ideas and the neuroscience revolution, several researchers have been directly affected by Jamesean ideas. For instance, as a student of Raymond Stetson (Harvard Ph.D., 1901) at Oberlin, Roger Sperry was first drawn to study the mind-body problem by reading James's *Principles of Psychology*, and by the Jamesean idea that "attainment of a genuine glimpse into the mind-brain relation would constitute the scientific achievement before which all past achievements would pale." Sperry's split-brain work was the result. See Polly Henninger, "Sperry's Place in the History of Psychology," paper presented at the annual meeting of the American Psychological Association, Los Angeles, August 12, 1994, pp. 2–3.

Likewise, for James's influence on another neuroscientific pioneer, see Karl Pribram, "Self-consciousness and intentionality: A model based on an experimental analysis of the brain mechanisms involved in the Jamesean theory of motivation and emotion," in G. Schwartz and D. Shapiro, eds., *Consciousness and Self-Regulation: Advances in Research* (New York: Plenum, 1976), pp. 51–100. And for a popular account of the mind-brain revolution that mentions the contemporary relevance of James's ideas, see Francis Crick and Christopher Koch, "The problem of consciousness," *Scientific American*, September 1992, pp. 152–59.

For more on James and his possible relation to developments in the neurosciences, see E. I. Taylor, "Radical empiricism and the new science of consciousness," *History of the Human Sciences*, February 1995.

ON TO NON-WESTERN EPISTEMOLOGIES

Some preliminary attempts in the Jamesean tradition to define the parameters of classical Eastern psychology for Western academic psychologists are Swami Akhilalanda, *Hindu Psychology: Its Meaning for the West*, introduction by Gordon Allport and a foreword by Edgar Sheffield Brightman (New York: Harper, 1946); Gardner and Lois Murphy, *Asian Psychology* (New York: Basic Books, 1968); J. Fadiman and R. Frager, *Personality and Personal Growth* (New York: Harper and Row, 1978); E. I. Taylor, "Asian interpretations: Transcending the stream of consciousness," in K. Pope and J. Singer, eds., *The Stream of Consciousness: Scientific Investigations into the Flow of Human Experience* (New York: Plenum, 1978), pp. 31–54.

The case for increased dialogue between scholars in comparative religions who are qualified to interpret the Asian traditions and Western psychologists has been made in E. I. Taylor, "Contemporary interest in classical Eastern psychology," in A. Paranjpe, D. Ho, and R. Rieber, eds., *Asian Contributions to Psychology* (New York: Praeger, 1988), pp. 79–122.

For materials developing James's connections to Asian psychology, see E. I. Taylor, "Psychology of religion and Asian studies: The William James legacy," *Journal of Transpersonal Psychology*, 10:1 (1978), pp. 66–79; idem, "Swami Vivekananda and William James," *Prabuddha Bharata: Journal of the Ramakrishna Society, Calcutta*, 91 (September 1986), pp. 374–85; and David Kalupahana, *The Principles of Buddhist Psychology* (Albany: State University of New York, 1987).

For primary psychological texts in some of the Asian traditions, see *Dignaga, On Perception: Being the Pratyaksapariccheda of Dignaga's Pramanasamuccaya, from the Sanskrit Fragments and the Tibetan Version*, trans. and annotated by Masaaki Hattori (Cambridge, Mass.: Harvard University Press, 1968). For an introduction to *pratityasamuttpada*, the Buddhist theory of causality, see Rune E. Johanson, *The Dynamic Psychology of Early Buddhism* (London: Curzon Press, 1979); and for a look at the Buddhist theory of conditioning, see the *Karmasiddhiprakarana* of Vasubandhu, a Sanskrit text for which we have only the Tibetan version, e.g., *Karmasiddhiprakarana*, trans. from the French by Leo M. Pruden (Berkeley: Asian Humanities Press, 1989).

We can only conclude from such diversity, as James himself once did, that in psychology as in life, "each person being a syllable in human nature's total message, it takes the whole of us to spell the meaning out completely."

INDEX

abnormal personality, 42
abnormal psychology, 4, 6, 7, 28, 29, 41
abnormal states of consciousness, 78
abreaction, 54
Absolute, the, 28, 83, 90, 134
Age of Theory, the, 152
agnostic positivism, 112, 124
Alcoholics Anonymous, 141
Aldrich, Mrs. B., 15
Allport, G. W., 9, 57
alternating personality, 60
ambulatory psychoneuroses, 23, 70, 79
American Academy of Arts and Sciences, 22
American Association for the Advancement
   of Science, 22, 99, 101
American Journal of Insanity, 41
American Journal of Otology, 18
American Journal of Psychology, 26, 41, 99
American Journal of Religious Psychology, 82
American Men of Science, 101
American Mind Cure philosophies, 86
American Philosophical Association, 74,
   128
American Psychological Association, 15, 74,
   99, 117, 128, 141, 150, 151, 152
American religious psychotherapies, 146
American Society for Psychical Research,
   19, 22, 24, 36, 47, 99, 101; Committee
   on Apparitions and Hallucinations, 23;
   Committee on Experimental Psychology,
   22; Committee on Hypnotism, 23; Committee on Mediumistic Phenomena, 48;
   Committee on Mediumship, 23; Committee on Thought-Transference, 22
Anaesthetic Revelation, 138
anatta, 147
Angell, J. R., 3, 73, 98, 111
anti-Jamesean movement, 98
applied psychology, 104, 105, 106, 144
Archives de Psychologie, 129
Aristotle, 58
association of ideas, 77
associationism, 27
associationist psychologists, 59
associationists, 31, 70
Atman, 62, 88

automatic writing, 19, 24, 53, 75, 80, 116
automatism, 135
automaton theory, 30
Avenarius, R., 5
Awakened Consciousness, 137
awareness, normal waking, 39

Baldwin, J. M., 41, 52, 97, 99, 149, 150
Beard, G. M., 17, 73, 146
behaviorism, 6, 7, 82, 141
beliefs, 123
Bergson, H., 125, 128, 135, 141; and radical
   empiricism, 136
Bernard, C., 14, 16
Bernheim, H., 23, 38, 54
Beth Israel Hospital, 74
Binet, A., 23, 42, 59, 73, 81
Blavatsky, H., 88
Blood, B. P., 91, 138, 141
Boring, E. G., 9, 15, 21, 97; on James, 9
Boston City Hospital, 23
Boston Evening Transcript, 55
Boston Museum of Natural History, 22
Boston Psychopathic Hospital, 74
Boston School of Abnormal Psychology,
   6, 76
Bourne, A., 36, 60
Bowditch, H. I., 22
Bowditch, H. P., 14, 16, 21, 22, 24, 28, 47,
   75, 97, 98
breathing, 86
Breuer, J., 23, 52, 53, 54, 55, 67
Brown-Sequard, C. E., 14, 16
Buddhism, 93; and Christianity, compared,
   94; Buddhist conception of personality,
   147; Buddhist meditation, 147

Calkins, M. W., 3, 74, 98, 146
Cambridge Metaphysical Club, 61
Cannon, W. B., 3, 17, 71, 75
Carpenter, W., 14, 29, 35
Cattell, J. M., 41, 52, 98, 99, 100, 101, 102,
   110, 149, 150, 151, 152
census on hallucinations, 73
cerebral localization, 16
chance, 124

character development, 77
Charcot, J. M., 16, 23, 38, 40, 42, 52, 54
Child Study movement, 98
Chinese religions, 93
chloral hydrate, 91
Christian Scientists, 46, 56
clairvoyance, 41, 102
Clark, W. H., 89
Clark University, 98, 99, 100, 146, 149
clinical neurology, 24
clinique, la, 15
cognitions, 3
cognitive psychology, 35
Columbia University, 149
Comte, A., 5
Congress of Experimental Psychology in
    Paris, 23
consciousness 3, 4, 5, 8, 10, 12, 14, 18,
    20, 24, 26, 28, 29, 30, 32, 34, 35, 39, 40,
    42, 46, 53, 54, 58, 71, 79, 81, 83, 84, 85,
    87, 90, 92, 96, 113, 116, 118, 125, 126,
    129, 130, 134, 135, 143, 145, 147, 149; be-
    yond the margin, 67; double, 43; field
    formula of, 87; habitual or empirical, 66;
    higher, 64; hypostatized into a category,
    126; infinite Mother-Sea of, 83; multiple,
    43; multiple states of, 39; spiritual evolu-
    tion of, 63; split, 66; stream of, 66; thresh-
    old of, 142; as an ultimate plurality of
    selves, 79; as an ultimate plurality of
    statis, 5, 92, 135
contagion within groups, 66
Cornell University, 108, 110
Critique philosophique, 27
cross-cultural comparative psychology of
    trance states, 94
crystal gazing, 23, 53, 80, 116

Dana, C. L., 22
Darwin, C., 5, 111
Darwinists, Social, 3, 5, 12
Delboeuf, J., 23, 27
Demon possession, 60, 68, 89
Demon Possession and Allied Themes, 89
depth psychology, 142
Descartes, R., 58, 73
determinism, 5
Dewey, J., 73, 97, 125
Dewey Decimal System, 73
Dharmapala, A., 62, 147
Die Religion des Buddha, 88
Dilthey, W., 61

dissociated states, 30
dissociation, 20, 23, 78, 79, 96, 147
Dissociation, Law of, 78
dissociative consciousness, 78
doctrine of relations, 35
doctrine of specific energies, 19
double consciousness, 75
dreams, 96, 124, 143
Dresser, H., 94
Dresser, J. and A., 94
DuBois, W.E.B., 75
dynamic psychology of the subconscious,
    66, 71, 147
dynamic psychotherapy, 9

Earth-soul, Fechner on, 137
élan vital, 135, 141
Eliot, C. W., 13, 28, 47, 84, 95, 99, 107
Ellenberger, H., 6, 53
Emerson, R. W., 3, 12, 61, 79, 86
emotions, 35, 86, 87, 119, 126
English mental testing, 101
Erkenntnisstheorie, 33
Essay Concerning Human Understanding, 58
État mental des hystériques, 52
Evans, R., 28, 149
Everett, C. C., 61, 62, 92
everyday waking consciousness, 116
evolution, 10
evolutionary functionalism, 12
"Exceptional Mental States" lectures, 65,
    89, 140, 141, 143
existentialism, 141
experience of activity, the, 128
experimentalism, 3, 4, 5
experimental measurements, 29
experimental physiology, 24
experimental psychology, 24, 107, 144
experimental psychopathology, 8, 21, 24,
    28, 35, 41, 78, 95
Experimentalist's Club, 151

Faith, 123
fall of the threshold, 145
faradic currents, 17
Fechner, G. T., 9, 99, 101, 137, 145; the day-
    light view, 137
feeling of effort, 18
Fifth International Congress of Psychology,
    Rome, 128, 129, 149
First International Congress of Experimen-
    tal Psychology, 50

Eugene Taylor, Ph.D., is a Lecturer on Psychiatry at Harvard Medical School, a Clinical Associate in Psychology at Massachusetts General Hospital, and an Executive Faculty member at Saybrook Institute. He is also author of *William James on Exceptional Mental States*.